FANATIC
HEART

FANATIC HEART

A Life of John Boyle O'Reilly
1844–1890

A. G. Evans

Northeastern University Press
BOSTON

First published in 1997 by the University of Western Australia Press.
Published in 1999 in the United States of America by
Northeastern University Press, by arrangement with
the University of Western Australia Press.

Library of Congress Cataloging-in-Publication Data
Evans, A. G. (Anthony G.)
Fanatic heart : a life of John Boyle O'Reilly, 1844–1890 /
A. G. Evans.
p. cm.
Includes bibliographical references and index.
ISBN 1-55553-395-7 (pbk.)
1. Poets, American—19th century—Biography. 2. Journalists—
United States—Biography. 3. Ireland—History—1837–1901—
Biography. 4. Irish Americans—Massachusetts—Boston—
Biography. 5. Convicts—Australia—Biography. 6. Fenians—
Biography. I. O'Reilly, John Boyle, 1844–1890. II. Title.
[PS2493.E93 1999]
811´.4—dc21
[B]   98-54846

Printed and bound by Thomson-Shore, Inc., Dexter,
Michigan. The paper is Glatfelter Supple
Opaque Recycled, an acid-free sheet.

MANUFACTURED IN THE UNITED STATES OF AMERICA
03 02 01 00 99   5 4 3 2 1

Out of Ireland have we come.
Great hatred, little room,
Maimed us at the start.
I carry from my mother's womb
A fanatic heart.

W.B. Yeats

TO CLAIRE
who was generous enough
to change her name
from Kelly to Evans

CONTENTS

CONVERSIONS

Historical biographies invariably present authors with the problem of how to refer to distances, measurements and other values in common use at the time of the events in the story but which have now given way to the metric and decimal systems. As imperial measurements are used throughout this work a simple conversion table is given below for those readers who may wish to check specific details in the text.

1 inch	2.54 centimetres
1 foot	30.5 centimetres
1 yard	0.914 metre
1 mile	1.61 kilometres
1 square mile	2.59 square kilometres
1 nautical mile	1.8 kilometres
1 ounce	28.3 grams
1 pound	454 grams
1 hundredweight	50.8 kilograms
1 ton	1.02 tonnes
1 pint	568 millilitres
1 bushel	0.0364 cubic metres
Fahrenheit (°F)	$°C = \frac{5}{9} (°F - 32)$

Australian currency changed from pounds, shillings and pence to dollars and cents in 1966. At the time of changeover the following approximate conversions applied:

1 penny	2 cents
1 shilling	10 cents
1 pound	2 dollars
1 guinea	2 dollars and 10 cents

At the time of publication the value of the US dollar was approximately A$0.78.

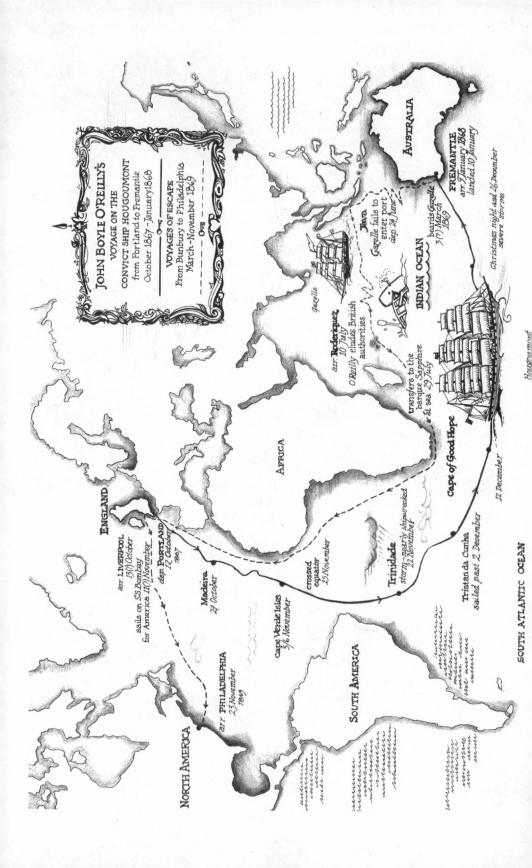

JOHN BOYLE O'REILLY'S
VOYAGE ON THE
CONVICT SHIP HOUGOUMONT
from Portland to Fremantle
October 1867 – January 1868

————

VOYAGES OF ESCAPE
From Bunbury to Philadelphia
March–November 1869

○——○

ENGLAND

arr. LIVERPOOL
15(?) October

sails on SS Bombay
for America 11(?) November

dep. PORTLAND
12 October
1867

arr. PHILADELPHIA
23 November
1869

Madeira
29 October

Cape Verde Isles
5/6 November

crossed
equator
15 November

Trinidade
storm – nearly shipwrecked
22 November

Tristan da Cunha
sailed past 2 December

12 December

NORTH AMERICA

SOUTH AMERICA

SOUTH ATLANTIC OCEAN

AFRICA

Cape of Good Hope

gazelle

arr. Roderiquez
10 July
O'Reilly eludes British
authorities

transfers to the
barque Sapphire
at sea 29 July

Gazelle fails to
enter port
dep. 24 June

Java

boards Gazelle
3(?) March
1869

INDIAN OCEAN

AUSTRALIA

FREMANTLE
arr. 9 January 1868
landed 10 January

Christmas night and 26 December
severe storms

Hougoumont

PREFACE

A short distance down a side road which turns west off the coastal highway running between Perth and Bunbury in Western Australia, about 15 kilometres north of Bunbury—and almost lost under the paperbark trees—is a simple, unadorned memorial to the Irish poet and patriot, John Boyle O'Reilly. It takes the form of a rough-hewn block of granite a metre and a half high with an engraved brass plate affixed near the top. The plate, now tarnished and difficult to read, tells us that it was erected in his proud memory and marks the place near where he hid and escaped from custody in 1869.

A much larger and more ornate memorial to the poet stands at a busy intersection near the Fenway in Boston, Massachusetts which was erected in 1896, six years after his death. Its style is baroque and it is richly embellished by Irish interlacings and emblems. On one face is a bust of O'Reilly, and on the other are three bronze figures: Erin in the centre has on her right hand the life-size figure of Patriotism, and on her left is Poetry, holding a lyre. Into the lap of Erin the two side figures scatter oak and laurel leaves with which Erin may weave a crown for her heroes.

There is yet a third memorial in stone, incorporating a bust of O'Reilly and surmounted by a huge Celtic cross, in the little graveyard at Dowth, County Meath, the village where he was born. Here a wreath-laying ceremony is held every year on the anniversary of his death, although his remains lie buried in Holyhood Cemetery, Boston.

And so John Boyle O'Reilly is remembered and revered on three different continents: in Ireland as a famous son, brave patriot and native poet; in

Australia as a convict, one of many unjustly transported in the middle of the 19th century and who made a daring and exciting escape which has become part of that country's folklore; and in America, where O'Reilly is honoured as a journalist, poet and philanthropic public figure, and who was accorded on his death in Boston in 1890 a rare civic funeral presided over by the cardinal archbishop.

John Boyle O'Reilly is one of the most attractive, heroic convicts to have lived and worked in Australia, albeit for only a brief time. His influence and his place in our history is of far greater significance than the few months he spent here might suggest. But in spite of this his story is not widely known. Most people know only his name and that he escaped on an American whaler. Facts about his early life and influences, and what happened to him when he left Australia, are forgotten or not known at all. Few are aware that he wrote the first West Australian poetry and a novel about the early days in the colony. The bare facts appear from time to time in books of essays, magazines, and newspaper articles; and a few of his poems—those on Australia—turn up in local anthologies. But his extraordinary, eventful life is eclipsed in this country by the later more popular and legendary episode of the *Catalpa*. Few realize that if O'Reilly had not succeeded in escaping from custody in 1869, and had not afterwards resided in Boston and helped plan the notorious *Catalpa* escape, the six Fenians who have become heroes of countless stories and ballads would not have found freedom. For this reason alone his story deserves to be told.

And yet no modern biography of O'Reilly has been published before. The first and only authoritative book on his life was written by his devoted friend and colleague on the *Pilot* newspaper, James Jeffrey Roche, and was published in New York in 1891. It has now become so rare and valuable that reference libraries are inquisitive about those who wish to consult it. Another important work on O'Reilly is the PhD thesis, 'Behind the Lighthouse', written by Dr Martin Carroll (University of Iowa, 1954). This covers in great detail, and with impressive scholarship, the sojourn of O'Reilly in Western Australia. Sadly, it was not published at the time, and in the forty years since it was written fresh material has been discovered. A third book, *The American Years of John Boyle O'Reilly 1870–1890*, is a doctoral dissertation by Francis McManamin, SJ which deals specifically, as its title suggests, with O'Reilly's life in America from 1870 until his death in 1890. Another work which was published in recent years is *The Fenians in Australia* by Keith Amos which includes a valuable chapter on O'Reilly. These four works are important sources and their help to me is sincerely acknowledged. Amos's exhaustive research into the political intrigue before the Fenians arrived in Western Australia forms the basis of my own chapter on the subject. In 1956 a popular novel was published, *Seek for a Hero*, by the American journalist William Schofield. The author relies heavily on Roche's work to reconstruct O'Reilly's life and adds fictional dialogue.

Apart from the works mentioned above little else exists. O'Reilly's name is often cited in books about the convict era and in the story of the *Catalpa*, but there is no contemporary work that features O'Reilly centre stage. The excuse for writing this book then—if one is needed—is to fill that gap and tell a remarkable story which has not been generally available. For many years I have been fascinated by O'Reilly and have believed him to be a greatly under-estimated figure, unsung not only in Australia but also in modern Ireland and America where he may be accounted more important. I have told his story as best I could when others have thought only of the *Catalpa* rescue. I have written modest radio programs about O'Reilly, and broadcast them when I was in a position to do so. I have collected material about him over many years, but it was not until Perth writer and historian, George Russo, very generously turned over to me his collection of research material and urged me to begin (providing constant encouragement along the way) that I felt able to tackle the subject. He may be said to be midwife to the work but, as in keeping with that noble profession, he is not to be blamed for the result.

Because O'Reilly is known—if he is known at all—solely for his daring escape on an American whaler, I have attempted to place his convict years in the context of his entire life. I have tried to discover his character and the formative influences, his friendships and experiences. In short, I have tried to discover what led him from being an impetuous youth by the River Boyne, to becoming a journalist on a British newspaper, a dashing career soldier in the British Army, a convict transported to the Swan River Colony, and eventually a newspaper editor and leading citizen of Boston. Although O'Reilly's later experiences in Boston wrought a change in his attitude to the Irish republican cause—he came to eschew violence and political extremism—he always remained an Irish patriot and became a spokesman, largely through his speeches and writings, for the emancipation of his country.

Because O'Reilly's poetry and fictional work is so revealing of the man—and no story of his life would be complete without studying them—I have quoted generously where they are relevant to the narrative. O'Reilly is revered as a poet of some consequence in Ireland, although clearly not of the first rank. His appeal is mainly through his patriotic fervour; his voice is that of the folk balladeer effusing a shared devotion to the motherland. A contemporary, wider audience might find much of his poetry too commonplace, too sentimental and lacking in technical craft. But the best of it is deeply moving and has a sincerity and wisdom that surely deserves to be remembered. A new volume of only his best poems, judiciously chosen and annotated, is much needed and would serve to restore his reputation.

In addition to George Russo, friends and correspondents who have generously given information, answered queries, and lent me material include: Walter McGrath of Cork, Ireland; Mrs Peggy O'Reilly of Drogheda; Kevin Cusack of Bryn Mawr, Pennsylvania, whose work on John Casey's diary of the *Hougoumont* voyage contributed significantly to my chapters on that episode; George E. Ryan, one-time editor of the *Pilot*; Keith Amos who put me on the right track and encouraged me; and Gillian O'Mara whose recent work deciphering O'Reilly's shorthand notebook shed new light on his attachment to Jessie Woodman. Gratitude must also be expressed for the help received from the staff of various libraries and museums: the Battye Library, Perth; the Mitchell Library, Sydney; the new library at Notre Dame University, Fremantle, where the rich collection of American works proved invaluable; John Atteberry in the John J. Burns Library and the staff of the O'Neill Library, both at Boston College; the Houghton Library, Harvard; the Boston Public Library; the National Library, Dublin; Ann Denison at the Preston Public Library; Stephan Bull at the Lancashire County Regimental Museum in Preston who provided valuable information about the 11th Lancashire Volunteer Regiment; the Kendall Whaling Museum and the New Bedford Whaling Museum, Massachusetts, for information about the *Catalpa* and the *Gazelle*. I also express my sincere thanks to the following who contributed much to the work and who have, in many cases, become my friends in the process: my generous hosts in Boston, Jane and Charles Walsh; Alfred Madden who shared with me his local knowledge and took me on an essential 'O'Reilly tour' of Boston; Professor Richard Boyle O'Reilly Hocking and his wife, Kaye, whose warm hospitality at their mountainside home in Madison, New Hampshire included access to the family archives; Greg Brophy in London who undertook important research on my behalf after I had returned to Australia; Professor Geoffrey Bolton who gave me important research advice; and Ms Margaret Pinto who translated relevant parts of the log of the *Gazelle* from Portuguese. Also of assistance were Liam Barry and Ormande Waters; Dorene Mackey who read an early manuscript draft and made valuable comments; and my wife, Claire, who read each chapter in turn and corrected embarrassing errors. Special thanks are due to my editor, Deborah Taylor, whose attention to detail and points of style has been invaluable. I should also like to thank the following for permission to reproduce photographs in this publication: Richard O'Reilly Hocking; Tony Stemp; Battye Library, Perth; Mitchell Library, Sydney; New York Public Library; New Bedford Whaling Museum; and the *Pilot* newspaper. I also acknowledge with gratitude a grant from the Literature Committee of the Western Australian Department of the Arts which enabled me to visit 'O'Reilly territory' in Ireland, Preston, and Boston.

These, and many others who are unnamed, have contributed to this story of O'Reilly. Thereby they have contributed to a rich episode in the early history of a colony subject to the Imperial Crown which retains strong links with a former colony of the Crown—Ireland.

A.G. Evans
April 1997

Part One

THE CRY OF THE DREAMER

1844–1867

The Boyne Valley from Dowth Castle. (Photograph by the author)

CHAPTER 1

CHILDHOOD BY THE BOYNE

*As children we drew in a burning hatred of
British rule with our mother's milk. Until
my father died, at over eighty, he never said
'England' without adding, 'God damn her!'.*

Elizabeth Gurley Flynn

THE River Boyne, rising in the Bog of Allen on the central plains west of
Dublin, winds north-eastwards through the peaceful landscape of County
Meath and reaches the Irish Sea 48 kilometres north of the capital. The scenery
on its banks is beautiful, but never grand.

Of the several notable rivers of Ireland, the Boyne possesses the richest
history and arouses the strongest loyalties among those who live in its region.
'So memorable in ancient history, and so rich in monuments of the past is it,
that we fear not to assert that the history of Ireland might be written in tracing
its banks.'[1] Foreign invaders, the Danes and the Normans, first entered the
country on its waters; and St Patrick landed at the Boyne's mouth, sailed upriver
to Slane, and there in AD 433 lit his beacon of Christianity—the Paschal Fire—
in defiance of the pagan king, Loeghaire.

But the Boyne was important long before the coming of Patrick. Ancient
kings and warring tribes had settled along its banks for over 8,000 years and
there remain today neolithic stone circles, massive cromlechs, and impressive
burial mounds considerably older than Stonehenge and the pyramids of Egypt.

At the first bridge across the river, 2.4 kilometres from the estuary and
6.4 kilometres from the sea itself, stands the ancient maritime town of
Drogheda, approachable at high water by vessels of moderate draught. The
author Frank O'Connor described Drogheda as a dreary little town perhaps on
account of its muddy estuary, town quays, and stone-grey buildings, but local
people claim that it is one of the most enjoyable historic towns on the east coast;
certainly its ancient town walls, the St Laurence Gate with two four-storey drum

towers, the 18th century warehouses, and the splendid Victorian viaduct high up over the river support this view. Drogheda is a lively, working city on the main railway line from Dublin to Belfast, redolent of history and enlivened each year by thousands of pilgrims who come to venerate Blessed Oliver Plunkett, the archbishop who was executed at Tyburn in 1681 on an unfounded charge of treason. His head is preserved in an ornate golden casket in St Peter's parish church on West Street.

Above Drogheda the moderately rapid waters of the Boyne are tidal for another 4 kilometres and follow a course north-west as far as Oldbridge. There, the river makes a sharp bend and doubles back on itself to form a loop; it then winds in a curve westward again to form a semicircle through a deep narrow valley. The steep sides hereabouts are covered with trees which stretch their arms over the dark water below. Leaving the valley the river wends north-west again, passing through rich meadows until it reaches Slane (13 kilometres west of Drogheda) whose battlemented manorial castle rises up high over the surrounding country.

All the country of the Boyne between Slane and Oldbridge is another place of pilgrimage, with a different object of veneration to Blessed Oliver's head at Drogheda. Tourists, on their way to visit the Stone Age passage graves at Newgrange, stop on the road to photograph the site of the great Battle of the Boyne which was fought on 1 July 1690. The grey obelisk, which once marked the battlefield 3.2 kilometres out of Oldbridge, was blown up by republican forces during the Civil War of 1922 and only the rock base remains, overgrown with shrub and ivy. Visitors can also see the glen named after William of Orange, whose superior forces mustered there, and enjoy the view south across the river to where the Catholic army of James II waited on the other side. The state of the Boyne's tide on that 1 July would have been crucial to William's success: at low water the greatest depth does not cover a man's shoulders and the width from bank to bank is scarcely 30 metres.

Lying almost midway between Oldbridge and Slane (about 7 kilometres west of Drogheda), in the curve formed by the river and on the north side of it, lies the village of Dowth. And a little distance away from the village, overlooking the water, are the ruins of Dowth Castle which dates from the middle of the 17th century. Close by are a ruined chapel, the old village church and graveyard, and the substantial brick-built Alms House dating from 1877 which replaced an earlier, smaller building. The castle itself, a tower-like structure, is one of several similarly styled castles in the region, looking less like the traditional crenellated pile commonly found in England and resembling more a tall, square manor house of three storeys. Its only castle-like feature is a small square tower at one end, with a parapet. Built of limestone and rubble with dressed stone framing

4

Dowth Castle and schoolroom today. The adjoining brick building was erected in 1887 after the departure of the O'Reilly family. (Courtesy of Tony Stemp)

the doors and windows, it has a vaulted cellar and fireplace in the west wall, and the two upper storeys have wooden ceilings. At the time of writing it was in a dilapidated condition, having been the home in recent years of backpackers, hippies and a group of Buddhists.

Dowth Castle must have looked much smarter early in the 19th century when the eccentric owner, the sixth Viscount Netterville, bequeathed it and its adjoining buildings together with sixty surrounding acres 'for the support of a charitable institution for poor desolate widows and orphans, with provision for educating and apprenticing the latter'. The castle was modernized for their use and became known as the Netterville Institute. The noble lord in making his will mentioned his wish that, 'the inmates should live in peace and good feeling with each other; that they must be clean, tidy and perfectly sober, and that they must attend when able to those who from sickness are unable to do this for themselves'.[2]

In 1836, five years after the National School system had been introduced by the British Government, a school which served not only the orphanage but also the families of the surrounding district was incorporated into the Netterville Institute. The old chapel was fitted out as a schoolroom at a cost of £44 18s 4d, two-thirds of the cost being met by the Schools Commissioners and one-third by the parish.[3]

The National School system was an attempt by the British Government to provide universal education in Ireland, and in so doing set an educational pattern that survives in modified form throughout Britain today. A national

The 16th century ruined chapel adjoining Dowth Castle which was used as the schoolroom during O'Reilly's boyhood. (Photograph by the author)

board, the Commissioners of Education, was established to make grants towards the construction of the schools and pay the teachers' salaries. The Commissioners issued lists of approved texts and made regulations for the conduct of classes and set standards of teaching. Each school had a local manager who was generally the priest if predominantly a Catholic school, or the local vicar if Protestant. By 1850 there were over 4,000 National Schools serving over half a million children.[4] The teaching (in the English language) was of a high standard; the textbooks published by the Commissioners, though not compulsory, were finely produced and became a popular series chosen and used by schools throughout the British Empire.[5]

The National Schools were bitterly resented by fervent nationalists who saw in the narrow English curriculum a deliberate attack on Irish language and culture:

> The National Schools were established for the express purpose of denationalising the children of Ireland. Certain textbooks, written by the daughters of Archbishop Wakely, were calculated to undermine Irish Nationality.[6]

Other judgements proved, with hindsight, less condemnatory. It is now generally recognized that the main achievement of the system was to bring numeracy and literacy to vast numbers of otherwise impoverished children; by teaching them English it enabled many of them 'to rise from the pit', and it opened the way for social and economic advancement.[7]

The first schoolmaster appointed to the Dowth National School, and who occupied the post for thirty-five years, was William David O'Reilly from Dublin. He came with the reputation of being a scholar and a fine teacher. The O'Reillys were a proud and ancient family, lords of Cavan for over a thousand years. They distinguished themselves as soldiers, prelates and scholars, and many of them fought in foreign lands when careers were denied them at home. William O'Reilly was a disciplinarian, strict with his pupils and his children, but his reputation as a fine teacher was somewhat dented later by school inspectors' adverse reports. In 1855 he was admonished for 'pupils' want of proficiency particularly in arithmetic and penmanship', and the following year he was fined £1 for the 'discreditably low state of the school'. In 1857 the Assistant Commissioner of the National School Board visited Dowth and reported that 'English dictation was extremely unfavourable. Only one boy exhibited any knowledge of geography. None of them could parse a sentence'. He did however add that the school was orderly, 'and in the point of discipline well regulated'. There were fifty-eight children on the roll at that time but the average daily attendance was thirty. The schoolmaster received an annual salary of £15.[8]

William O'Reilly had married Eliza Boyle in Dublin before his appointment to Dowth. A woman of considerable intellect and talent, Eliza and her family were proud of her famous forebear, the revolutionary John Allen, who had been associated with Robert Emmet's rising in 1803 before fleeing to France to become a colonel in the French Army. The patriotic quest for freedom and brave soldiering were part of the family tradition.

When the O'Reillys moved to Dowth to live in the castle Eliza was appointed matron of the orphanage, a job she managed with efficiency and affectionate concern for the inmates between raising her own family of eight children. The firstborn, a daughter, was baptized Margaret on 14 January 1841 in the parish of Rathkenny. A year later a son was born and baptized William Joseph on 10 August 1842.

Two years later when Eliza was pregnant a third time, Daniel O'Connell, the Irish hero and Member of Parliament for County Clare, addressed a mass anti-Act of Union rally in the Dowth district. William O'Reilly was a friend and admirer of 'the Liberator', as he was popularly known, and decided that if the child was a boy he would be called Daniel O'Connell. Determined though he was, Eliza defied him and insisted that he be named after *her* people. And so he was. Their son was born on 28 June 1844 and baptized John Boyle in Rathkenny parish on 18 July of that year.[9]

Eliza Boyle, John's mother, painted in Ireland by an unknown artist.
(Courtesy of Richard O'Reilly Hocking)

1844 may hardly be accounted a propitious year for entry into the world if, as was the case, that world happened to be rural Ireland. The Census Commissioners in 1841 reported that nearly half of the families of the rural population were living in windowless mud cabins consisting of a single room. 'There never was', said the Duke of Wellington, a native of County Meath and near neighbour of the O'Reillys, 'a country in which poverty existed to the extent it exists in Ireland'.[10]

Of the many causes of that sad state of affairs perhaps the most important was the relationship between landlord and tenant: large tracts of land, owned by absentee landlords, were let out at a fixed rent to a middleman who sublet as he chose. In practice farms were split into smaller and smaller holdings, and with profit being the only motive there was no security for the peasant farmer as a consequence. Irish farmers had no contracts and landlords could raise rents at will. The more the tenant improved the land the more likely he was to receive a demand for higher rent. John Stuart Mill observed:

> The whole agricultural population can be evicted, either at the expiration of a lease or, in the far more common case of their having no lease, at six months' notice. In Ireland alone, the bulk of the population wholly dependent on the land cannot look forward to a single year's occupation of it.[11]

Another contributory cause of poverty was the increase in population. The census taken three years before John Boyle O'Reilly was born showed the population had reached over eight million; Disraeli declared Ireland to be the most densely populated country in Europe at that time. The reason for the increase is partly explained by the Irish people's love of children but also because children of the poor were regarded as a necessity, the only insurance against destitution in old age.

The increasing population, pressing ever harder on available land, despaired of finding work. The majority of Irish farms were too small to require labourers (having been divided and subdivided for profit) which left over three-quarters of the workers without regular employment. Unless a family could be sure of a small patch of land on which to grow potatoes to feed themselves, husband, wife and children starved. And then in 1845 an already bad situation turned into catastrophe. In that year, when John Boyle O'Reilly turned one year old, the Irish potato crop was attacked by a microscopic living organism able to reproduce itself with lightning speed: the entire crop failed.

> The people of Ireland, gazing over their blackened fields, despaired. They were already exhausted. What resources they possessed had been used up, and death from starvation was not a possible but an immediate fate.[12]

No event in the recent history of Ireland so fuelled a sense of injustice and burned into the consciousness of generations of Irish patriots as the Great Famine of 1845-49. Within a space of five years thousands died a miserable death and over a million people fled, mostly to America, others—a substantial number—to Canada and Australia. Many graphic and deeply disturbing accounts exist of the widespread misery and starvation endured by a majority of Irish people at that time. From the mountain of written evidence one of the most shocking accounts is surely Nicholas Cummins's letter to *The Times* in November 1846. He had witnessed scenes in the west of Ireland which were 'such as no tongue can convey the slightest idea of'. In one of the hovels he had found

six famished and ghastly skeletons, to all appearances dead, were huddled in a corner on some filthy straw, their sole covering what seemed a ragged horsecloth, their wretched legs hanging about, naked above the knees. I approached with horror, and found by a low moaning that they were still alive. They were in fever, four children, a woman, and what had once been a man. It is impossible to go through the detail. Suffice to say that in a few minutes I was surrounded by at least twenty such phantoms, such frightful spectres as no words can describe, either from famine or from fever. Their demoniac yells are still ringing in my ears and their horrible images are fixed in my brain. The same morning the police opened a house on the adjoining lands, which was observed shut for many days, and two frozen corpses were found lying upon the mud floor, half devoured by rats.

Although the south and west of Ireland provided the most dramatic reportage, the O'Reilly family's county of Meath in the east was not spared. As one local farmer wrote: 'Awful is our story concerning the potatoes. I do be striving to soil them in the boiling. I trust no harm will come from them'.[13]

To what extent the O'Reilly family was affected by the Famine is difficult to know. Probably they were spared its worst excesses because William O'Reilly was assured of his salary paid by the Education Commission. He did not depend on growing potatoes, as many of his neighbours would have done, and the Alms House was reasonably endowed. But the poverty and the want all around them must have been deeply distressing, and no doubt added to that sense of injustice and rebelliousness which John Boyle carried with him for most of his life.

In whatever quarter of the world an Irishman sets his foot, there stands a bitter, an implacable enemy of England. There are hundreds of thousands of the population of the United States of America who are Irish by birth, or by immediate descent; and be it remembered, Irishmen settled in the United States have a large influence in public affairs. They sometimes sway the election of the

Legislature, and may even affect the election of the President of the Republic. There may come a time when questions of a critical nature will be agitated between the Governments of Great Britain and the United States; and it is certain that at such a time the Irish in that country will throw their whole weight into the scale against this country.[14]

From his infancy John was not just the village teacher's son but also his pupil, living conveniently within the shadow of the schoolroom. Compared with the majority of poor Irish children, he would have had a relatively comfortable childhood and a happy one. The Irish are devoted to their children and family feeling is exceptionally strong; John retained a deep love for his parents, more especially for his mother, although he parted from them both at a young age.

When not in the schoolroom he romped, hunted, swam and fished in the River Boyne, and was invariably accompanied by his beloved pet spaniel. He wrote lovingly of the dog in later life and admitted that his possession of it made him the happiest and proudest boy in all Ireland. Years later, as an exile and successful journalist in Boston, O'Reilly remembered those days in a letter written to Father Anderson of Drogheda:

> I send my love to the very trees and fields along the Boyne from Drogheda to Slane...the pictures that I carry forever in my brain and heart—vivid as the last day I looked at them.
>
> If you go into the old graveyard at Dowth, you will find my initials cut on a stone on the wall of the old church. I should like to be buried under that spot.[15]

From time to time the young John may have given hints of exceptional qualities to come, but there is evidence that his behaviour was much like any other village boy of his age: boisterous, energetic, and sometimes disobedient. His sister remembered that as a child he was noted for his winning qualities and that his greatest charm was his manner:

> From earliest childhood he was a favourite with everybody, and yet the wildest boy in Dowth. If any mischievous act was committed in the neighbourhood, John was blamed, yet everybody loved him and would hide him from my father when in disgrace.[16]

Such disgrace followed upon one occasion when he and his friends played a trick on the new curate appointed to the parish. The priest was on his way to visit an old Irish-speaking parishioner, Mrs Dan Henry, when he stopped to speak to the boys. 'Can any of you tell me how I'll say "God Save you" in Irish to Mrs Henry?' he asked. John spoke up and said it was easy and rehearsed the

The River Boyne below Dowth Castle where the young John Boyle played and swam.
(Photograph by the author)

priest with the words: 'Droch rath ort, a bhean a tighe'. The priest thanked his young tutor and, repeating the words lest he forget them, went on his way. The story continues as originally told by an old farmer of the district who, as a young boy, was a member of John's gang in Dowth:

> As soon as his Reverence was out of sight, John cried "Come on lads, across the fields to the back of Mrs Dan's and we'll be in time for the fun". Soon we heard the sound of the priest's cheery voice as he stepped across the threshold: "Droch rath ort, a bhean a tighe". The first sound we heard after that was the sound of broken delph [sic], where Mrs Dan had let a cup fall from her hand in wonder and fear.
>
> "Musha, Glory be to God, Father jewel, what did I do to you at all, at all, for you to curse at me like that?"
>
> "Curse at you, Mrs Henry! Why what have I said?"
>
> "You said 'Bad luck to you, woman of the house' Father, and if that is not a curse, I don't know one."
>
> His Reverence said nothing for a few moments, and then began to laugh. He explained how it had happened...we watched him go down the road, but you may be sure we didn't let him see us.[17]

John discovered the attractions of the opposite sex at an early age, and if his love poems are any indication then he had several sweethearts in the district. In 'Boyhood Days'[18] he recalls how he loved to play along the Boyne's banks, to roam freely with his schoolmates and collect birds' eggs, and how he told his boyish love to a little brown-haired maid: 'And planted first on Mary's lips a lingering lover's kiss'.

There is later evidence, both from his own poetry and his friends' reminiscences that John Boyle was romantic, sensual, and successful with women. His nature was to commit himself passionately to causes, to people, and to things that he took to his heart. His first biographer, James Jeffrey Roche, wrote that: 'He loved nature, and he loved art, but he better loved mankind'.[19]

His early love of nature and an empathy with living things is well illustrated in the simple poem 'At School', in which he recalls those carefree days, and hints that learning from nature is just as important and rewarding as learning in the schoolroom:

> The bees are in the meadow
> And the swallows in the sky;
> The cattle in the shadow
> Watch the river running by.
> The wheat is hardly stirring;
> The heavy ox-team lags;
> The dragon-fly is whirring
> Through the yellow-blossomed flag.
> And down beside the river,
> Where the trees lean o'er the pool,
> Where the shadows reach the quiver
> A boy has come to school.
> His teachers are the swallow
> And the river and the trees;
> His lessons are the shallows
> And the flowers and the bees.[20]

From his earliest years he also loved stories from Irish history; he often sat round the fire listening to the adults recounting legends and nationalistic episodes:

He never tired listenin' to talk about Robert Emmet an' when my father'd stop talking the question'd often be, 'Will there ever be a risin' again Tom?' 'Maybe there would, avic, maybe there would', is what my father'd always say to him, an' then the lad'd begin lookin' into the fire the same as if there was no one at all near him, and sorra word he'd say the whole night.[21]

John's father was in a position to ensure that his sons commenced studies at an early age. He recognized that John was quick-witted, of above average intelligence, and had a sensitive nature. John attained a high standard of proficiency in basic subjects, particularly literature and history, a proficiency far in advance of his years: surprising, perhaps, in view of the adverse school inspectors' reports received by his father.

> He'd be sitting along the edge of the river bank reading out loud to us—he'd always read or tell us something about Sarsfield, or Emmet, or Wolfe Tone. I think it was his voice that put a charm on us. He could make us cry too, when he'd recite a poem, and he had dozens of them off by heart.[22]

With educated parents, and in surroundings rich with historical significance, young John imbibed not only formal learning from his books but also that wider knowledge—the lore of Ireland—which is nurtured by a spiritual attachment to the landscape and its people, and an awareness of human suffering. For a sensitive child whose first window on the world looked out across meadows to the Boyne—his playground being the scene of the infamous battle—it is little wonder that he grew up marked with a fierce patriotism and devoted his life to the cause of justice and freedom.

Few events in the long, painful saga of repression and injustice marking Anglo-Irish history rank so bitter in the collective Irish memory as the Battle of the Boyne in 1690. Young John would have relived the battle by day in the meadows, and at night listened to its legends at his father's knee. He would have heard how the deposed Catholic king, James II (O'Reilly later wrote of him as 'the pusillanimous monarch'), made a last desperate bid to retain the throne of England and Ireland; supported by Catholic Ireland he rallied his army, a force of some 25,000 men, and faced Dutch-born William III across the Boyne.

William had landed at Carrickfergus with an army of 36,000 men comprising raw English recruits, foreign Protestant mercenaries, and his own countrymen: Protestant Europe (the Orangemen) versus Catholic Jacobites. William deployed his army so that a large force made a strong frontal attack fording the river near Oldbridge, but sent a smaller force (his right wing) across the river upstream near Slane. James guessed, incorrectly as it turned out, that the main battle would be on his left flank, and moved the bulk of his small force in that direction. Divided, the Jacobites were then so thinly spread that they could not hold the line at the Boyne crossing. Although James's Irish Dragoons fought bravely in the centre the Dutch forced their way across the river sustaining only minor casualties.

Too soon the battle was lost. James fled with the remnants of his army and crossed the English Channel taking with him Ireland's best soldier, Patrick

Sarsfield, to command his bodyguard. The memory of James's debacle is still bitterly remembered even to the present time. 'The outcome of that day', wrote Professor G.M. Trevelyan in A *History of England*, 'subjected the native Irish to persecution and tyranny for several generations to come'.[23]

The infamous Battle of the Boyne was not the only tragic event which embittered the consciousness of those who lived in that part of Ireland. The town of Drogheda is synonymous with the repressive campaign of Oliver Cromwell forty years previously when Irish patriots, attempting to throw off the English yoke, were cruelly crushed, the clergy executed, and the Catholic majority subjected to draconian penal laws. These provided that no Irish Catholic could vote or serve on a jury, enter the army or navy, teach in school, carry a gun, or own a horse to the value of more than 5 guineas. No Irish Catholic could marry a Protestant or buy land from a Protestant. No Irish Catholic could enter a university, become a lawyer, or work for the government. No Irish Catholic could have more than two apprentices. No Catholic church could have a spire and every Irish Catholic had to pay tithes for the support of the established Protestant Church. The Irish language was forbidden and schools became almost unknown.

It was not until 1828 and the passage of the Catholic Emancipation Act in Westminster that these repressive laws were repealed; but the injustice of them was never forgotten. This sad history, indisputably one of cruelty, mayhem and injustice, was, in the countless retellings from generation to generation, exalted into glorious legend. Such provided the tinder for the fire of revolutionary zeal which inflamed John Boyle O'Reilly and his companions in their subsequent adventures. Some may think that the sixteen years of emancipation before John's birth were long enough for the wounds to have healed. But parents and grandparents of his friends and neighbouring children would have lived under those same laws and their culture had been repressed by them. Just as in our own time the children and grandchildren of those who suffered in the Nazi death camps are determined that the world shall not forget a terrible event fifty years in the past, so the bitterness of those post-penal years in Ireland becomes understandable.

When John was around eleven years old, his older brother William, an apprentice at the *Drogheda Argus* newspaper, contracted tuberculosis and was forced to return home.[24] If a contemporary description of Drogheda by Sir William Wilde is accurate we need enquire no further for an explanation of the young apprentice's condition:

> Drogheda has been noted for its ecclesiastical establishments, and the ruins of several still remain, but they are scarcely approachable, owing to the quantity of filth by which they are surrounded. The Magdalen Steeple...is surrounded by the

most miserable hovels, inhabited by the most wretched portion of the population, and not only is the adjoining locality a disgrace to the town, but the very site itself stands more in need of the efforts of a Sanitary Commission than any other place we know of in the British dominions.[25]

John, more robust than his elder brother and still at school, volunteered to take his place in order to save the family's investment of £50 premium. His generous offer was accepted although this meant curtailing his schooling. Before dawn he would trudge the four and a half miles into Drogheda to be at the newspaper office by 6.00 a.m. He took an hour's break for breakfast at 9.00 a.m. and another at 2.00 p.m. for dinner. It was back to work again at 3.00 p.m. until 7.00 or 8.00 p.m. before trudging back to Dowth for his supper. A strenuous regimen for a child of eleven years, but not unusual in those days.

Although his formal schooling was over, he continued to learn much from the stimulating environment of the newspaper office. He was being educated through his newspaper by studying articles on local history, politics and contemporary events. The *Drogheda Argus* was an independent weekly paper which was published every Saturday, a closely packed broadsheet of six columns per page in the style of the day, without headlines and contributions unsigned. It was a forthright supporter of an Independent Irish Party at Westminister and called for protection for Irish tenant farmers when reporting regularly on abuses of absentee landlords. John would have formed many of his political beliefs from typesetting and reading the editorials:

> There is not a more favoured class to be found under the canopy of heaven than the landlord class of Ireland. In other countries there is a controlling power by which the land-holders are made to feel that their position is one of responsibility, to be maintained for the mutual benefit of their retainers and themselves; but in Ireland the landlords have an irresponsible control over the people placed under their care with which they maintain a despotism oppressive and iniquitous.[26]

Also he would have learnt to appreciate literary expression and poetry which was a popular feature in Irish papers of those days. Roche, relying on conversations he had had with O'Reilly in later life, wrote that the young John saw his first poems printed in the pages of the *Argus* and received payment for them, supplementing his meagre wage. Because all such contributions were unsigned it is impossible to trace them.

Much of the *Argus* poetry of that time strikes us now as too sentimental and overly simplistic, but it is intriguing to wonder whether a verse, such as the following, was the work of the immature O'Reilly. Compare it, for example, with his poem 'At School', already quoted on page 13.

16

> The Springtime of love
> Is both happy and gay
> For Joy sprinkles blossoms
> And balm in our way
> The sky earth and ocean
> In beauty repose
> And all the bright future
> Is coleur de rose.[27]

Those years at the *Argus* were more than a technical apprenticeship; they constituted his university where he could develop a facility with language, a love of poetry, and his literary talent.

John Boyle O'Reilly's period of working on the *Drogheda Argus* came to an untimely end in 1859 with the death of the proprietor. His indentures discharged, he returned home to Dowth and suddenly found himself with little prospect of suitable employment. He was then about fourteen years of age.[28]

From time to time the O'Reilly family in Dowth Castle received visits from a relative, Captain James Watkinson, whose ship the *Caledonian* frequently berthed at Drogheda. Watkinson came from Preston and had married a sister of John's mother, Christiana Boyle. With John at a loose end looking for work, it is no surprise to find that he was invited to sail on the *Caledonian* in August 1859 in order to visit his aunt and uncle in Preston.

Sooner or later the thoughts of all unemployed young Irishmen turned eastwards across the Irish Sea towards industrial England, and in this John Boyle O'Reilly was no exception.

CHAPTER 2

THE YOUNG JOURNALIST

There is no profession so complete and rounded as ours,
and none so far-reaching in its scope. The rawest youth
who pens a police report is one end of a line which
extends, still vibrating, until it becomes radiant in the
editorial rooms of the Atlantic Monthly.

John Boyle O'Reilly

JOHN Boyle O'Reilly's years spent in the North of England from 1859-63 formed a happy and tranquil period of his life. In America in later years he wrote nostalgically of his time there: 'To me every impression of Preston has kept its sharp outline...I loved it and the friends I made there [were] better than any I have since known'.[1]

The Lancashire port town was a home away from home for expatriate Irishmen and in some ways was a mirror image of Drogheda, the two towns being directly opposite each other on either side of the Irish Sea some 120 nautical miles apart. Each is located on a river some distance from the mouth of the estuary: the Boyne on one side, and the Ribble on the other. Both rivers find their way to the Irish Sea through a picturesque hinterland important in agriculture and history. In the 19th century trading ships plied back and forth across the Irish Sea and the forty cotton factories of Preston, the pride of industrial Lancashire, relied much on a supply of cheap Irish labour. Blake's 'dark satanic mills' provided tempting though sweated labour for half-starved emigrants from across the water.

The population of Preston (about 20,000 in the middle of the 19th century) was strongly Catholic. Its name is said to be derived from 'Priest's Town', not only because of the Irish influx but also because the gentry clung to the old faith during the Reformation, and at a later date the district remained Royalist during the English Civil War. O'Reilly might have speculated grimly that he had left one town, Drogheda, once ravaged by Cromwell's forces, to embrace yet another

18

which had suffered similar cruelty at his hands. In 1648, Cromwell had stormed Preston killing 1,000 Royalists, and taking 4,000 prisoners.

The Watkinsons' home, 81 Barton Terrace, was at the end of a row of respectable Georgian houses in Deepdale Road about a mile from the centre of town. The terrace and house still exist although No. 81 has become known as 54 Deepdale Road, and the front window, unlike those of the other houses in the terrace, has been enlarged which disfigures its Georgian proportions. The deceptively small frontage hides four bedrooms on the first floor and two reception rooms and a kitchen below. At the end of Deepdale Road, almost within sight of the house, stands the County Prison which the young O'Reilly would have passed on his way to work every morning—a grim and as yet unrecognized omen of his life to come. In the other direction, a short walk from the house, was the parish church of St Aloysius where he attended mass with his aunt on Sundays.

John Boyle seems to have led a full social life. In the winter months he became involved in amateur theatricals and at Christmas time organized parties and stage performances for local children and young relatives who often stayed in the house.[2] In the summer he sailed a boat on the Ribble and walked in the

54 Deepdale Road (on the right of the photograph). The window on the ground floor has been redesigned in recent years. (Photograph by the author)

surrounding countryside. On one occasion he walked as far as Ribchester and Stoneyhurst—a round trip of about 26 miles. He remembered that particular day as 'one of the happiest of my life'.[3]

Despite Preston's emerging industrial role at that time it retained a small town atmosphere and appearance. The industrial suburbs, the new housing estates, and the network of roads and motorways were far in the future. The countryside was at its doorstep and Walton-le-Dale, south of the Ribble, was a peaceful village described in O'Reilly's novel, *Moondyne*, as comprising 'one quiet main street having three or four short side streets that lead in the summer days into sweet meadows and orchards'.[4] There is more than a hint of O'Reilly's fictional village in the Walton of today. One of the little cottages that fronts the south bank of the river may well have been the one he imagined as the home of his heroine Alice Walmsley. By bicycle, Walton-le-Dale is only a few minutes from Deepdale Road.

How soon after his arrival O'Reilly found work on the *Preston Guardian* is uncertain, but his experience on the *Argus* and his winning personality would have counted much in his favour when applying for the job. 'No one could know him without becoming his friend; and it was impossible to be his enemy once you experienced the spell of his affectionate personality.'[5]

John Boyle, then barely sixteen, worked hard and conscientiously, first as a compositor and later as a reporter; the hours were less demanding than he had experienced during his apprenticeship.

The *Preston Guardian*, a conservative broadsheet, appeared weekly on Saturdays, price threepence ha'penny. A supplement appeared on Wednesdays which was free to subscribers; to others the cost was a penny. Although the paper carried cable news from London and elsewhere it was popular with the businessmen and mill owners of Preston and the surrounding towns of Clitheroe, Burnley, Accrington and Lancaster. It was read for its trade and financial announcements and the closely packed advertisements on the front page. Among the regular items of local news on which John Boyle would have cut his teeth—flower shows, a new harmonium for the local school, guild meetings, and the Mayor's dinner—there were grim reminders of the mortal dangers faced by lowly workers, victims of the industrial revolution: a young girl was hit in the temple by a shuttle thrown from a loom and died four hours later; three men painting the roof of Birmingham railway station fell 50 feet to their death when the scaffolding collapsed; a fireman on a steam train fell onto the track and was crushed under the wheels; five lives were lost in a mine explosion. The litany of death was unremarkable for the times, and was repeated weekly.[6]

O'Reilly's pride in his profession and the high ideals he set for himself which guided his later conduct as a newspaper editor, were first moulded in these formative years on the *Guardian*. Addressing the Boston Press Club on 8 November 1879, he said:

> For all time to come, the freedom and purity of the press are the test of national virtue and independence. No writer for the press, however humble, is free from the burden of keeping his purpose high and his integrity white. The dignities of communities are largely entrusted to our keeping; and while we sway in the struggle or relax in the rest-hour, we must let no buzzards roost on the public shield in our charge.[7]

About a year after his arrival in Preston, on 26 June 1861, O'Reilly did something which although much in character with his love of physical activity, comradeship, and outdoor sports, ultimately was to change the direction of his life. He walked into the militia storehouse near the prison at the end of Deepdale Road and enrolled in the 11th Lancashire Rifle Volunteers: he became a part-time soldier.

In the 1850s Britain looked nervously across the English Channel at the rumblings of war in Europe: France and Austria were fighting in Lombardy; Prussia was mobilizing, and a Napoleonic invasion of Britain was thought so likely that Lord Palmerston, the British Prime Minister, began a massive fort-building program on the south coast. As a result there arose a popular demand for general mobilization and a campaign ensued for the recognition of volunteer units. In response the government took the cheapest option and sanctioned the formation of these units on condition that they 'furnish their own arms and equipment' and 'defray all expenses'.

Units were set up in counties all over England, and nowhere more enthusiastically and prolifically than in Lancashire where each large town boasted not one but several units—Liverpool, Manchester, Blackburn, Rochdale and Bolton being among the leaders. The Preston corps, the 11th Rifles, was formed in October 1859 under Major W. Goodair. Only those who could afford a modest subscription towards the cost of uniform and arms were able to join which tended to exclude 'the working-class element'.[8] Evidently O'Reilly could afford to pay. A typical charge was 5 guineas for officers and a guinea for 'the men' which was often paid in instalments.

There is no suggestion at this stage that this gentle Irish journalist-poet, interested in amateur theatricals and a lover of bicycling, swimming and other sports, joined the militia for revolutionary activities. At sixteen it was too soon for him to have had plans to win over soldiers for Fenianism. That would occur in Dublin several years later. O'Reilly probably joined for no other reason than that he enjoyed good company (many volunteers would have been fellow expatriates), an active outdoor life, camps, manoeuvres, and a chance to become familiar with firearms. A militia unit in those days would have had the attractions for adventurous youth which scouting was to have fifty years later.

O'Reilly would have attended rifle practice at the 11th Lancashire Volunteer Regiment range at Hutton Marsh, and would certainly have been a participant in the 1862 Great Volunteer Review and Sham Fight on Preston Moor when 3,200 volunteers from various local units took part, watched by a crowd of 30,000 members of the public. A mock battle took place with skirmishing and artillery fire as well as crashing volleys from the companies, the overall effect only being spoilt by the collapse of one of the spectator stands which resulted in panic and injuries to some of the occupants. This proved to be a good news story for reporter-rifleman O'Reilly who, conveniently, happened to be on the spot.

O'Reilly may not have been a revolutionary volunteer soldier, but the young Irishman was being influenced by revolutionary ideas. He took an interest in politics and studied accounts of abortive attempts to liberate his country in the past. His studies would have taught him that a recurring factor in these failures was a conspicuous lack of military experience among those who took part. He mixed freely with friends who were close to new political movements in Ireland and America, groups of conspirators who were planning an assault on the ruling government. It is therefore likely that O'Reilly chose a practical way of preparing himself for action by training as a soldier. Like so many of his countrymen, he dreamed of setting Ireland free: not merely independent of British rule, but absolutely free. In short, he dreamed of Ireland becoming a republic.

The reasons why O'Reilly decided to leave Preston sometime in the spring of 1863 are unclear. He resigned from the 11th Rifles on 16 April of that year and returned to Dowth soon afterwards. In doing so he gave up his comfortable home in his aunt's house, his evident success and solid advance-ment on the *Guardian*, his friendships, and his membership of the militia even though 'those days...were the happiest and brightest of my life'.[9] Roche in his biography suggested that by then his period of preparation was concluded and his political feelings had matured. Consequently he wished to play a part in one of the patriotic revolutionary movements taking shape in his own country. Among his Irish friends in Preston there would have been talk—highly exaggerated talk, no doubt—of imminent revolution, glory, and success across the water. A young man of O'Reilly's poetic and patriotic temperament would have naturally wanted to be part of that triumph. Roche also wrote that despite heartache and tears, indicative that he did not want to leave Preston, O'Reilly obeyed a call from his father to return to the family and apply for a job on some Irish paper.

If the last reason has any credence, once home John must have quickly persuaded his father that his future lay not in working for a newspaper, but in becoming a soldier. His experience in the militia in Preston had whetted his appetite. Within two months of his return, on 1 July 1863, he enlisted as a trooper in the 10th Hussars then stationed in Dublin. This proud regiment, also known as 'The Prince of Wales' Own' (the future Edward VII was colonel-in-chief), was noted for its dashing uniforms of blue with gold trimmings and the men's fine physical appearance, valour, and high standard of conduct.

Trooper O'Reilly was evidently a model soldier, popular among the men and respected by his officers. He was soon the life and soul of the barracks, infecting his comrades with his own cheery good nature. He performed in concerts and sang his own songs and Irish ballads. He revelled in military life and discipline and, like all Hussars, took a pride in his splendid appearance. He was so proud of it that he later admitted he often rode out of his way when on special courier duties in order to pass in front of large shop windows wherein he could admire his reflection.[10]

But was O'Reilly secretly playing a part as a modern spy would do in the Cold War? Was he establishing himself as a trusted member of the regiment so that he could fulfil his real purpose all the more successfully? John Devoy, his friend and fellow Fenian, denied that O'Reilly had revolutionary intentions at the outset and wrote: 'he enlisted because, like many other Irishmen, he liked soldiering...he was more than two years in the Regiment before he did any work for the movement'.[11]

Life in the Hussars at that time was tranquil enough, consisting mainly of parades, guard duty, ceremonial functions, and manoeuvres. In theory at least, a British regiment was not an occupying force on a war footing. Since the Act of Union in 1801 Ireland and England were, in a practical sense, one country— a fact hotly contested by most Irishmen. The old parliament in Dublin had been dissolved and Irish members were elected to Westminster. According to law Ireland was as much a part of Britain as Wales was, and the home government would have argued that it was as natural to have regiments posted in Dublin as in Cardiff.

In reality the authorities were troubled by the bitterness and active campaigning among sections of the Irish people for a repeal of the Union. They had feared a popular rising following Daniel O'Connell's mass meetings in the 1840s. Additional troops were drafted from England, barracks were fortified and provisioned to withstand siege. But in spite of the tension Irishmen, ironically always a mainstay of the British Army, were encouraged to join up, and many of them who did were untroubled by conflicting loyalties. True, there were occasional outbreaks of nationalistic fervour: patriotic skirmishes which were

23

mismanaged and ill-prepared and ended, like the rebellion of 1848, in defeat and humiliation. However, all this was to change from about the time O'Reilly joined the Hussars; and although he was not a key figure, he was to play an important role in the republican cause.

CHAPTER 3

THE REBEL SOLDIER

A man is not the slave of circumstance
Or need not be, but builder and dictator;
He makes his own events, not time nor chance;
Their logic his: not creature, but creator.

John Boyle O'Reilly

ON 17 March (St Patrick's Day) 1858, a year or more before O'Reilly left for Preston (and so certainly without his knowledge), a secret revolutionary society was formed in Dublin which was to have a direct bearing on the future course of his life.

A group of rebels, among them some who had escaped after the unsuccessful nationalist rising of 1848, met to create a united league of Irishmen whose aim was to rise up in arms when the signal was given, to put an end to British rule and to establish a truly independent republic. The ideals were similar to those of previous groups who had failed miserably, but this new movement had good reasons for optimism: they were not alone. A similar group had been formed at the same time from among Irish emigrants and sympathizers in New York. With the expectation of financial support, arms, and military advice being freely pledged by their brothers across the Atlantic, where the American War of Independence was still a living memory, there seemed a fair chance of success.

The Irish group was headed by James Stephens who, after the 1848 rising, had fled first to America and then to Paris. It was in Paris, so lately the home of revolution, that Stephens resolved to try again: to return to Ireland and organize a secret society based on French Jacobin principles. It was to be a popular movement embracing existing patriotic societies such as the Phoenix Movement in the south-west; agrarian organizations like the Ribbonmen in the Midlands; and public organizations such as the St Patrick's Brotherhood and the National Petition Movement. It would appeal to labourers and craftsmen; farmers and fishermen; shop assistants and commercial travellers; clerks and trade unions; in short, it was to have a democratic, proletarian character. But this new movement, unlike its predecessors, was to be organized on military principles, with James Stephens as commander-in-chief.

Intended to be highly secret, the new organization required an oath of allegiance from members, and was built on a complicated structure of cells known as 'circles'. Each circle was commanded by an 'A', considered equal in rank to a colonel and the apex of the pyramid; under 'A' were nine 'B's, equivalent in rank to captains; under each 'B' were nine 'C's, equivalent to sergeants; and under each 'C' were nine 'D's, equivalent to the rank and file and forming the base of the pyramid. Each circle therefore should have numbered 820 men, but in practice this figure was often exceeded. They called themselves the Irish Republican Brotherhood (IRB), but later adopted the American preferred title, 'Fenians'. The ideals and methods became known universally as 'Fenianism'.

Spurred on by the patriotic zeal of Stephens and his assistants, Thomas Clarke Luby, Jeremiah O'Donovan Rossa and John Devoy—all of whom toured the country on recruiting missions—the IRB, or 'the organization' as it was referred to among the members, flourished. Stephens was a leader successful in inspiring hope where previously hopes of freedom had been dashed. He brought promises of help from America and spoke of military action in the near future. He talked of the Republic as if it already existed; indeed members pledged loyalty in taking the oath, not to the Brotherhood, but to 'the Republic':

> I...do swear allegiance to the Irish Republic, now virtually established; that I will take up arms at a moment's notice to defend its integrity and independence: that I will yield implicit obedience to the commands of my superior officers, and finally I take this oath in the spirit of a true soldier of liberty. So help me God.[1]

During the first five years of its existence, the IRB spread remarkably successfully through the whole of Ireland. Enthusiasm, however, far exceeded military proficiency. Henry McCarthy, an official from the Brotherhood in the United States, reported after a visit to Ireland in 1864 that there were about 60,000 organized, earnest men impatient for action. He then went on to say that only 15,000 were armed, and then only with a few rifles, a number of fowling pieces and thousands of pikes.[2] While one is inclined to smile at the 'Dad's Army' approach, it is hardly different from the Home Guard in England training with broomsticks at the beginning of World War II. The pikes were manufactured in Dublin in small quantities and sent to various centres in the country. Unlike broomsticks they might have proved an inconvenience to mounted troops if placed in the ground at an angle to form a defence against horses, but it is doubtful whether they could have been a successful weapon against a fully armed regiment of Hussars.

The IRB spread to Britain and a strong contingent was formed in Scotland. Members of the organization could be found wherever there was a significant proportion of Irish in the population. (According to the census, the Irish-born population in Scotland in 1865 was 204,000.) The IRB was also strongly represented in the North of England and in London itself. Various estimates were bandied about concerning the total number of Fenians, and no doubt the strength of the organization was greatly inflated due to both Irish partisanship and a wish to inspire fear in the hearts of the enemy. One figure given in a consular report from America to the Home Office in London—and given credence at the time—stated there were 400,000 secret Fenians in Ireland and another 18,000 on mainland Britain, all waiting for the word to rise up in arms.[3] James Stephens himself estimated a total membership of around 80,000 in Ireland and Great Britain together by the year 1865, and this figure is usually accepted.[4]

When it was first put to Stephens that the British Army in both Ireland and England would be a valuable recruiting ground for the IRB, he refused to consider it. He feared that when the critical moment came army loyalty would triumph over the call to commit treason—treason followed by the death sentence if discovered. Later he came to the opinion that the vast majority of Irishmen in British regiments, with their superior military training, their equipment and their discipline, were vital to the IRB and that they could, with the right approach, be persuaded to fight for the new Republic rather than stand against it. It is an intriguing irony that in the middle of the 19th century (and indeed in most later periods in history) the British Army, whether at war or at peace, relied to a great extent on a large Irish recruitment. In 1860 for example, the proportion of Irish serving in British regiments was estimated to be a little under a third of all rank and file troops. In Ireland alone at that time there were some 26,000 regular troops, and the proportion of Irish in regiments in the home country seems likely to have been higher.[5] A rich recruiting ground indeed!

Our attention now turns to John Devoy, close associate of John Boyle O'Reilly throughout his life, and one of the inner circle of the organization being a confidant of the commander-in-chief. He was twenty-three years old at that time, handsome, with a dark complexion and of stocky build. He presented an enigmatic figure playing the role of the secret agent; to all appearances he was a well-known and respected young businessman. His business, however, was revolution. Devoy had been appointed by the IRB command to be in charge of recruitment from the ranks of the British Army. His dark eyes and iron-firm jaw displayed an authoritative if rather severe expression. From the beginning of operations Devoy had served as a Fenian 'centre' with the equivalent rank of colonel in County Kildare; he was then called to Dublin by his chief. Like so many leading Fenians he gave his entire loyalty to the movement, even to the extent of serving a period in the French Foreign Legion which he regarded as a necessary training for action. He inspired confidence and affection among those he commanded and later, as an exile in America, he never forgot his responsibility towards those who had suffered a longer and harsher imprisonment than himself.

The two men previously appointed to be in charge of recruitment – a one-time seminary student, Pagan O'Leary, followed by William Roantree – had been arrested. On this evidence the job was judged a dangerous one. In October 1865 Stephens wrote to Devoy appointing him as replacement. His allowance from the organization was set at £3 a week to cover all expenses including 'travel and refreshment to any soldier you may have to meet'.[6] Stephens added an injunction that Devoy be prudent: 'You owe me this, to justify the appointment of so young a man to so responsible a post'.[7]

Stephens could not have made a better choice. Devoy was resourceful and canny, and an efficient administrator. Because he could not personally visit all the military stations throughout Ireland, he appointed local men as his lieutenants who came regularly to Dublin to report and receive fresh instructions. Devoy himself concentrated his efforts on the capital.

In 1865 Devoy estimated that there were 8,000 sworn members of the IRB among the ranks of the 26,000 regular troops in Ireland. In addition there was the militia, numbering 12,000 men, of whom more than half were Fenians. Of the garrison of 6,000 soldiers in Dublin, 1,600 were sworn members of the organization.[8]

Devoy did not have a regular office or headquarters but planned his activities from several 'safe' addresses in the city. One of them survived until quite recently, a little public house in Clare Lane off Clare Street, not far from Merrion Square. Peter Curran was the landlord and a 'friend', which in the code of the times signified a member of the IRB. Another safe address was Hoey's public house in Bridgeford Street, not far from the Royal Barracks. In these and other pubs Devoy organized meetings in back parlours and received, secretly, troopers in their uniforms who came to swear allegiance, not to the Queen but to the new Republic.

Devoy first sought O'Reilly at Island Bridge Barracks in the western outskirts of Dublin. 'I had been working for some weeks on the regiment before I even knew of his existence', he wrote, 'and none of my predecessors had any knowledge of him'.[9] Devoy posed as a relative of O'Reilly's and, together with a companion, enquired of the troop sergeant major his whereabouts. The sergeant was 'a bluff hearty Englishman of the best type' who insisted on giving the visitors a cup of tea. 'He praised O'Reilly to the skies, said he was the best young soldier in the regiment and predicted a great future for him.'[10]

The two visitors, regretting that they had to trick so honest a fellow, were directed to Victoria Barracks on the other side of the Liffey. There they found Trooper O'Reilly in the stable tightening the saddle girths of his horse prior to setting off for the vice-regal lodge with a dispatch for the Lord Lieutenant. Devoy described O'Reilly then as a handsome, lithely-built young man of twenty years, immaculately turned out in the dark blue uniform of the 10th Hussars: gold-braided across the chest, a shiny black busby set at a jaunty angle on his head, and the bearskin held by a linked brass chain catching under the lower lip; there was also the suspicion of a black moustache on his lips. As O'Reilly sprang into the saddle there was no time for discussion then, but an appointment was made for later that evening; a meeting was to take place at one of Devoy's safe houses.

Whether O'Reilly took the Fenian oath that night, or whether he had been a member of the organization earlier, is not clear. What is clear is that he was quickly enlisted as an IRB agent in his regiment for the purpose of recruiting members. And singularly successful he proved to be, bringing eighty men to Devoy over a period of time. He organized them into troops and drilled them, and also obtained possession of keys and access to stores of arms. O'Reilly, by his charm, bravery and resourcefulness, managed to undermine the traditional loyalty of the whole regiment, and earned the wrath of his commanding officer, Colonel Baker, for having done so.

O'Reilly's abilities were quickly recognized by John Devoy who thought he had a

> good military head...his ideas about the capture of Dublin, and the way to get out of the city, in case we failed, were all practical. Mere boy that he was, he believed that the blow should be struck in Dublin, where our organisation was the strongest and our membership of the British army was largest.[11]

O'Reilly himself provides a graphic picture of the excitement—and danger—of those clandestine meetings in rooms set aside for them above the smoke-filled bars of backstreet Dublin hotels. On one occasion the rebels sat late in council when they were startled by the sound of heavy military boots mounting the stairs outside. Their faces grew tense, teeth were clenched, and they grasped their revolvers in the expectation that, having been betrayed, they would be confronted by an armed guard sent to arrest them.

> A moment after, the door opened and a man in scarlet walked into the room—all knew him well. With full equipment, knapsack, rifle and bayonet, and sixty rounds of ammunition, Hassett [Private Thomas Henry Hassett of the 24th Foot] had deserted from his post and walked straight into the ranks of rebellion. He

was quickly divested of his military accoutrements; scouts went out to a neighbouring clothing store, and soon returned with every requisite for a fully-fledged 'civilian'. The red coat was voted to the fire, and the belt and arms were stored away with the religious hope in the coming fight for an Irish Republic. The next evening one more was added to the group of strangely dressed men who smoked and drank their 'pots o' porter' in a certain house in Thomas Street. The men were all deserters and the last arrival was Hassett. All vainly watching for the coming fight, the poor fellows lived in mysterious misery for several weeks.[12]

With the wholesale recruitment of soldier Fenians and the society still managing to work relatively secretly (the government was suspicious but not well informed) coupled with the presence in the country of large numbers of Irish-American army officers, the time was never more opportune for an armed rising. The psychological moment had arrived.

Stephens had promised that 1865 would be the year of action. He was under great pressure from the American wing, and seemed to be working towards it. As untiring and zealous as ever, he visited branches of the IRB all over Ireland and Scotland in that year, addressing them and preparing them for the signal. It was expected by many of his officers that the Fenians would be 'in the field' before 1 January 1866.[13]

But, unaccountably, Stephens hesitated. In the opinion of many, if he had struck any time in the autumn of 1865 the IRB would have ended British government in Ireland within three months. Stephens—the leader, creator, and inspiration of Fenianism, and a man with a gifted and compelling personality who was neither impulsive nor hot-headed and a born conspirator—bungled it at the critical time.

His men felt betrayed by his failure to act. Devoy wrote years later: 'The signal never came, and all his [O'Reilly's] and other men's risks and sacrifices were thrown away through incompetent and nerveless leadership'.[14]

The game was lost in that autumn of 1865. The government, becoming alarmed at the open talk of rebellion, accumulated evidence and finally made a surprise raid on the offices of the indiscreet Fenian newspaper, the Irish People. Records were seized, arrests were made and the authorities resorted to one of the oldest tricks of counter-revolution—the use of the double agent, or, as he was called in Ireland at the time, the detested 'informer'.

CHAPTER 4

'A Terror to the Throne'

People crushed by law have no hopes but from power.
If laws are their enemies, they will be enemies to laws;
and those, who have much to hope and nothing to lose,
will always be dangerous, more or less.

Edmund Burke

IN 1864 Mr Kelly, water bailiff of Clonmel and a zealous Catholic and patriot, presented himself to the Fenian conspirators in his locality in Tipperary. He showed great enthusiasm for the cause, and when his credentials were checked he was appointed an officer and authorized to form a circle. So zealous and convincing was Mr Kelly, and so apparently sincere in his dealings with recruits, that he quickly made many converts to the Brotherhood. He personally administered the IRB oath.

For the best part of a year Mr Kelly remained, to all appearances, a hard-working, patriotic Fenian organizer, privy to secret Fenian tactics and plans. Not only did he receive the most confidential instructions from the IRB command, but he initiated training, meetings and forays in his area.

But in reality Mr Kelly was Head Constable Talbot, a common policeman, whose duty was to collect evidence of the IRB conspiracy which he did with remarkable efficiency. This he passed on to his superiors and, when the time came, he acted as the government's chief witness at the trials of the military Fenians. After the trials he was held in such loathing by the populace generally that he was gunned down in a crowded Dublin street by an agent of retribution.[1]

There were other informers: simpler, less professional men than Talbot, but nevertheless useful to the government in quashing the republican movement. Inevitably among so many troopers, a few who lacked the courage and commitment to the republican cause were mistakenly invited along to meetings at the safe houses at which O'Reilly, Devoy and others assembled. Such a one was Private Patrick Foley of the 5th Dragoon Guards.

Foley first met O'Reilly and Devoy at Hoey's public house on 14 January 1866 after having admitted to an interest in Fenianism. Also in the group, and recognized by Foley, were James Wilson and Martin Hogan, deserters from the 5th Dragoons and both wearing civilian clothes at that time. Neither the experienced Devoy nor O'Reilly suspected Foley and welcomed him on that and subsequent occasions. Foley, who took the oath with the intention of becoming an informer, was present at meetings when plans were discussed for the general rising which was so eagerly anticipated in the coming weeks. On the mornings following these meetings, Foley would report the proceedings verbally to his commanding officer.

Nor was Foley the only informer building up a case against Devoy and the military Fenians. A private named Maher of the 1st Battalion, 8th Regiment attended the meetings and took the Fenian oath with the intention of carrying information to the authorities. He was present the night Devoy and O'Reilly, sketch map of the barracks in hand, discussed plans for hamstringing the Dragoons' horses (snipping the tendons in the hind legs so as to disable them) on receiving the signal for rebellion.

It was inevitable that the British Government would pounce sooner or later; the mounting spirit of rebellion, the barely disguised clandestine meetings, and the information supplied by informers could no longer be ignored. Action when it came was swift and efficient.

> Every Irish-American that could be found was arrested, every civilian that was suspect or believed to be dangerous, and some of the army Fenians were uncovered, and arrests followed.[2]

On 22 February detectives and uniformed police stormed Pilsworth's public house in James Street after having been tipped off, probably by Foley who was one of the group arrested and later released. O'Reilly was not there on that occasion but Devoy was. His arrest was particularly calamitous to the military Fenians: their organization disintegrated rapidly from that moment. Other arrests followed. When Trooper John Boyle O'Reilly, on duty at Island Bridge Barracks, looked out from the window across the parade ground and saw to his alarm one of his fellow conspirators being led under escort to the guardhouse, he whispered to his companion, 'My turn will come next'.[3] And it did. He too was marched across the same parade ground within forty-eight hours. Initially he was confined to a cell in the guardroom for twenty-six days from 6 March, and he forfeited his pay which at that time was 1s 3d per diem.

At the end of this period, in accordance with strict service procedure, he was taken before his colonel, Valentine Baker, to be charged. The colonel shook his fist in the face of the prisoner and roared: 'Damn you, O'Reilly! You have ruined the finest regiment in the service'.[4]

Official army records show that from 1 April John Boyle O'Reilly was absent from duty musters and 'In confinement, awaiting trial'.[5] For three months the prisoner languished in Arbor Hill Military Prison, Dublin while the authorities went on collecting evidence, making more arrests and corroborating reports. Exhaustive efforts were made to extort a confession from the prisoner, to extract from him information about his fellow conspirators. He was warned that if he did not cooperate he would face the death sentence if convicted; but if he did cooperate he would be allowed to go free. However, O'Reilly was not for sale.

He spent his time writing patriotic songs and ballads, one a sentimental poem describing an old clock on the wall of his schoolroom in Dowth Castle. The poem tells of a return visit to his school some years after he had left when he observed the clock had been replaced by a modern Yankee piece. Although much of O'Reilly's poetry is now hard to find, 'The Old School Clock', sentimental and poignant, is one of the better known of his works and occasionally turns up in anthologies:

> 'Twas a quaint old clock with a quaint old face,
> and great iron weights and chain.
> It stopped when it liked, and before it struck
> it creaked as if 'twere in pain.
> It had seen many years, and it seemed to say,
> 'I'm one of the real old stock',
> To the youthful fry, who with reverence looked
> on the face of the old school clock.
> What a terrible frown did the old clock wear
> to the truant who timidly cast
> An anxious eye on those merciless hands,
> that for him had been moving too fast!
> But its frown soon changed, for it loved to smile
> on the thoughtless, noisy flock,
> And it creaked and whirred, and struck with glee,
> Did that genial, good humoured old clock.
> Well, years had passed, and my mind was filled
> with the world, its cares and ways,
> When again I stood in that little school
> where I passed my boyhood days.
> *My old friend was gone!* And there hung a thing
> that my sorrow seemed to mock,
> As I gazed with a tear and a softened heart
> at a new-fashioned Yankee clock.

> 'Tis the way of the world. Old friends pass away
> and fresh faces arise in their stead.
> But still 'mid the din and the bustle of life
> we cherish fond thoughts of the dead.
> Yes, dearly those memories cling round my heart,
> and bravely withstand Time's rude shock;
> But not one is more dear or more hallowed to me
> than the face of that old school clock.[6]

This and other verses were secreted in a ventilator of the cell and miraculously survived to find their way, by a circuitous route, back into the hands of the author in America many years later. That he could choose such a commonplace subject for his poem while he was in prison facing, for all he knew, the death sentence, is surely an indication of the casual attitude he must have had to his situation at that time.

Towards the end of June 1866, the mess of the 85th Regiment at the Royal Barracks, Dublin was formally rearranged to accommodate the proceedings of a court martial. Since practically all units on service in Ireland had been infiltrated by Fenians lately arrested, all were involved in a series of trials. O'Reilly's turn to face his judges came on the 27th of the month—the day before his twenty-second birthday. The president of the court was Colonel Sawyer of the 6th Dragoon Guards; the prosecutor was Captain Whelan of the 8th Regiment who was assisted by a Queen's Counsel. The prisoner was defended by Mr O'Loughlen who was assisted by a solicitor with the unlikely name, under the circumstances, of John Lawless.

Court proceedings began with the charge being read out against the prisoner:

> Having at Dublin, in January 1866, come to the knowledge of an intended mutiny in Her Majesty's Forces in Ireland, and not giving information of intended mutiny to his commanding officer.

'How does the Prisoner plead?' was the routine question from Colonel Sawyer. 'Not guilty, Sir', replied Mr O'Loughlen.[7] Captain Whelan was then invited to open the case for the prosecution, and addressed the court:

> The enormity of the offence with which the prisoner is charged is such that it is difficult to find language by which to describe it. It strikes at the root of all military discipline, and, if allowed to escape punishment which it entails, would render Her Majesty's Forces—who ought to be the guardians of our lives and liberty, and the bulwark and protection of the constitution under which we live—a source of danger to the State, and all its loyal citizens and subjects would

become the prey and victims of military despotism, licentiousness and violence. Our standing army would then be a terror to the throne, and a curse, not a blessing, to the community...

Whelan went on to remind the court of its duty to carefully weigh the evidence put before it, and that this evidence would prove the prisoner was an active member of the Fenian conspiracy. Furthermore, it would prove that he had endeavoured to induce other soldiers to join him.

The prosecution case against O'Reilly rested on the testimonies of the informers, Constable Talbot (alias Kelly), Patrick Foley and Maher; and of other soldiers who, while not active informers, had frequented the public houses where the Fenians met, but had not taken the oath. They had observed what was afoot, but had not reported it. One by one they denied complicity and although one suspects that they may have been sympathetic to the republican cause, in the witness stand at least, they acted as loyal soldiers of the Crown.

The first witness, Lance Corporal Fitzgerald of the 10th Hussars, admitted that he had met O'Reilly in Hoey's public house sometime in November and O'Reilly had been with Devoy at the time:

We three sat down together and I asked Devoy who was carrying on this affair. He said, 'Stephens'. I asked whether there were any arms and ammunition. He said there was. And they were getting lots every day from America. I asked who were to be their officers. He said it was to be so carried on that privates did not know their non-commissioned officers, nor they their officers.

Fitzgerald went on to describe how Devoy and O'Reilly had left the room and after a few minutes O'Reilly came back and said that Devoy wanted to speak to him alone, down in the yard. Fitzgerald went downstairs and Devoy addressed him: 'I suppose O'Reilly has told you what I want with you?'. Fitzgerald told the court that he had replied to Devoy, 'I do not know'.

Fitzgerald then testified that Devoy said they wanted him to join the Fenians, and to do so it was necessary to take the oath. This confirms the general policy of the IRB that the oath was always administered by a civilian, the head of a circle, and never by a serving soldier. Fitzgerald, according to his testimony, said he refused to take the oath and the two men returned upstairs to O'Reilly. The president of the court then asked Fitzgerald what he meant by constantly using the words 'this business' and he replied: 'I mean the Fenian conspiracy'.

Occasionally throughout the prosecution case O'Reilly, as was his right, objected to questions being put, such as when conversations were reported at which a third person was not present. Generally these objections were overruled.

At least one prosecution witness proved less than satisfactory. Private McDonald of the 10th Hussars said he had been to Pilsworth's public house about Christmas time, but surprised the court by saying he did not know the names of those who were there and that there was no conversation relating to Fenianism. Evidently this was not what the president expected him to say and McDonald was reminded sternly that he was on oath to tell the truth. McDonald continued to be evasive.

Further witnesses were called including Privates Denis Denny and John Smith, both of the 10th Hussars, and they described how they had met O'Reilly in private hotel rooms where they played cards, smoked and talked of revolution.

The most damning evidence, as to be expected, was given by the informers Foley and Maher. First one and then the other took the stand, forming the climax to the prosecution's case. They reported Fenian meetings and conversations and named those present. Foley said that he had 'most decidedly taken the oath with the intention of breaking it', and Private Maher said he had taken the oath 'out of curiosity to see what the Irish conspiracy, or republic, as they called it, was'.

Maher's evidence concluded the case for the prosecution. At that point the prisoner's guilt, as charged, seemed pretty firmly established. The procession of witnesses telling their stories of illicit meetings, oath-taking and Fenian intrigue in the smoky bars and upstairs private rooms of Dublin's backstreet public houses, all clearly implicated O'Reilly.

So far the trial had lasted three days. The court was then adjourned until 7 July to give the defence time to prepare its case.

CHAPTER 5

PRISONER 9843

I never saw sad men who looked
With such a wistful eye
Upon that little tent of blue
We prisoners call the sky,
And at every happy cloud that passed
In such strange freedom by.

Oscar Wilde

THE unforgiving, punitive machinery of British military justice closed around Trooper O'Reilly like iron pincers when the tribunal reassembled on Saturday, 7 July 1866.

The prisoner was marched into the makeshift courtroom and the defence presented its case. Counsel began by thanking the assembly for the patient consideration they had bestowed on the prosecution's case throughout the trial so far, and stated that the prisoner had no doubt that those qualities would be exhibited in consideration of the points which would be submitted to them for his defence. Counsel for the defence declared that:

There is only one charge which the court has to consider and that is: 'Having come to the knowledge of an intended mutiny...'. To sustain that charge the prosecutor should prove, first, that there was a mutiny actually intended; second, that he—the prisoner—had a knowledge of that intention; and third, that he possessed that knowledge in January 1866, and did not communicate it to his commanding officer. The prosecutor was bound to prove each and every one of these allegations, by evidence on which the court might safely act.

A confident opening but one not supported by ensuing argument. The defence case was weak from the start but whether this was because of incompetence on the part of those advising O'Reilly, or perhaps their prejudice, or a feeling that the game was lost anyway and the defence was merely a matter of form, it is hard to know. The arguments put forward rested mainly on pointing out discrepancies between various witnesses, and the contradictions between two of them, namely Privates Denny and Smith. Denny, it was alleged, had clearly committed perjury. Of the known informers who had given evidence it was asked:

> What was the amount of credit to be given to those men, when they both took the Fenian oath, the one, as he said, through curiosity; the other with the deliberate design of informing?

The prisoner, through his defence counsel, reminded the court that the commanding officer, Colonel Baker, had testified to his good character. Then the captain of O'Reilly's troop, Barthorp, was called. He stated in answer to questions that he had known the prisoner for three years and that his character was good.

Although the prosecution case had taken three days, O'Reilly's defence was concluded within one day. The court then adjourned until the following Monday.

When it reassembled on 9 July the outcome of the case must have been evident to everyone, not least to O'Reilly, the one who was to lose most by it. Captain Whelan, the prosecutor, was invited to respond to the defence, and proceeded to refute the claim that his witnesses were unreliable. He insisted that they were all trustworthy and credible, and argued that the discrepancies which had been pointed out in their evidence were such as would naturally arise, and only proved that they were telling the truth.

The deputy judge advocate then proceeded with his summing-up:

> The court should bear in mind that the existence of an intended mutiny should be proved before the prisoner should be found guilty of the charges upon which he was arraigned. The court should also bear in mind that it was for it to prove charges and not for the prisoner to disprove them.

He then referred to the question of whether the prisoner had knowledge of an intended mutiny, and said it was up to the court to prove this. Because O'Reilly did not give notice of such a mutiny to his commanding officer, it became a subject of enquiry whether any such mutiny was intended. The deputy judge advocate went on:

> On this point they had the evidence of Head Constable Talbot, and they should attentively weigh it. Assuming that it [a mutiny] was intended, and that the prisoner was aware of it, and an accomplice in the design, they had then no less than eight witnesses to prove that complicity.

He then went minutely and lucidly through the evidence, pointing out to the court where it was favourable to the prisoner, or bore against him. Finally, he advised those who had the task of returning a verdict:

> [Y]ou may feel very great suspicion of the prisoner's guilt, and yet if you are not satisfied that the charge is proved home to him beyond rational doubt, no amount of suspicion will justify conviction. Apply to your consideration of the evidence the same calm, deliberate and faithful attention and judgement which you would apply to your most serious affairs. The law demands no more, and your duty will be satisfied with no less.

O'Reilly's trial was conducted by the highest category of court martial, known as a general court martial, which was reserved for the most serious cases, rather than the lesser category termed 'regimental' or district courts martial. These were limited in the penalties they might impose whereas the general court had power to punish by death or penal servitude. It consisted of not less than nine officers, each of whom must have had not less than three years service, with five of those nine holding the rank of captain or above. At the conclusion of the deputy judge advocate's address, these nine retired to consider their finding.

They were not long about it. The officers returned to the court that same afternoon and all were in agreement. Their only delay was to ask Adjutant Russell of the 10th Hussars to give testimony to the prisoner's character. Russell pleaded successfully for leniency on behalf of the youthful prisoner, in as much as the formal death sentence was commuted to twenty years penal servitude. Other military Fenians who were sentenced in this series of trials received life imprisonment.

Although there were some aspects of the trial that may seem to us shoddy and unfair—the president's biased questioning of some of the witnesses and the irresolute defence case, for example—it would be unreasonable to expect that the authorities could have come to a different conclusion. O'Reilly was a soldier in the British Army, voluntarily drafted, who had taken an oath of allegiance to the Crown. He had broken that oath. Fifteen years later, when O'Reilly was editor of the Boston *Pilot*, he went as far as admitting in an editorial that '[the] courts-martial were fairly constituted, and that justice was done them by their judges'.[1]

What might seem unjust was the procedure whereby the prisoner was marched out of court and escorted to Mountjoy Prison without being informed of the verdict or the sentence, adding much to his mental punishment. According to custom, prisoners were not informed of the verdict or the sentence until the day on which the humiliating ceremony of being drummed out of the regiment took place. In O'Reilly's case this was set for two months after the trial.

Only in name, certainly not in nature, was Mountjoy Prison a mount of joy. Its curious title was derived from an Irish peer, Viscount Mountjoy, on part of whose estate it was built. Traditional in design, it consisted of four grey, four-storey cell blocks radiating from a central square tower like the spokes of a wheel. Around the three sides of each block were the 'galleries', the metal walkways which gave access to the rows of cells. Outside in the open air was a giant circular cage bounded by railings of a style common in Victorian zoos. Instead of elephants or tigers behind bars there were prisoners pacing around the perimeter watched by an armed guard, for this was the exercise yard.

On Monday, 3 September O'Reilly attended his drumming out ceremony in the Royal Square, Royal Barracks. Several thousand troops paraded that day: the 10th Dragoon Guards; the 2nd Battalion, 3rd Regiment; the 75th Regiment; the 92nd Highlanders; and the 85th Light Infantry. With full military pomp and brass bands O'Reilly, for the last time dressed in the full uniform of which he had once been so proud, was marched in to face his old comrades. The charge, his guilt, and his sentence were then formally read out, and to the accompaniment of a roll of drums, the prisoner was stripped piece by piece of his military uniform and clothed in convict's dress. He was then marched away under escort back to Mountjoy Prison.

The rough, grey woollen convict garb of buttoned tunic and trousers, the close-shaven hair, and the chains to which he was shackled as he marched

Mountjoy Prison, Dublin in the 1860s. Prisoners exercising in the cage.

John Boyle O'Reilly in convict uniform, Mountjoy Prison, Dublin, 1866.
(Courtesy of the Larcom Collection, Rare Books and Manuscripts Division,
The New York Public Library, Astor, Lenox and Tilden Foundations)

through the streets of Dublin were not sufficient to dampen the irrepressible good spirits and humour of the newly convicted prisoner. In Ireland at the time, the Fenian prisoners would have had something close to the status of heroes among the populace; they were self-styled political prisoners and their cause was judged by the majority to be just. This confidence and pride in their status had given O'Reilly and his fellow prisoners strength in those first weeks of imprisonment; thus the poet Fenian had scratched defiant verses on the wall of his cell together with the postscript: 'Written on the wall of my cell with a nail, July 17th 1866. Once an English soldier; now an Irish Felon; and proud of the exchange'.

In a letter written to his family about this time O'Reilly displayed his inner courage of heart and forestalled any criticism there might have been over his actions:

> I hope I shall be very happy; and even if I am separated from you all for years, I'll pray morning and night for your happiness.
>
> Never grieve for me, I beg you. God knows I'd be only too happy to die for the cause of my country. Pray for me, pray also for the brave true-hearted Irishmen who are with me; we are all brothers who are suffering.
>
> Men who do not understand our motives may call us foolish or mad; but every true Irish heart knows our feelings, and will not forget us.[2]

But those spirits were to be sorely tried and nearly—but never finally—broken by the many months of much harsher incarceration that lay ahead. In English prisons there would be no hint of glory; on English soil he would be regarded by populace and officials alike as a dangerous traitor.

Two other military Fenian prisoners had been committed along with O'Reilly in July: Sergeant McCarthy and Corporal Thomas Chambers. On 4 September, shackled together once more, all three were marched through the streets of the city to a waiting ship, and transported to England; thence to London for a few days transit in Pentonville, North London; and then to Millbank, within sound of the chimes of Westminster.

When Millbank was completed (just fifty years before O'Reilly and his companions arrived) it was considered a model establishment: an enlightened improvement on the older, overcrowded, foully dirty, pestiferous dens described by Dickens and others, and which were the rule rather than exception. A wave of change had swept through the English penitentiary system by the mid-19th century, fired by the great reformers such as John Howard, John Neild, Jeremy Bentham, Elizabeth Fry, and Dickens himself, culminating with the publication of *Little Dorrit* in 1855. As a result of the campaigns of these and others who realized that the old system was a disgrace, land was purchased by the government beside the Thames (the site of the present-day Tate Gallery) and a great new stone structure was erected on Bentham's ideas. Six vast blocks of cells radiated from a central hexagon from which every cell was visible (the design on which Mountjoy had also been based). Every prisoner had his own cell which was a maximum of 12 feet by 8 feet—contemporary sources referred to them as 'spacious'.

Millbank may have been a vast improvement on what had gone before, but it still remained a grim, heartless place of punishment. At that time the reformers, concerned by the corruption, disease and opportunities for further crime inherent in the old system, believed that the best course lay in segregating prisoners by giving them their own cell, and that 'seclusion, employment, and religious instruction' effected penitence and eventual rehabilitation. Dickens was among the few who rejected this particular reform and saw the ghastly reality of what solitary confinement entailed:

I hold this slow and daily tampering with the mysteries of the brain to be immeasurably worse than any torture of the body; and because its ghastly signs are not so palpable to the eye and sense of touch as scars upon the flesh; because its wounds are not upon the surface, and it exhorts few cries that human ears can hear; therefore I the more denounce it, as a secret punishment which slumbering humanity is not roused up to stay.[3]

O'Reilly's cell had a stone floor and bare whitewashed walls. The bed was made of three planks raised off the floor by 3 inches at the foot and 6 inches at the head, so that he slept on a slant. The only other item was a bucket with a lid which contained water for washing and served as a stool on which to sit while picking oakum or coir. Daily rations in Millbank included 8 ounces of bread and three-quarters of a pint of cocoa for breakfast; 4 ounces of meat and a pound of potatoes for dinner; and for supper each night, 6 ounces of bread and a pint of 'skilly' containing oatmeal.

But the severest punishment of Millbank was the silence, broken only by the clanging of cell doors and the Westminster chimes every quarter of an hour, all day of every day of every week for the seven months that O'Reilly and his companions were incarcerated there. Michael Davitt, a contemporary of O'Reilly's who was confined to Millbank about the same time, wrote later:

Oft in the lonely watches of the night, it [the sound of the chimes] reminded me of the number of strokes I was doomed to listen to and how slowly those minutes were creeping along! The weird chant of the Westminster clock will ever haunt my memory, and recall that period of my imprisonment when I first had to implore Divine Providence to preserve my sanity and save me from the madness which seemed inevitable through mental and corporal tortures combined.[4]

Prisoners were forbidden to talk among themselves or to warders, even during the one-hour exercise period each day. This consisted of walking in single file around the quadrangle, with sufficient distance between each prisoner to preclude whispering, followed by a period turning the crank handle of a pump which worked the water system. O'Reilly recalled, some years later, being afraid of associating with the worst of violent criminals (there was no segregation of political prisoners from criminals) when they met for chapel, parade, or exercise. He was particularly afraid of one, a brutal-looking corpse-faced lag, and he described the circumstances of his change of heart:

> I turned towards the centre of the yard, where ran the series of cranks arranged with one handle for two men facing each other. When I got to my place I was face to face with the Corpse-man, and when he turned sideways, I saw his left eye through the scoop in his cheekbone. The officers stood behind me. There were three of them to the gang of twenty men, and their duty was to watch so that no communication took place between the prisoners. I felt that the Corpse-man wanted to talk to me, but he kept his hidden eyes on the officers behind me, and turned the crank without the movement of a muscle in his face. Presently, I heard a whisper, 'Mate', and I knew it must be he who spoke, although still not a muscle seemed to move. I looked at him, and waited. He said again, in the same mysterious mutter, 'Mate, what's your sentence?'.[5]

In spite of the ban on talking there were still other methods of communicating. For example, O'Reilly described in a letter written from prison—possibly from Millbank—how the inmates would knock on the walls of their cells at night as a signal to one another to pray together for their country's freedom: 'Men who, a few months ago were careless, thoughtless soldiers, are now changed into true patriots, however humble'.[6]

We may wonder how O'Reilly managed to survive such an inhuman, harsh regimen and yet remain sane at the end of seven months. The explanation may have been in part due to his youth—he was in his twenty-third year—and his good physical health. He still possessed the optimism of youth. He was imbued with an unshakeable love of his country and a belief in the rightness of its cause. His morale was surprisingly high; his mind ceaselessly active. And he had the poet's imagination and sense of enquiry so that all experiences, however dull they might be to most of us, inspired him with a sense of wonder and mystery. There was also a touch of youthful brashness in the young O'Reilly, amounting to cockiness. Most important of all, he was sustained by a deep, simple religious faith. In Millbank he was required to read religious books daily, and he studied *The Imitation of Christ* by Thomas à Kempis. Therein he might have found solace in the author's advice on the subject of solitude and the advantages of shutting out the tumults of the world: 'Thou shalt find in thy cell what thou shalt often lose abroad', and, 'Thy cell, if thou continue in it, grows sweet; but if thou keep not to it, it becomes tedious and distasteful'. And O'Reilly, although a loyal, practising Catholic all his life, must have been struck by the irony of these words: 'In silence and quiet the devout soul goes forward, and learns the secret of the scriptures'.

In April 1867 O'Reilly and his two companions, Sergeant McCarthy and Corporal Chambers, were transferred in chains to Chatham where the regime of solitary confinement was replaced by heavy manual labour. Here, on the south bank of the Thames estuary on the north Kent shore, they were set to work on the enlargement and extension of the naval dockyard. The place and the time conjure up the images of river fogs, a marshy landscape, and convicts in chains so graphically drawn by Dickens in *Great Expectations* which had been published six years before O'Reilly's experience of the place.

Within a few weeks they were on the move again, to Portsmouth, where similar work was being carried out by convicts. According to Roche, while at both Chatham and Portsmouth, O'Reilly attempted to escape. We have no further details, only that on each occasion he was quickly recaptured and sentenced to a diet of bread and water. It is interesting that the escapes were not reported in O'Reilly's official record (and perhaps leads to some doubt that they took place at all), a puzzling omission given the meticulous reporting of all incidents in the prison service at that time. When O'Reilly arrived in Australia a year later his conduct was recorded simply as 'good' which had an important bearing on later events.[7]

By far the worst privations that O'Reilly suffered in English prisons were the four months experienced in grim Dartmoor where he was sent next in midsummer 1867, prior to transportation. The fortress at Princetown in the centre of high windswept, boggy moorland in Devon, beloved of fiction writers because of its mysterious and isolated location, was built in 1809 to house French prisoners captured in the Napoleonic wars. It had fallen into disuse in the intervening period and was reconstructed and reopened in 1850. Here, prison gangs under close supervision spent their days digging drains on the marshes and quarrying stone on the moors.

In one of his novels set in a future year, O'Reilly described life there in this way:

> In the centre of its wide waste of barren hills, huge granite outcrops, and swampy valleys, the gloomy prison of Dartmoor stood wrapped in mist...Its two centuries of unloved existence in the midst of a wild land and fitful climate, had seared every wall-tower and gateway with lines and patches of discolouration. Originally

45

built of brown stone, the years had deepened the tint almost to black in the larger stretches of outer wall and unwindowed gable...Through the thick drizzle of the early morning the convicts were marched in gangs to their daily tasks; some to build new walls within the prison precincts, some to break stone in the round yard encircled by enormous iron railings fifteen feet high, some to the great kitchen of the prison, and to the different workshops. About a third of the prisoners marched outside the walls by the lower entrance; for the prison stands on a hill, at the foot of which stretches the most forsaken and grisly waste in all Dartmoor.[8]

O'Reilly's two companions, McCarthy and Chambers, who were not sentenced to be transported, survived twelve years of prison torture with a large part of their sentence being spent in Dartmoor. They both died as a result of their sufferings, McCarthy shortly after release and Chambers a few years later, but clearly as a result of his imprisonment. O'Reilly, remembering their Dartmoor days, wrote when he learned of Chambers's death:

For months they [McCarthy and Chambers] toiled in the drains which were only two feet wide, and sunk ten feet in the morass. It was a labour too hard for brutes, the half-starved men, weakened by long confinement, standing in water from a foot to two feet deep, and spading the heavy peat out of the narrow cutting over their heads. Here it was that Chambers and McCarthy contracted the rheumatic and heart diseases which followed them to the end. McCarthy had left a wife and children out in the world whose woes and wanderings throughout the years had racked his heart even more than disease had his limbs. When at last the cell door was opened, and he was told that he was free, the unfortunate man, reaching towards his weeping wife and his children grown out of his recollection, fell dead almost at the threshold of the prison.

Chambers lingered until Sunday morning, his body a mass of aches and diseases that antagonised every moment and puzzled all the skills of the doctors. 'They don't know what is the matter with me', he said with a smile...'but I can tell them. They never saw a man before who was suffering from the drains of Dartmoor'.[9]

Yet O'Reilly appears to have survived comparatively unscathed and one day, according to Roche, made his third unsuccessful break for freedom.

Armed sentries were normally stationed on certain elevated parts of the moor to watch the gangs of prisoners at work in the drains, and to signal the approach of fogs which from time to time rolled in from the sea to envelope the entire moor in a thick grey blanket. The Dartmoor fogs, in both fact and fiction, were an opportunity for escape, and it was important for the warders to round up the gangs and gather them inside the prison walls before the fogs arrived.

On one occasion when a fog was signalled, O'Reilly remained hidden in the drain—and waited. When all his fellow convicts had been returned to the prison and the fog gave him sufficient cover, he made his way quickly beyond the boundaries of the prison towards the coast. Wearing a rough suit of clothes which he had secretly made from the coarse sheets in his cell, he evaded his pursuers for two days and nights, hiding on one occasion on the roof of a house, and later remaining up to his neck in water in a dyke communicating with a river. But escapees from Dartmoor were statistically doomed, and O'Reilly was not among those very few who succeeded. While he was in the water one of the tracking party, some way off, spied a ripple through his field glass and ordered guards to investigate. Soon the plucky fugitive, suffering from exposure and hunger, was discovered in the river and marched back under escort to Dartmoor where he languished for twenty-eight days in the punishment cells on a diet of bread and water. This serious breach of discipline, like the earlier escapes, was unaccountably omitted from O'Reilly's record.

It would have been early in the October of 1867 that O'Reilly first heard rumours that his time in English prisons was drawing to a close and he would shortly be sailing for Australia:

Australia! The ship! Another chance for the old dreams [of escape]; and the wild thought was wilder than ever, and not half so stealthy. Down the corridor came the footsteps again. The keys rattled, doors opened, and in five minutes we had double irons on our arms, and were chained together by a bright strong chain. We did not look into each other's eyes; we had learned to know what the others were thinking of without speaking. We had a long ride to the railway station in a villainous Dartmoor conveyance, and then a long ride in the railway cars to Portland. It was late at night when we arrived there. The ceremony of receiving convicts from another prison is amusing and 'racy of the soil'. To give an idea of it, it is enough to say that every article of clothing which a prisoner wears must at once be sent back to the prison whence it came. It may be an hour, or two, or more, before a single article is drawn from the stores of the receiving prison— during which time the felon is supremely primitive. To the prison officials this seems highly amusing; but to me, looking at it with a convict's eye and feelings, the point of the joke was rather obscure.[10]

Chambers and McCarthy had been left behind in Dartmoor but O'Reilly was united with others at Portland who had lately arrived from Ireland and were now awaiting transportation. One brought news of his elder brother, William, who was serving a sentence in Dublin for Fenian activities. (William, suffering from ill-health since childhood, was to die in captivity while O'Reilly was in Australia.)

Another prisoner awaiting transportation in Portland was the Fenian, John Casey. In his diary he described how some 120 prisoners were inspected by the surgeon superintendent on 7 October and issued with clothes for their coming voyage. On 8 October they were required to work as usual until 9.00 a.m. and were then summoned inside and addressed by the prison governor and a naval officer. Permission was asked of the governor for the men to bid goodbye to comrades who were staying behind. At first he refused, but then relented, 'all men very much affected'.[11]

In the prison yard they all assembled in lines, and were reviewed again by the governor and the doctor. Chains were attached to them once more and the political prisoners separated from the criminals. There were others in the yard that day who looked strangely out of place among the convicts and the prison guards: 'They had bronzed faces, and careless sailors' dress'.[12] These strangers were the crew of the *Hougoumont*, then riding at anchor in Portland harbour, and they were there to superintend the embarkation.

CHAPTER 6

FENIAN FEVER

_____

*A Fenian privateer might destroy all the government
buildings on Rottnest, sink a merchant vessel or two, and
destroy all Fremantle without landing or losing a man
merely because there is not even a gunboat to prevent her.*

George Walpole Leake

BEFORE O'Reilly is escorted aboard the *Hougoumont*, let us take the opportunity to consider briefly the extraordinary political and administrative strategies
governing transportation at that time which were being played out by two
departments of State in London—the Colonial Office and the Home Office—
and the Swan River Colony. These strategies go some way to explain the long
delay between the conviction of the Fenians in Dublin and their eventual
departure from England.

When Western Australia was explored and founded by Captain Stirling in
1829, the settlers boasted of their 'free colony' in contrast to New South Wales,
so notoriously of convict beginnings. Twenty years on, after a period of struggle,
stagnation, and bitter wrangling, the colony's viability was in doubt, due in part
to the absence of a pool of cheap labour. Driven by necessity, the leading
colonists sent a plea to the home government to allow penal settlement. The
importation of convicts was seen to be the only hope.

The British Government reacted favourably when the request was received in
London and moved with unprecedented speed: the opportunities for sending
England's criminals to distant parts of the world had been drying up. New South
Wales had abolished transportation in 1840 and the whole subject of transportation was, by then, a hotly debated controversy. Tasmania ceased transportation in
1853; neither South Australia nor Victoria were convict states. Although opinion
was by no means unanimous among settlers the influential property holders in the
colony managed to force the issue by lobbying the Governor.[1] The first ship
bearing its human cargo—the *Scindian*—arrived off Fremantle on 1 June 1850.

In the eighteen years that followed Western Australia benefited greatly from convict workers; and not merely from the essential public works that they made possible but also because many of them were given tickets-of-leave, granted pardons and went on to become respectable, successful citizens.[2] However, by the 1860s mounting pressure from anti-transportation groups (together with rising costs of shipping and surveillance) shifted public opinion back again. Transportation, it was decided, had served its purpose and therefore would cease in 1867. The home government's decision that no more convicts would be sent to the colony after November of that year had been conveyed to Governor Hampton in Western Australia as early as 1865, the year before O'Reilly's arrest.[3]

On 16 September 1867, just six weeks before transportation was due to cease, the British Secretary of State for the Colonies, the Duke of Buckingham, informed Hampton that a convict transport was being chartered to carry 280 male convicts to Fremantle. It is of considerable significance that he did not mention in his dispatch (which would have arrived in Western Australia after the departure of the *Hougoumont*) that sixty-two Fenians would be included in that number; and of that number seventeen had been British soldiers. As the Colonial Office's firm policy at the time was to exclude military Fenians from transportation we are left asking the question: why were seventeen military Fenians—including O'Reilly—ever sent to Western Australia? Did Buckingham deliberately hide the facts so as not to alarm Hampton, or did he simply not know they were on board? William Burgess, an Irish Protestant West Australian pastoralist who attacked the decision to dispatch the Fenians, alleged that Governor Hampton had been asked to accept the Fenians at an earlier date but 'had refused to have them as it would only draw upon the colony an American raid to liberate them, and he had no means to resist'.[4] If this allegation were true, then it would appear Buckingham had withheld the important information deliberately. Another more plausible explanation is possible: that the Home Office, fearing objection, failed to inform the Colonial Office of what it was about. In a dispatch to the Under-Secretary at the Colonial Office, T.F. Elliot, dated December 1867, Hampton expressed his concern about rumours that Fenians were being sent to the colony. Elliot added a marginal note for his chief, virtually agreeing with Hampton but saying that he was absent from the office at the time the decision was made, and no references or papers could be found. The Duke of Buckingham added his own excuses:

When I became aware of the intention of the Home Office to send out Fenian Convicts to W.A. I pointed out the probable insecurity and communicated personally with the Home Secretary. The reply was that none but prisoners of no importance were to be sent...[5]

The Times broke the news in London on 10 October that convicts were boarding the *Hougoumont* in the Thames; that the ship was bound for Fremantle, Western Australia; and that twenty-three Fenians were among their number. More would join the ship at south coast ports. The announcement alerted West Australian visitors in London at the time and one of them, C.P. Measor, wrote to several London papers attacking the wisdom of including Fenians:

> We know from Manchester and other instances what the folly of Fenianism will dare, and a considerable number of turbulent spirits are among the miscreants [on the *Hougoumont*] who have now left their country for their country's good. A few months ago we might have thought the police-van mania an impossible ebullition of the lawless mind; but a scene of carnage on the ocean, and resistance there to lawful authority, is quite as much within the range of possibility where a mixture of desperate men of the worst criminal type with Irish-American rowdies who consider themselves martyrs constitutes three-fourths of the living beings cooped up in a convict ship. It will be a mercy if the *Hougoumont* reaches the Swan River without some frightful scene.[6]

The reference to the police van incident in Manchester alluded to the daring rescue by Fenians in that city of two of their leaders, Colonel Kelly and Captain Deasy, as they were being conveyed from court to prison in broad daylight. One of the guards was killed and five Fenians were later arrested and sentenced to death. The Manchester incident and other Fenian attacks were widely reported in Australian papers so that colonists were inclined to believe that all Fenians were violent men bent on acts of terrorism, and that the colony was lucky to be far away from the scene of the troubles.

When home mail arrived in Fremantle in December confirming that some of these same Fenians were even then approaching the coast, alarm akin to panic broke out among the settlers; there were protest meetings, rumours and letters to the papers:

> Perhaps a shipload of more daring reckless men never floated on the ocean, and the probability of an attempt being made to seize the ship on her passage out is far from unlikely. Should such however not be the case, and they arrived here and are placed within the walls of the Establishment what a continual source of anxiety they will prove to the authorities and the inhabitants.[7]

On 18 December, some three weeks before the arrival of the *Hougoumont*, a deputation led by two wealthy English pastoralists, William Brockman and Samuel Phillips, confronted Governor Hampton. They advised him strongly of the feelings of the majority of settlers whom they claimed to represent, and argued that Fenians in their midst would pose a threat to the security of the colony.[8]

Hampton told the deputation that their fears were greatly exaggerated, but agreed to ask the Admiralty in Sydney to send an armed vessel to protect Fremantle in the unlikely event of a Fenian vessel being sent to rescue the convicts, this being the settlers' chief fear. Privately, he must have had his own misgivings based on the information he was receiving from some of his advisers. Captain Charles Manning, for example, a leading land-holder and commander of a West Australian volunteer force, wrote to the colony's military commanding officer and the letter was passed on to Hampton:

> For some months past I have had hints given me of a probable rising among some of the Bond people and the inmates of the convict establishment, of their holding possession of the town for a few hours, and seizing vessels in the harbour, carrying off what booty they could secure and such women in their raid as they might take a fancy to. Now, Sir, no one in this Colony knows better than I do the daring audacity and disregard of life of American ruffians. Two or three of them as leaders, could, before the *Hougoumont* discharged her surplus stores, have full possession of her, sail her away with such of our wives and daughters they might please to select and three or four hundred convicts that assisted them in their enterprise...[9]

Fear among the colonists was not allayed by Hampton's assurances. Late in December he received further evidence of the extent of their alarm. Edward Newman, a wealthy British merchant and member of the Town Trust, called for immediate measures to prevent Fremantle from being sacked and bombarded, and hinted that some colonists were planning to prevent the Fenians from being landed when the ship arrived.

Fremantle was the centre of the storm. As the port of disembarkation and the home of the gaol where the Fenians would reside, its citizens naturally believed they were the ones in mortal danger. Perth on the other hand, being 10 miles upriver, seemed blissfully safe and unconcerned. Neither did it escape their notice that the Governor, who also appeared unconcerned—or at any rate less concerned than they were—lived in Perth. For this reason no doubt Hampton, in a dramatic gesture, moved himself and his family from Government House to Fremantle:

> I at once removed to that town with my family and establishment, publicly announcing my intention to remain there until the Fenians were disposed of; at the same time quietly endeavouring to allay the apprehension of the residents, and without attracting their attention making every practical arrangement which

52

the means at my disposal would admit of for promptly dealing with any contingency that might arise.[10]

Not all colonists shared the concerns of the alarmists. The Catholic chaplain of Perth prison, Father Matthew Gibney, and another prominent Catholic, J.T. Reilly, called on Hampton a few days before the *Hougoumont* arrived and assured him that there was no cause for concern. They asked that the Fenians be kept in one group, and said that if they were treated fairly like other prisoners they were sure not to give trouble.[11] There were others, representing the liberal view, who believed that it was a small minority of Irish Protestant and English immigrants who had exaggerated the threat thereby importing and maintaining all the old Anglo-Irish bitterness.

Thus the colonists waited, watching the western horizon for the first sign of a sail: some believing that a period of rape and pillage was about to descend on them; some ready to believe that the Fenians would certainly be no worse, and perhaps even better behaved, than the average convict. And doubtless there were a few citizens of Irish descent, highly amused at the distorted stories of Fenian terror, half-hoping that some of them were true.

As they wait, let us return to England in October 1867 where the *Hougoumont* is sailing around the coast of Kent escorted by the gunboat *Earnest*. There are thirty-six Fenians on board. Others join in Portsmouth and yet more in Portland, including John Boyle O'Reilly.

CHAPTER 7

ON BOARD THE *HOUGOUMONT*

Who, as he watches her silently gliding,
Remembers that wave after wave is dividing
Bosoms that sorrow and guilt could not sever,
Hearts that are broken and parted for ever?
Or deems that he watches, afloat on the wave,
The death-bed of hope, or the young spirit's grave?

John Boyle O'Reilly

PRISON cells do not normally afford scenic views from their barred windows but if John Boyle O'Reilly could have glimpsed his surroundings from the high vantage point of Portland, where he was temporarily incarcerated, his poetic heart would surely have been impressed.

The Isle of Portland, more accurately to be described as a peninsular, is a wild and precipitous headland rising 150 metres above the sea, thrusting out into the English Channel from the Dorset coast 13 kilometres distant. The headland, or 'Bill', is joined to the mainland by a narrow ridge of shingle, Chesil Bank. Rising from the sea like a sleeping giant Portland Bill presents an awesome barrier to vessels plying up and down channel, and unless ships have business in the harbour or in nearby Weymouth, they give it a wide berth. Many a sailing ship has been lost in the turbulent waters of famous Portland Race off the southern extremity.

The Bill makes an ideal site for a prison, being inaccessible from the sea and approachable only by way of Chesil Bank. It also seems an ideal site for a naval anchorage, being naturally protected from the south, west and east by two great curving breakwaters like pincers which were built of Portland stone quarried by the convicts. In October 1867 the view from high up on Verne Hill, looking north-east, would have taken in the vast expanse of the harbour dotted with the masts and spars of ships at anchor. There would also have been iron-built, steam-powered vessels in the harbour as they were beginning to make their appearance in the navy by the 1850s and 1860s.

On the morning of 6 October the Portland fleet was joined by two newly arrived ships: the gunboat, *Earnest*, and the transport, *Hougoumont*. Both had sailed from Sheerness on the Thames with their human cargo of Fenians and other assorted convicts. O'Reilly described the *Hougoumont* as 'riding within the dark shadow of the gloomy cliff, upon which is built one of the greatest of the English imperial prisons'.[1]

The *Hougoumont*, named after one of the sites of the Battle of Waterloo, was a Blackwall frigate of 875 tons built in Burma in 1852. Like others of her class she was four-masted with three foremasts each having six square sails and the fourth mast, a mizzen. She was a sleek, handsome vessel, 167 feet in length and 34 feet wide; the bowsprit carrying a jib and three staysails added to her overall length. She had been chartered to the French Government during the Crimean War, and afterwards resumed service as a cargo ship and transport. Without disguising her name, O'Reilly described her in his fictional account of the voyage as, 'a large old-fashioned merchant ship of two thousand tons burden; a slow sailer, but a strong and roomy vessel'.[2]

On charter to the British Government in 1867, the *Hougoumont* had been modified to carry convicts. Its upper deck had been partitioned into three areas by means of 9-foot high wooden barriers. The barriers had doors so that sailors could pass through while working the ship, but there were soldiers with loaded rifles posted to prevent the convicts from using them.[3] The lower deck was similarly divided into three sections, the iron-reinforced bulkheads having holes in them so that the guards could fire their carbines on the prisoners if the need arose. The non-Fenian convicts and the soldier Fenians were accommodated in

The convict ship Hougoumont. (*Courtesy of the Battye Library, Ships' Index C.88*)

a section amidships; the civilian Fenians in the after section; and the crew in the forward section. Each section had its own hatchway with a ladder to the upper deck, and the two serving the convicts were enclosed by iron cages from floor to ceiling. In order to pass from the lower to upper deck it was necessary to first enter the cage through an iron gate guarded by an armed sentry and then climb the ladder. The arrangement gave plenty of air and a good deal of light below, the only obstruction being the bars. 'The convicts below never tired of looking upwards through the bars, though they could see nothing above but the swaying ropes and sails, and at night the beautiful sky and the stars.'[4]

In the prison yard the contingent joining the *Hougoumont* had been checked and secured to their chains with twenty men to each chain. The gates were then opened, and the order given, 'Forward there!'. With a loud jangling of iron the men moved forward painfully, awkwardly, under armed escort. O'Reilly was there amongst them, no doubt thankful that his experience of English prisons was at an end. Casey, in his diary, recounted that they talked among themselves during the walk to the pier and that the officers repeatedly reprimanded them. It was a Tuesday; the weather was fine with occasional showers. Crowds collected on the wharf to see them go.

A paddle-driven steam pinnace was waiting to take the prisoners on board the transport at anchor some distance from the quay. Just as the column of shuffling men reached the gangway to go on board the steamer, a woman's piercing shriek rose up from the crowd on the wharf. It was a young Irish girl, the sister of one of the prisoners, Thomas Dunne, who had come from Dublin in the hope of seeing her brother before his exile. She burst through the crowd and threw herself around the neck of the poor man in chains, sobbing and screaming all the while.

> Poor Dunne could only stoop his head and kiss his sister—his arms were chained; and that loving heart-broken girl, worn out by grief, clung to his arms and his chains as they dragged her away; and when she saw him pushed rudely to the gangway, she raised her voice in a wild cry: 'Oh, God! Oh, God!' as if reproaching Him who willed such things to pass. From the steamer's deck we saw her still watching tirelessly and we tried to say words of comfort to that brother—her brother and ours. He knew she was alone, and had no friends in wide England...[5]

The steamer's manoeuvre alongside the *Hougoumont* was not without incident. The bow of the tender collided with the hull of the larger ship, damaging the smaller vessel. When the excitement subsided the convicts clambered aboard, though how precisely they would have done this while still in chains is not clear. Lined up on deck, the chains were knocked off and then they were ordered below. As they climbed down the hatchway, surrounded by the iron grill as if they were entering a cage, prisoners already on board since Sheerness and Portsmouth pushed and jostled on the other side of the bars to get a look at the new arrivals. O'Reilly observed:

> As I stood in that hatchway, looking at the wretches glaring out, I realised more than ever before the terrible truth that a convict ship is a floating hell...There swelled up a hideous diapason from that crowd of wretches; the usual prison restraint was removed, and the reaction was at its fiercest pitch. Such a din of diabolical sounds no man ever heard. We hesitated before entering the low-barred door to the hold, unwilling to plunge into the seething den. As we stood thus, a tall gaunt man pushed his way through the criminal crowd to the door. He stood within, and stretching out his arms, said, 'Come, we are waiting for you'. I did not know the face: I knew the voice. It was my old friend and comrade, Keating.[6]

Keating led O'Reilly through another door amidships where he came face to face with his fellow Fenians—his brothers—who were housed apart from the criminals: 'Great God! What a scene that was, and how vividly it arises in my mind now!'.

O'Reilly's joy at being united with his comrades can hardly be exaggerated. Their common heritage, their shared patriotism and belief in the republican cause, their shared imprisonment, their humour and their support of one another was to sustain them and ameliorate their sufferings in the months ahead. Intensely and incorrigibly gregarious as the Irish people are generally recognized to be, these articulate Fenians could have experienced no greater deprivation than to be isolated from the company of friends.

Among those who greeted O'Reilly that first day on the *Hougoumont* and who were to remain part of his inner circle of friends throughout the voyage, and beyond, were: John Flood, aged thirty-two, a Wexford man who had studied law and was sentenced to fifteen years penal servitude; Thomas Duggan from Cork, the oldest of the group at forty-four and a teacher by profession, sentenced to ten years penal servitude; John Sarsfield Casey from Mitchelstown, County Cork, aged twenty-three and who wrote patriotic newspaper articles under the nom de plume 'Galtee Boy'; Denis Cashman from Waterford, aged twenty-seven, a clerk who left a wife and three children in Ireland with whom he was later united in Boston where he became business manager on O'Reilly's newspaper; and Edward John Kelly, aged twenty-seven, a carpenter from Cork, who also joined O'Reilly in Boston at the end of his sentence.

Of the 280 convicts on board sixty-two were Fenians—known as political prisoners—and of these seventeen were military Fenians, including O'Reilly. The ship's complement included forty-two crew, forty-four pensioner guards, and eighteen pensioners' wives and their twenty-five children. There were also warders and their children, two chaplains, and a surgeon totalling 431 beings under the command of Captain William Cozens. It is almost impossible for us to imagine today the overcrowding on a ship of the *Hougoumont*'s size and the extraordinary discomfort that must have been the lot of all on board over a period of three months or more. We may get some idea by visualizing the interior of a modern intercontinental Boeing 747 flying between the United Kingdom and Australia with a full load of passengers—approximately the same number as sailed on the *Hougoumont*; and yet the open deck space on the ship would have been less than the area in the Boeing passenger cabin.[7]

Crowded conditions aboard a convict ship similar to the Hougoumont.

The guards on the ship, some of whom had served in the same regiments as the Fenians, were generally well disposed towards the Irishmen and allowed the military Fenians, officially classed as criminals, to associate with the civilians during the day; and after a period of time they even allowed O'Reilly (contrary to the rules) to remain with his companions at night.

During the remainder of that day they exchanged news and talked of the 'perfidy and treachery of Stephens' in his reluctance to call for a rising and his subsequent escape from Ireland. But when evening came, their bitterness on this subject gave way to their native ebullience and shared love of Irish music and poetry.

After supper our friends entertain us with some well known songs of our dear native land and once more we roam in spirit—over green fields and sunny hills by the sparkling streams and through the romantic old ruins of old Erin. 8 o'clock to bed. No sleep for us talking all night—a new life this to that of Portland.[8]

In that first of many concerts aboard Mr O'Reilly presented a recitation, a poem entitled 'In Memory of the French Prisoners', and we can judge from this that already the military Fenian was allowed to mix with his civilian counterparts.

For the next three days the *Hougoumont* remained at anchor preparing for her voyage. On Wednesday the governor of Portland Prison came aboard and 'very graciously bid us adieu. How different his manner [is] to us compared to a month since'.[9]

On Saturday, 12 October, with the last of the free passengers aboard, the stores loaded and the convicts securely confined down below, the crew weighed anchor at 2.55 p.m. The *Hougoumont* was towed out by the *Earnest* between the port and starboard arms of the breakwaters of Portland in an easterly direction. Making a great sweep until they were facing west and well clear of danger, the two ships gave the Shambles rocks and Portland a wide berth. Then the *Hougoumont*'s sails were set for her course down channel towards Ushant and the *Earnest* dropped her towline. And so the last ship to leave English shores conveying convicts to Australia bent to the breeze, and more than 300 souls who were aboard ship for the first time began to experience the disturbing motion of the waters. The gunship *Earnest* remained in attendance, on the alert for a rumoured attempt to rescue the Fenians on board.

On the first morning at sea the Fenians were allowed on deck. The weather, though fair, had the ship rolling on her way down the English Channel and John Casey recorded that he felt seasick. Father Delaney, the Catholic chaplain, said mass and Casey served with difficulty. Delaney was a 33-year-old devout Dublin priest who courageously volunteered to accompany the Fenians on their voyage, and was to become a great friend and solace to them. In service in Western Australia he built a new church and the first Catholic school in Albany. He went on to serve parishes in Perth, Fremantle, Guildford and Geraldton before retiring as chaplain to St Joseph's Orphanage in Perth, where he died in 1893.

Below decks the Fenians made themselves as comfortable as possible. They were divided into groups of eight, forming a mess, and one member was appointed captain of the mess to collect provisions and act as spokesman. Breakfast usually consisted of ship's biscuit and tea or hot chocolate. Dinner served in the middle of the day was usually pea soup, salted beef and preserved potatoes. A glass of wine was issued at 2.00 p.m. each day, and gruel at 4.00 p.m. A convict also received a pint of water each day, an occasional tobacco issue, and fruit when available.

At the beginning of the voyage O'Reilly had to sleep in the main convict section of the ship, being a military Fenian. It is not known for certain how soon he was allowed to spend all his time with the others, but if the first night's concert is any indication, it seems most of the guards were indulgent towards him. His description of life on board in his novel *Moondyne* conveys a grimmer picture:

> The first few days of the voyage are inexpressibly horrible. The hundreds of pent-up wretches are un-used to the darkness of the ship, strange to their crowded quarters and to each other, depressed in spirits at their endless separation from home, sickened to death with the merciless pitch and roll of the vessel, alarmed at the dreadful thunder of the waves, and fearful of sudden engulfment, with the hatches barred. The scene is too hideous for a picture—too dreadful to be described in words.[10]

Five days out from Portland the *Hougoumont* encountered heavy weather in the Bay of Biscay, and in the midst of the unpleasant motion the cry went up 'Sail Ho!'. It was supposed the much hoped for Fenian cruiser was bearing down on them to effect a rescue. When the rumour circulated the bulwarks were crowded with anxious, excited prisoners waiting for their deliverance. To give substance to their hopes the approaching vessel appeared not to display identification, and while the Fenians held their breath in anticipation the crew of the *Hougoumont* studied her with some anxiety, the captain with his glass to his eye. The excitement, especially amongst the Fenians, became near hysterical.

In an instant, their hopes crashed; the Union Jack was spied fluttering on the yard and a friendly cheer could be heard from her decks. The 'Fenian cruiser' turned out to be none other than an English merchant ship bound for Liverpool with a cargo of rice.

On 19 October, midway across the Bay of Biscay, the storm reached its peak. Wind howled with violence through the rigging, fierce squalls tore the canvas to shreds, and heavy seas crashed over the decks. Two days later the ship was within sight of the coast of Spain, the weather abated, and the Fenians stood at the rail in the warm sunshine admiring the distant mountains through the haze.

> I felt as if I never would weary of admiring the grand majesty of those noble mountains, and while I inwardly cursed the power which held my own dear land in bondage, I sighed for the time when her sons would emulate the example of the chivalrous Spaniard.[11]

The second week at sea brought a different complexion to the voyage. Mediterranean warmth, blue skies, calmer seas and light breezes, with opportunities for meetings and social intercourse, softened the bitterness of the Fenians' predicament. 'The mild airs of the warmer latitudes surprised and delighted those who had only known the moist climate of Britain', wrote O'Reilly.[12] The ship forged on at around 8 to 9 knots, and on 25 October was on the same latitude as the Azores and about 550 miles from Cape St Vincent. The Fenians were charmed by the vivid sunrises and sunsets—'unknown in our latitudes'—and watched shoals of porpoises playing in the waters around the hull.

On 24 October they debated the best means of amusing themselves during the voyage. Denis Cashman proposed theatricals, but this idea was subsequently abandoned because they judged there was insufficient space available for a stage. They did, however, begin a series of concerts in the evenings which proved popular throughout the voyage. Programs were compiled of duets, traditional Irish ballads, and recitations of poetry. John Boyle O'Reilly played a prominent part in most of them by singing and reciting his own ballads.

O'Reilly's ballad poetry of that period was unashamedly sentimental, expressing an idealized bond with, and longing for, the homeland. An early poem, 'Farewell', is characteristic and one of his better known:

> Farewell! Oh how hard and how sad 'tis to speak
> That last word of parting—forever to break
> The fond ties and affection that cling round the heart,
> From home and from friends and from country to part.
> 'Though it grieves to remember, 'tis vain to regret.
> The sad word must be spoken, and memory's spell
> Now steals o'er me sadly. Farewell! Oh farewell!
>
> Farewell to thy green hills, thy valleys and plains,
> My poor blighted country! In exile and chains
> Are the sons doomed to linger. Oh God, who didst bring
> Thy children to Zion from Egypt's proud king,
> We implore Thy great mercy! Oh stretch forth Thy hand,
> And guide back her sons to their poor blighted land.
>
> Never more thy fair face am I destined to see;
> E'en the savage loves home, but 'tis crime to love thee.
> God bless thee, dear Erin, my loved one, my own,
> Oh! how hard 'tis these tendrils to break that have grown
>
> Round my heart. But 'tis over, and memory's spell
> Now steals o'er me sadly. Farewell! Oh, Farewell![13]

Not all the songs sung by the Fenians on the *Hougoumont* were nostalgic or political in intent. There were comic songs and recitations, and Irish dancing accompanied by the banjo; but the concert always concluded with the whole company singing, in unison, Tom Moore's 'Let Erin Remember', which had the status of a national anthem for the republicans:

> Let Erin remember the days of old,
>   Ere her faithless sons betrayed her;
> When Malachi wore the collar of gold
>   Which he won from her proud invader;
> When her kings with standard of green unfurled
>   Led the Red-Branch Knights to danger;
> Ere the emerald gem of the western world
>   Was set in the crown of a stranger.

It is not difficult for us to imagine those ebullient Irishmen who, if only for a short space of time, became oblivious of their cramped quarters, and innocently sang and danced uninhibited by the stares, the curses, and the harsh rebukes of their criminal neighbours between decks.

On 25 October the *Hougoumont* was about level with Casablanca on a course west of the Canary Islands. By then O'Reilly must have been allowed to mix freely with the main body of Fenians because Casey noted in his diary that they discussed reciting Brutus and Cassius in the concert that evening, 'but I believe he doesn't take much interest in it'. O'Reilly was popularly known to his friends on board as 'Jack'. Shakespeare did not figure in the concert program until the following evening, but it was not Jack O'Reilly but John Kenneally, a clerk from County Cork, who recited 'To be, or not to be'. It is surely a comment on the memory training and the education of these men that they were able to present programs made up of around eighteen songs and recitations in daily shipboard concerts throughout the voyage, and without recourse to music and reference books. It is possible that Father Delaney, before he sailed, thoughtfully packed such items in his luggage for the entertainment of his flock, but judging from the volume of material used throughout the long voyage he could have brought only a small part of it.

Jack O'Reilly's contribution to the concert on 29 October was his poem 'The Old School Clock' (quoted on page 33), and from then on he appeared regularly, either with one of his own works or telling a traditional story.

On the 26th, the day was enlivened when one of the criminal convicts received forty-eight lashes, administered by the boatswain—the first recorded punishment of the voyage—for having attacked and beaten a fellow convict 'most inhumanely'. He took his punishment without wincing and the other prisoners cheered him at the last stroke. He was then placed in irons.

Late that same night after the last notes of 'Let Erin Remember' had died away and the singers had clambered into their bunks—or in some cases, into their hammocks—the ship was struck by a violent squall. Everyone was awakened by the noise of the jib being smashed to pieces and the great spruce foreyard becoming entangled in the shrouds. Fear and confusion reigned below. The noise of a storm as heard in the hold of a wooden sailing ship is greatly amplified—the effect akin to being inside a bell. The helpless prisoners, locked in their compartments while the ship tossed about like a cork, panicked. Because of the pitch darkness, the confined space and the lack of means of escape, it would have been psychologically far worse for those below than for those on deck. On deck at least, one might have retained the illusion of being able to help oneself. To add to the panic the word circulated that the crew, themselves overcome with fear, had refused to go aloft to stow the sails which provoked a situation of the utmost danger. A ship with sails furled can ride out a storm in relative safety; but over-canvassed with sails flying in the wrong position, she can be driven into the waves, capsized, or her masts can be brought crashing down on deck.

Worse was to come. In the midst of the crisis members of the crew were heard screaming through the storm: 'Breakers ahead!'. Not for the first time on a sailing ship did the entire company fear for their lives—and not without reason. The officers were immediately ordered aloft in place of those who had disobeyed earlier commands. The ship laboured and rolled dangerously in the troughs, the waves pounded over the gunwales, and the timbers creaked ominously. By midnight, although the seas were not much calmer, the danger appeared to be over; the crew returned to their duties and the sound of their mournful shanties could be heard by the prisoners below.

When daylight came, all was quiet; the sails were reset and the mutinous sailors of the night before put in irons. There, visible in the morning light on the port side, but now safely distant, were the breakers which had come near to wrecking the *Hougoumont*: waves crashing on the rocky shore of the isle of Madeira.

CHAPTER 8

THE WILD GOOSE

I will aim to console you for the past, to cheer
you for the present, and to strengthen you for
the future. But it becomes not so shy a bird
to promise too much...

John Flood

THE restless, resourceful spirit of John Boyle O'Reilly, which had already been responsible for three escape attempts in English prisons, was not to be quenched by being confined on board ship.

His friend Denis Cashman, writing of O'Reilly after his death, recalled that he was father to a scheme to capture the ship, guards, convicts and all, and alter course for America.[1] And as they crossed the tropic of Cancer in calm weather at the beginning of November—having first established themselves as a compliant, cultured group—the Fenians might well have been in the best position to carry out the plan then. The ship was sufficiently distant from Britain for a mutiny to remain secret, at least long enough for them to alter course and reach the east coast of America. John Flood, according to Cashman, was a first-class navigator. A small group secretly discussed plans and resolved to 'try the experiment' providing they could get all the other Fenians to cooperate.[2]

Jack O'Reilly was undoubtedly the ringleader and would have gone through with it. He was fearless, and probably considered he had nothing to lose and much to gain by taking action. But others did not support him: some with shorter sentences looked forward to their release and eventual return to Ireland. If a mutiny were staged and proved successful all would have had to remain permanent exiles in America. If a mutiny failed those responsible would surely have suffered death from the halter which, as they were painfully aware, was kept in readiness on the foredeck to swing mutineers and murderers over the side before releasing them bound and blindfolded into the water.

It is fascinating to imagine a different story if such a mutiny had taken place. A swashbuckling enterprise would have had much appeal for the Fenians at the time, an event to enter the history books which would rival the rescue of Stephens from a Dublin gaol after the 1848 rising, or the daring rescue of the Fenian prisoners in Manchester at the time of the *Hougoumont* voyage. It might have eclipsed the mutiny on the *Bounty* which had occurred seventy-eight years previously. From what we know of O'Reilly's character, both before the voyage and subsequently, we can be sure that, as a soldier, he would have passionately supported the scheme and led the charge. But others were older and perhaps wiser, and believed that freedom would come to them long before the end of their sentences and without the need for violence—a belief which proved correct.

At least we can be sure now that the subject of mutiny was thoroughly debated. Cashman recorded in his diary how the inner circle went below to 'attend school'. This was part of the 'improvement' process which penal reformers insisted upon whereby a period was set aside for instruction and religious education. But Cashman reported that it was a bit of a farce with everyone sitting around doing nothing. It may have been at those times that the idea of mutiny was floated. Again according to Cashman, another consideration which weighed heavily against mutiny was the problem of restraining and controlling over 200 criminal convicts, some of whom were violent and deemed not be trusted.[3] In the event, O'Reilly's enthusiasm for escaping had to be stilled and kept in readiness for a more suitable occasion.

Thoughts of mutiny laid to rest, the conspirators turned their energies towards a more peaceful, creative pastime: the production of a weekly newspaper. A series of preliminary meetings was held to plan the enterprise. Tom Duggan was appointed chairman; John Flood, editor; Jack O'Reilly, subeditor; and John Edward Kelly, manager. Others closely involved were Cashman, Casey, Michael Cody and Joseph Noonan—the same 'inner circle' which was largely responsible for the daily concerts.

In the meantime, the *Hougoumont* continued on a south-westerly course, passing the Cape Verde Islands on 5 and 6 November. She was now twenty-six days out from Portland and had covered approximately 4,000 miles, an average of 150 nautical miles per day. The weather had become insufferably hot, and it was particularly so between decks; moreover the ship was becalmed for long periods, this being the region of the doldrums. The Fenians seemed to have spent most of their days resting, reading and talking on deck:

If it was disagreeable on deck with the hot sun pouring down its molten rays day after day upon the heads of the unfortunate passengers, who were stretched in every conceivable position on the forecastle, imagine how much worse it was in the hold, where the air was stifling and oppressive. There was no draught through the barred hatches. The deck above was blazing hot. The hot pitch dropped from the seams, and burned flesh as it fell. Water was the one thought in all our minds.[4]

One afternoon a turtle was seen asleep on the calm surface of the sea and the second mate, with six men, put out a boat and harpooned it. They had great difficulty hauling it up the side of the *Hougoumont* as it weighed about 2 hundredweight. A second turtle was sighted soon afterwards and the boat put out again, but on this occasion the animal escaped. Later, a huge shark was seen following the ship, 'its green eyes glistening with a fierce expression through the blue waters'. And then a flying fish landed on deck, 'it was black, and about the size of a herring'. These and other distractions—common experiences of all who travelled south on sailing ships—together with preparations for the publication of their newspaper, kept the Fenians well occupied. 'I expect to be rather busy for the voyage', wrote Cashman on 7 November.

The heat became oppressive and, what was worse, affected the condition of their food. The hot chocolate, which they were served every morning, was judged undrinkable and the seven Fenian mess captains requested to see the doctor. At first their request was refused but after they had thrown their chocolate overboard he had a change of heart. Dr William Smith, the surgeon superintendent, was evidently swayed by their complaint because he ordered that hot chocolate should henceforth be served every fourth morning and tea on the other three. He also granted them a much needed increase in the water ration to 14 pints between eight men each day.

On Tuesday, 5 November a crude ventilating system was brought into service whereby air was pumped between decks by means of canvas bags and this was judged to provide great relief below. But it was short-lived. Food continued to be affected by the heat and several men threw their meat overboard.

On 7 November a meeting of the newspaper committee finalized details for the first edition and decided on a name. Several suggestions were considered but the final choice rested on the *Wild Goose*, proposed by their manager John Edward 'Ned' Kelly. 'The Wild Geese' was the name given to Irish soldiers of earlier generations who had found service in European armies when forced into exile from their own country. Thus, not only was the paper honouring those soldiers, but also subtly implying that the Fenians on the *Hougoumont* were themselves in the tradition of Wild Geese. Father Delaney had managed to supply a sufficient quantity of paper, pens and ink, and it was arranged that the first number would appear on Saturday, 9 November.

John Casey suffered from sickness and spent much of his time in his bunk or lying on deck. His diary entry for 7 November, like so many others, gives an impression of lazy days spent conversing or reading:

> Sick today eat no breakfast. Listened to an interesting conversation on Mesmerism and Electro-biology. Soldadoes [soldiers] giving lessons on fencing—Breeze light. Intensely hot but little cloudy. Impossible to remain in sunshine on deck—very pleasant to sit in shadow of mainsail as its flapping gently fans me. Great confusion on deck caused by a chase after a rat who escapes beneath the forecastle.[5]

On Saturday, 9 November the day dawned very hot again, with a beautiful sunrise and the ship making little headway at 4 knots. Some of the convicts danced on deck to guitar music during their recreation period, or whiled away the time playing cards, dominoes and chess. Down below O'Reilly, the subeditor, and his copublishers were working hard to complete the paper for release that evening: 'Printing all day. 6 Mess is turned into a publishing office'. That evening, amid general congratulations and enthusiasm, the *Wild Goose* made its debut. In respect of this event, the usual concert was cancelled so that O'Reilly could read the journal aloud to his comrades.

The *Wild Goose* was handwritten on both sides of four full sheets of white paper and folded in the centre to form an eight-page booklet. Each page consisted of two columns with the headings in bold copperplate and the neat, legible articles written by a number of hands. The layout consciously followed the style employed in printed journals: an ornate masthead on the front page incorporated the name in bold capitals and was festooned with shamrocks, and beneath was a subtitle in Gothic letters, 'A Collection of Ocean Waifs', which was the artistic work of Denis Cashman. A bold but less ornate repetition of the name 'Wild Goose' appeared on the centre pages and underneath was the epigraph 'They'll come again when south winds blow' along with the day and date.

The tone was literary rather than political and there was a strong element of humour. John Flood, in his statement to readers on the front page of the first edition, personified the Wild Goose—'I have flown to cheer you on your weary way with my homely notes'—and went on to express the purpose of the paper:

> I will aim to console you for the past, to cheer you for the present, and to strengthen you for the future. But it becomes not so shy a bird to promise too much, nor must I flatter myself that I shall be as welcome to you as one of more melodious throat or gaudier plumage. Yet welcome I trust I shall be here where all else is strange, and that each new weekly visitant may be still more welcome—

welcome not alone for the news it brings to keep your memories green, but also that it may prove of interest to all to watch the changing flight of the flock, and read the mystic story they grace as they pass on their airy flight to the shores of that far, strange land of our destined exile.[6]

The first episode of a serial entitled 'Queen Cliodhna and the Flower of Erin—a Tale of our Pagan Ancestors' occupied three columns of pages two and three. This was written by Tom Duggan who had been a schoolteacher prior to his arrest and was particularly knowledgeable on ancient Irish history. The second column of page three featured satirical paragraphs supposedly on the latest news:

From the Supernatural Spheres, Nov. 1. A tremendous banquet given to the Gods last night by Bacchus which showed they Hallow-e'en earthly festivities. Jupiter took soda-water and brandy this morning and a similar report has been maliciously circulated concerning the ox-eyed lady. Pheobus quite choleric; kicked Cholas out of the sky for breathing too heavily; indisposed towards evening, and retired to bed rather early.

Nov. 2. Venus winked at the man in the moon. Diana threatened to scratch her eyes out. Celestial Court greatly scandalised.

Marine Regions, Nov. 9th—Squalls ahead. Neptune thinks he has enough of Finny Uns in his dominions, and is incensed at the thought of a fresh influx of those turbulent beings. When they reach the line, he is determined to hook them, if they don't hook it.

The Markets

Tobacco not to be had at any price: holders unwilling to part with the commodity.
Great demand for potatoes and plum duff.
Water scarce and of an inferior quality.
Pork rather higher than usual and still advancing.
Biscuits getting livelier.
Chocolate a drug on the market.
Tea rather flat.—Oatmeal steady.[7]

The humorous trend continued on page four with answers to imaginary correspondents, the question being implicit in the answer given. The answer to 'Peter's' query, for example, was, 'yes; all Scilly people are English'. And to an 'Enquirer': 'very little is known of the first settlers of central Africa; but the supposition that it was colonised by an Irish Chieftain named Tim Bucktoo, appears to us to be a popular error'. And to a 'Constant Reader': 'We don't believe it possible to Cozen the Captain out of all the Sheep Shanks made by the crew; neither do we think they would improve the soup'.

Seriousness returned again in the editorial occupying the second column of page four, the two columns of page five and the first paragraph of page six. Under the heading 'Home Thoughts', John Flood exhorted his readers to accept their situation stoically and to seek consolation in religion. At the same time he asked them to remain true to their homeland:

> We love the little island that has pleased God to make our motherland. In her few smiles, in her many tears, and in her countless sufferings we love her. The blessed hope of turning again to her genial soil, and to the dear ones we left behind, will give us strength to bear and brave the worst; and until then, thro' pain, and regret, and sorrow, we will still look back and pray for her and for them with the true unswerving love known only to exiles.[8]

Of additional interest is the observation that the first paragraph was written in an upright, precise copperplate, and the editorial was then continued in a less formal hand which may be recognized as that of O'Reilly. Two poems occupied most of page six under the general ongoing, richly ornamented heading, 'Emerald Spray'. The first was 'Farewell' by O'Reilly written on the day, or soon after the day, of the *Hougoumont*'s departure from Portland (already quoted above on page 61); and the second was 'Prison Thoughts', written by John Kelly in Millbank and signed with his nom de plume, 'Laoi'. The final page, eight, featured a satirical piece about Australia which made much play on their lack of information and included an amusing but barbed reference to British colonization:

> This great continent of the south, having been discovered by some Dutch skipper and his crew, sometime between the 1st and 19th centuries of the Christian era, was, in consequence, taken possession of by the Government of Great Britain, in accordance with that just and equitable maxim, 'What's yours is mine; what's mine's my own'. That magnanimous government, in the kindly exuberance of their feelings have placed a large portion of that immense tract of country at our disposal, generously defraying all expenses incurred on our way to it, and providing retreats for us there from the inclemency of the seasons and the carnivorous propensities of the natives.[9]

The final column of the paper was taken up with wry notices and general information such as concerts being resumed on Monday the 11th; the Southern Cross being visible nightly in the south; and baths (probably saltwater showers) being allowed on deck early each morning. Finally, at the foot of the column, was the formal imprint:

Printed and published at the office, No. 6 Mess, Intermediate Cabin, ship 'Hougoumont' for the editors, Messrs John Flood and J.B. O'Reilly, by J.E.K. Registered for transmission abroad.[10]

Production of the *Wild Goose* in such adverse conditions was a considerable achievement and demonstrates the resourcefulness of the group, their literary talents and a determination not to be defeated by their circumstances.

On that first Saturday of publication, midway between the coast of Africa and Brazil, the Fenians assembled below deck under the dim yellow glare of the one available lamp and listened intently to O'Reilly's reading of the only copy. The *Wild Goose* lifted their spirits, and they greatly enjoyed the event which was to be repeated over the next six weeks as the paper ran to seven editions.

CHAPTER 9

IN SOUTHERN LATITUDES

———

Away, away the vessel speeds, till sun and sky alone
Are round her, as her course she steers across the torrid zone.
Away until the North Star fades, the Southern Cross is high,
And myriad gems of brightest beam are sparkling in the sky.

John Boyle O'Reilly

THE day after publication of the first *Wild Goose*, Sunday, 10 November, the weather continued hot and humid with an occasional heavy tropical shower. Mass was celebrated by Father Delaney at 11.00 a.m. with a choir organized and trained by Denis Cashman. 'The congregation praised the performance—we sang some beautiful pieces.'[1]

On the same day, the Fenians demonstrated that for all their good behaviour and their courtesy among themselves, they were not prepared to be subservient or kowtow to petty authority. When receiving their wine ration on deck each day they were required to acknowledge their names when called by answering, 'Sir!' or, 'Here Sir!'. But unlike the other prisoners, all of them refused to use the title 'Sir'. This led to a row with the officer concerned and the Fenians were ordered below. They were remonstrated with, cajoled and threatened; but they stood firm. Finally, it was the officer who gave in:

> He expostulates with them—in vain—upon second consideration gives us wine.
> As men we will stand on our dignity...we will never sir any man on board.
> Officer ferocious.[2]

On Monday, 11 November the weather became rough with frequent squalls but this did not prevent one of the Fenians from playing 'Garryowen' and 'The Last Rose of Summer' on the cornet, on deck. On 12 November the *Hougoumont* was sailing under reefed topsail and rolling in heavy seas. The heat had become intense as they neared the equator and the easternmost tip of Brazil.

An incident on 13 November indicates the fair but good-natured approach to discipline and punishment on the *Hougoumont*—at least in the matter of lighter offences. (And in the matter of serious offences there seemed to be few.) One of the non-Fenian convicts was caught stealing tobacco from his messmates, and also biscuits which were intended as food for a pig on board. He was reported to the surgeon superintendent.

Dr Smith, RN turned him over to be tried by a special commission of his fellow convicts, much to the amusement of all spectators on deck. O'Reilly has left an account of the trial, published in the second issue of the *Wild Goose*:

> Samuel Wiggins was this day arraigned before 'Judge Lynch' and a discriminating jury under the following indictment: For that being instigated by the devil and a love of plunder, he did on 12th November 1867, feloniously and avariciously attempt to steal one stick of tobacco of great value, to wit, of inestimable value, the property of Obediah Taylor. And that being instigated as aforesaid, he did, on 12th day of November 1867 feloniously and voraciously steal and eat the rations of a fellow passenger, to wit a small black pig; and further that said pig having resisted, he, said Wiggins, did maliciously and ferociously assault with his fists said small black pig: Whereby said small black pig received and suffered great bodily pain and injury, to wit a black eye, and a swelled head from the effects of which said small black pig yet suffers.[3]

O'Reilly, the reporter, enjoyed embellishing the comedy as much as the spectators must have enjoyed the actual event. Witnesses were called to testify to Samuel Wiggins's character which was sadly lacking in honesty. Eyewitnesses described how the defendant attacked the animal while it was at its tub devouring biscuits. There does not seem to have been much defence offered for poor Wiggins, and when the 'judge' asked the 'jury' for a show of hands if they found him guilty, the verdict was unanimous with the judge himself 'putting up two very unwashed specimens'. His 'Lordship' then proceeded to pass sentence— that the prisoner be tarred all over by the gentlemen of the court and then locked in the water closet for three hours, afterwards to be washed and scrubbed with a hair broom.

A week later a similar trial was staged when a second convict was accused of stealing tobacco. A court of fellow convicts was appointed as before; a 'military guard' armed with broomsticks and staves paraded on deck. 'The trial was conducted in admirable style, but the prisoner was acquitted, the proof not being sufficient.'[4]

The concert on the evening of the day of the first trial included two items by O'Reilly: a song, 'They Call us Aliens', which was sung by John Flood who was reputed to have an excellent voice; and a recitation, of 'In Memory of the French Prisoners', this being a repeat performance of the poem heard in the first concert aboard.

The *Hougoumont* crossed the equator on 15 November, thirty-four days out from Portland; the ship was still heading towards the coast of South America and progress was slow. It was very warm again on the 16th and towards evening they passed a double-funnelled paddle-steamer, a mail ship en route from Melbourne to England.

It being a Saturday, the second edition of the *Wild Goose* made its appearance. Among its features were the second episode of Tom Duggan's serial, the report of the Samuel Wiggins's 'trial' by O'Reilly, and a leader from John Flood exhorting the Fenians to be self-reliant:

Self-reliance! What a host of strength is in the mere name! 'Tis but to say 'I will', and already the battle is more than half won. Why not then, call it to our aid? And we shall find our imaginations and our souls strengthened, and our grey goose quills, as if by magic, imbued with a prose both to amuse and instruct; and, once invoked, let us never again lose such an ally, so that growing daily stronger in its strength, we may be enabled to fight life's battles bravely out.[5]

As in the first number, two poems were printed under the heading 'Emerald Spray'. The first was 'The Green' by O'Reilly, consisting of seven eight-line stanzas in praise of the colour green. The poet reflects that the colour is not only dominant in nature, but is also the symbolic colour of Ireland. In the first five verses he praises green which is so evident and important in all the seasons of the year; in verses seven and eight he considers how cherished the colour has become to those who love Ireland:

Oh! Fairest and best of the colours on earth,
How I love thy gentle smile!
Thy bright warm hue in my heart gives birth
To dreams of my own Green Isle.
To my childhood's home my memory runs,
O'er every well-known scene;
Ah! Deep in the hearts of her exiled sons
Is the love of their beautiful green.

'Tis never extinguished. It never decays.
It came with their earliest breath;
'Tis a light that is holy and pure, whose rays
Are vanquished alone by death.

God grant that the dawn of the morning is nigh
When o'er Liberty's ranks will be seen
Their heart-cherished sunburst rise gleaming on high
From its glorious field of green.[6]

The final page, as before, contained jokey news items including a dispatch supposedly from a special correspondent in Fremantle: 'A grand reception is being prepared for the Wild Goose, by her feathered friend, the Swan'.

On Sunday the 17th, the ship's position was 450 miles south of the equator. They had reached their furthest point west, longitude 32°, about 120 miles from the Brazilian coast. The choir performed at 11 o'clock mass and the Fenians were upset when Father Delaney included prayers for Queen Victoria. The day was burning hot. Casey was still sick and weak, and unable to retain any food in his stomach.

Rats were becoming a nuisance on board and they were so numerous that several were chased around the deck in broad daylight. But they were most feared at night when they crawled over the sleeping men in their bunks. Chloride of zinc was sprinkled between decks in an effort to get rid of them.

Heavy rain fell during the night of 20 November and throughout the next day, forcing the prisoners to remain below deck. The ship, almost becalmed, was deluged with water; it dripped from the rigging and the sails, and the air and the rough furniture and bedding below became damp and unhealthy. Casey was again sick in his bunk suffering from a severe cold and sore throat; and Cashman was homesick and spent the day reading and re-reading his wife's letters.

On the morning of Friday, 22 November the uninhabited island of Trinidade came into view through the haze. (This forbidding, barren place rises from the ocean in irregular precipices of sterile rock; its chief claim to fame rests on the sojourn there of the astronomer Halley in 1700.) While still close to the island the *Hougoumont* was struck by a fierce storm. The ship suddenly became unmanageable as it was tossed about on the surface of a furious ocean. The sea crashed over the gunwales and all the timbers creaked.

Several huge waves dashed across the ship, almost capsizing her, and shaking every timber in her. In an instant two sails were torn to shreds. There were not enough hands on board to set everything to rights. Six or eight prisoners mounted aloft in the midst of the wind and rain, and succeeded after some difficulty, in taking in the mainsail which had been fluttering to the wind.[7]

As suddenly as the storm had arisen so the wind dropped again and the sea became unnaturally calm. They were caught in the eye of the storm. Masses of dark watery clouds covered the sky and the ocean became steel grey. All souls on the ship waited in the eerie stillness for the second onslaught which they knew must follow. Sure enough, within a few minutes a low ominous rumbling was heard. The rain began to fall in torrents and the squall burst with redoubled fury causing the sea to rise to mountainous heights which threatened to engulf the little ship. 'We got knocked about like old boots.'[8]

At about 5.00 p.m. the storm abated; all became calm again. But as the slight wind was dead ahead the ship was hardly making way. With the rock-bound coast of the island still only about 2 miles distant the danger of drifting onto it was only too obvious. Cashman decided that the best thing he could do in the circumstances was to turn in and dream of his dear Kate and three children.

The following day was Saturday, the danger was passed and the Fenians looked forward to the reading of the third edition of the *Wild Goose*. When the time arrived for Jack O'Reilly to present it by the light of the lamp in the evening, he began with the continuation of the serial by Tom Duggan. Then followed a long, personal reminiscence of Independence Day celebrations in America written by John Edward Kelly. Those listening dreamed of their own independence day, and envied America's achievement. O'Reilly would have also read his own poem on page six, 'Mary', written to a youthful love:

> I see thee Mary, now before me
> As I saw thee long ago;
> Dreams of youth are rushing o'er me
> With resistless rapid flow.
> Time and worldly cares have found me,
> Each has left its mark behind.
> Still those day dreams hover round me,
> Saddening treasures of the mind.
> Far from childhood's home I wander,
> Sorrows come and disappear;
> Still when on the past I ponder
> Thou are present, Mary dear.[9]

By the last week of November the *Hougoumont* was well south, crossing the tropic of Capricorn during the 23rd on a south-easterly course. The weather had grown cool, even cold, and albatrosses were a common sight. One of the guards attempted to shoot one, but although he was a good shot, he fortunately failed after five or six attempts. Sea lore regards killing these giant, friendly birds as bringing bad luck upon the ship, as described in *The Rime of the Ancient Mariner*.[10]

On the last day of November 1867 the fourth *Wild Goose* was published. In this edition O'Reilly's signed contribution was a four-stanza sentimental poem extolling mothers' love. One wonders to what extent it was prompted by an intense longing for his own mother, the mother from whom he parted when he was twenty and who was to die while he was in exile in Western Australia.

> Time cannot break the sacred chain,
>   But adds a strengthening link;
> Nor can the ingrate's sharpest pain,
>   Those tender feelings sink.
> Oh, no! That bond round every chord
>   Thy infant fingers wove.
> Thy mother's heart is always stored
>   With deep undying love.[11]

He also contributed an unsigned piece under the pseudonym 'Boyne', a homily entitled 'First Steps' on the general theme of the importance of making the right decision at the start of any enterprise. 'In the lives of all men there is a certain point—a moment it maybe—fraught with the influences of the most material importance to our future happiness and well being'. And he went on to quote, 'There is a tide in the affairs of men, which, taken at the flood, leads on to fortune' from Shakespeare's *Julius Caesar*, words which were to become prophetic for O'Reilly at a later date. Quotations from Shakespeare might not strike us as being an accomplishment of a common soldier but is further evidence of O'Reilly's exceptional literary education.

In contrast to the serious, moralistic tone of most of the material in the issue, at the end of Boyne's article was punning advice on how to make whiskey:

Take a large sized key, whisk it rapidly through the air for about two hours. Place it in a hogshead. Add a proportionate quantity of water. Let it ferment, then bottle, cork, and seal for use. A wineglass full every morning fasting, good for lockjaw.[12]

By Sunday, 1 December the *Hougoumont* was at latitude 35° south of the equator, midway between the continents of South America and South Africa. On deck Father Delaney preached his sermon on eternity and the choir 'sang a beautiful Kyrie'. Five finback whales were sighted, estimated to be about 30 feet long. On 2 December the ship was heading for Tristan da Cunha at 10 knots under full canvas. Preparations were made on deck for a rendezvous with American whalers which called at the island; Captain Cozens evidently intended to replenish his supplies of fresh water and other provisions. As they neared the coast a mist descended, the wind freshened, and the captain changed his mind. This may have been because of the dangerous reefs, or poor visibility, or that he wished to take advantage of the favourable winds. A more plausible explanation may have been that he feared associating with American ships sympathetic to the Fenians. Whatever the reason, the *Hougoumont* sailed on without sight of the island in the mist, and in doing so made the entire voyage to Fremantle without calling at any port on the way.

Publication of the *Wild Goose* evidently found favour with those in authority on board because, in recognition of its positive influence, a new privilege was extended to the staff of the paper. From this time forward they were permitted to remain on deck until 7.30 p.m. Denis Cashman had 'a splendid walk and chat' with Jack O'Reilly and John Flood. Poor Casey was still wretchedly sick and remained below.

On Saturday, 7 December the ship was close to 1,000 miles south-west of the Cape of Good Hope, on latitude 40°. The morning was cloudy with rain intervals, and the wind buffeted the ship in fitful gusts. At first the sea was very rough. Later, the day took on a strange, ominous aspect. Everything became still; the sky was a dull leaden colour; the surface of the ocean took on a glossy appearance; there was not a breath of air. The *Hougoumont* was truly 'as idle as a painted ship upon a painted ocean'. The more superstitious among the passengers looked about the horizon for the approach of the Flying Dutchman. (The legend tells of a ghostly Dutch ship which haunts the waters around the Cape and is a presage of disaster.) Casey, somewhat recovered from his sickness, was amused to note the look of terror on their faces.

At about midday the rain poured down in torrents and continued for three hours, yet the sea still remained flat calm and the air cold, thick and still. At 6.00 p.m. the sails were shortened and everything both on deck and aloft was made ready for a wild night. An hour later the ship sailed under closely reefed topsails and the hatchways were battened down. At 8.00 p.m. the prisoners retired for the night but two hours later were awoken by a dull warning sound, growing louder and louder until it seemed to burst over the ship. In a few moments the sea was boiling in fury and a gale of terrific violence raged. Sleep was out of the question. The pandemonium on deck caused by waves dashing against the side of the vessel and the wind thundering through the rigging, raised panic in the minds of the convicts imprisoned and helpless below.

> Peering through the grating, the sight which met my eyes I shall not easily forget. The night was dark to blackness. Not a sound was heard save the howling of the wind. The waters appeared like huge dark rocks, towering above us, and threatening to engulf us in their midst.[13]

Despite the storm and the fierce rain during daylight hours, the fifth edition of the *Wild Goose* arrived on schedule. As well as the usual features—including an editorial by John Flood which continued his theme of the Wild Geese—there were three poems, two of which were dedicated to Jack O'Reilly; one of them by Flood and the second by Cashman. Both were entitled 'Friendship'. In Cashman's poem he declares he longs for friendship and understanding when he feels depressed, alone, and away from his family. He looks into the faces around him:

> Again I look with anxious glancing,
> And seek one friend among them all.
> Ah! Now a dear friend is advancing;
> He saw and understood the call.[14]

O'Reilly's own poem in that edition was entitled 'Memory', in which he looks back nostalgically to his boyhood days on the banks of the Boyne when he played, fished and searched for birds' nests. He also recalls his first love, his first 'lingering lover's kiss'. The object of his affection was a 'little brown-haired maid' named Mary. As this is the second loving reference to her in a poem we can assume that his romantic attachment to Mary once had serious and lasting intent:

> I pray that God may guard thy steps,
>   and bless thee, Mary dear.
> I'll never see thee more, but yet I know
>   thou'lt drop a tear
> For him who loved thee first of all,
>   who first thy lips impressed
> And told thee how he loved thee, with
>   thy cheek upon his breast.[15]

As the *Hougoumont* sailed south by east into the roaring forties, giving the Cape of Good Hope a wide berth, the weather grew cold and damp. The Fenians had difficulty keeping warm at night. On 11 and 12 December the ship was racing along, the best sailing days of the entire voyage; on each they covered a distance of 230 nautical miles. The pace slackened on Friday, 13 December when they found themselves enveloped in a dense, cold fog; the ship wallowed in a heavy sea. Work on the sixth issue of the *Wild Goose* progressed under difficulty. Then came a taste of the traditional roaring forties—reefed sails, a westerly gale and a grey, mountainous following sea. Seabirds screamed as they skimmed the broken surface of the waters. Plates and mugs were tossed about below, and at mealtimes the orderlies had the greatest difficulty negotiating the ladders while carrying food. At 2.00 p.m. visibility was scarcely 200 yards. The gale continued as the ship, with every timber creaking, crashed her way through the massive waves which broke over the gunwales. The evening was exceedingly cold, but by 6.00 p.m. the wind had eased a little and the waves relaxed their fury. Somehow—and it would seem to us impossible under those conditions—the sixth edition of the *Wild Goose* was published on time.

John Flood's editorial was in three parts: 'A Look Within' which dealt with self-analysis; 'Gentle Words' on persuasiveness; and 'The Useful', which suggested means for the pooling of practical knowledge. The style is frankly didactic and grandiloquent, and to the modern reader it will seem stilted and tedious. But in the context of the situation they were in, where they looked for firm moral leadership, a mentor, and morale-boosting advice, John Flood's essays in the *Wild Goose* were received with respect and gratitude. Jack O'Reilly's poem of the week was 'The Old School Clock'. In this issue he also contributed the first of a two-part descriptive, historical essay on the valley of the River Boyne. (The second part failed to appear in the seventh and last *Wild Goose*.)

The next day, Sunday, 15 December, was cloudy and bitterly cold. For the first time the ship's bell was used to summon the faithful for a Catholic service. There was no mass but they were given communion. Denis Cashman and the choir sang a litany and the 'Tantum Ergo'.

All agreed that the saddest day of the voyage was 16 December. It was a rough morning, dark, wet and cold, reminiscent of a winter's morning in Ireland. A poor Irish convict named Thomas Corcoran, not one of the Fenians, died at 6.00 a.m. from natural causes. The burial was held that evening at 6.00 p.m.

The ship rolled severely on account of the sails being furled in anticipation of the ceremony. The convicts, in readiness, ranged themselves in two lines along the starboard side of the ship. A procession approached headed by two acolytes and Father Delaney in his robes. Next came six convicts bearing the body sewn up in a canvas bag. The 'Misereri' and the 'Te Deum' were intoned and the body, covered with a flag, was placed in a slanting position over the side. At the conclusion of the prayers it was allowed to slip free from under the flag into the water below.

> He sinks immediately in consequence of weights attached to his feet. Cannot but meditate on the certainty of Death and the uncertainty of life. Cannot think without emotion of dying in a far distant land away from friends, home and kindred without a single hand to sooth and comfort me in my last moments.[16]

The Fenians were much affected by this melancholy event and alluded to it in their diaries and subsequent writings. Cashman wrote that he and Jack had a long chat in bed that night on the subject.

The *Hougoumont* reached her furthest point south on Wednesday, 14 December at latitude 49°, roughly 3,000 miles north of the Antarctic Circle. The deck was white with frost in the morning and the daytime temperature only reached five degrees Fahrenheit. During the night the lookout had given the dreaded cry, 'Iceberg ahead!', but fortunately it proved a false alarm. Being so bitterly cold, and the ship being in the southern latitudes, danger from icebergs would have been ever present.

The surgeon superintendent announced that the next issue of the *Wild Goose* was to be the last and that all paper was to be given up the following week and everything set in order for arrival at Fremantle. The editorial committee decided to make the edition a special Christmas double issue, and Cashman set about designing an elaborate seasonal masthead for it. Friday the 20th dawned piercingly cold, but the prisoners were obliged to remain on deck all day which they felt was cruel and unnecessary. In the evening they worked hard to complete the Christmas *Wild Goose*, and the choir started rehearsing carols for the services.

On Saturday, 21 December, 800 miles south-west of the Kerguelen Islands and, as Casey wryly recorded, 'midsummer's day' in the southern hemisphere, the noon temperature struggled to two degrees Fahrenheit. The temperature below deck was hardly of more comfort, but the event to warm the Fenians' spirits was the publication of the splendid sixteen-page double issue of the *Wild Goose*, 'the best number yet'.[17]

CHAPTER **10**

JOURNEY'S END

Day after day, in the mild southern air, the ship glided slowly on, and still the watchers on the crowded deck saw no sign of land. From morning light they leant on the rail, looking away over the smooth sea to where the air was yellow with heat above the unseen continent.

John Boyle O'Reilly

THE title page of the Christmas *Wild Goose*—or the masthead—is an impressive example of decorative art in its own right, all the more to be admired when we know the gruelling circumstances under which it was created. Forming a semicircle, the words 'Christmas Number' in ornate letters are entwined in holly branches. The word 'of' beneath it is also set in decoration, probably mistletoe, and 'The Wild Goose' is wreathed in shamrocks. Beneath this is the subtitle, 'A Collection of Ocean Waifs', written in Gothic letters with just a little more care and decoration than in previous issues. And finally, in meticulous copperplate are the words: 'The right of translation and reproduction is reserved'. There is nothing amateurish or homemade about the work; the whole effect is stylish and well crafted. Denis Cashman, as well as being a writer, was also a talented calligrapher.

Like Christmas editions of literary magazines today, the *Wild Goose* was packed with solid seasonal reading matter including a Christmas short story; a double ration of poetry on Christmas themes; a guest appearance by Father Delaney with words of moral advice; and a personified, valedictory message from the Wild Goose himself taking affectionate leave of his readers:

The end of your uneventful but rapid passage quickly approaches, and already your hearts are beginning to quicken with anticipation at what may be your future in the new land you are fast nearing. I know not what may be in store for you. I cannot pierce the inexorable veil of the future, drawn alike for me and for you; but bidding you a long farewell most likely, however we may wish it, never to meet again, I say to you—Courage, and trust in Providence.[1]

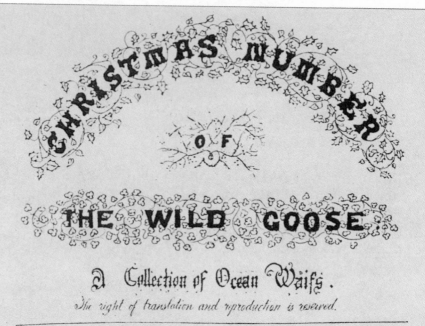

The Wild Goose *journal 'published' on board the* Hougoumont, *Christmas edition 1867.*
(*Courtesy of the Mitchell Library*)

There were three contributions from Jack O'Reilly including two long narrative poems. The first was 'The Flying Dutchman' which recounted the legend of the spectral ship. The second was entitled 'Christmas Night' in which 'the old north wind' was personified as a jovial traveller blowing over the countryside. He visited various places and observed festive celebrations, and then came upon a 'prison, all massive, and silent and stern, its darkening shadows cast' and the old north wind saw 'not a sign of mirth'. The third poem was a simple five-stanza carol for singing on board ship:

> Then brothers! Though we spend the day
> Within a prison ship,
> Let every heart with hope be gay,
> A smile on every lip!
>
> Let's banish sorrow, banish fears
> And fill our hearts with glee.
> And ne'er forget in after years
> Our Christmas on the sea.[2]

The final page concluded, as usual, with humorous paragraphs including a notice headed 'To be disposed of by private treaty', and underneath: 'The good will and interest in the Copyright and Plant of the Wild Goose, together with a valuable mass of unpublished manuscripts—apply the Editors'.

Although the Christmas *Goose* was published by the due date, the 21st, it seems from the diaries that O'Reilly delayed the traditional public reading of it until Christmas Day. The Fenians' energies were given over to preparations for the festivities, albeit those festivities would be limited on board a convict ship. Each mess saved some of its daily food ration and the choir practised regularly. But a damper on their efforts to celebrate the feast in an Irish fashion was the run of stormy weather, interspersed with all too short periods of calm, which dogged them over the next ten days.

The *Hougoumont* reached its furthest point south on 22 December at latitude 49°, close to halfway across the Southern Ocean; and hereafter the roaring forties would live up to their name. Dawn on Christmas Eve showed no hint of what was to come in the days ahead. The sky was clear and sunny, the sea moderate and of a splendid deep green. The air was cold and bracing. The ship's carpenter fitted a new mast to the ship's longboat in preparation for the arrival at Fremantle: the end of the voyage was in sight and this raised everyone's spirits.

By mid-afternoon the breeze had dropped and the sails hung limply; a deathlike stillness prevailed. The choir rehearsed 'Adeste Fidelis' and other Christmas music. At 6.30 p.m. the prisoners went below, leaving behind them sombre clouds and a stormy-looking sea. Sails were taken in, in anticipation of foul weather ahead. The Fenians formed a circle and passed the evening singing songs of home and reminiscing about family gatherings in recent years. They agreed that even in the restrictive conditions aboard ship they were better off than some of their comrades in solitary confinement in Portland, Millbank, or Dartmoor. When the hour came for turning in to their bunks it began to rain heavily on deck, the ship pitched and rolled alarmingly, and the sea rose.

A storm raged all that night and on Christmas morning the ship was still being tossed about like a cork on the waves; not a good beginning to the day and it was too rough to celebrate mass. The prisoners, some of them preferring to remain in their bunks, sang 'Adeste Fidelis'. With great difficulty Father Delaney made his rounds administering Holy Communion. Breakfast of sweetloaf followed which was 'rather a delicacy to convicts'. By that stage in the voyage the Fenian prisoners' stomachs were largely unaffected by the motion of the ship—with the possible exception of Casey—and so they were able to enjoy a special dinner of 'salt horse and plum duff' and a double ration of wine at 2.00 p.m. In the afternoon Jack O'Reilly read aloud the Christmas *Wild Goose*, but the weather was still rough with no relief in sight. On Christmas night the *Hougoumont* travelled through the darkness with only three sails set as the storm continued to rage. It had been a disappointing Christmas Day. The *Hougoumont* was then about 500 miles north-east of the Kerguelen Islands, on course for Fremantle, and logging a little over 200 miles in twenty-four hours.

On Boxing Day the sun rose brilliantly in a cloudless sky but the wind and the sea still lashed the ship violently. On the 27th conditions abated and a spell of mild and sunny weather brought a brief respite from the storms. But the calmer conditions were short-lived. More bad weather dogged them on Saturday the 28th when the sea broke over the decks, washing down the hatchways. That night they were all awakened by the terrible rocking of the vessel, the roaring of the sea, and the howling of the wind in the rigging. Every moment, it seemed, the ship must be swamped. The sea poured over the gunwales and streamed down the hatchways, flooding between decks. Sleep was impossible. 'Never got such a rocking as last night. Bones are quite sore. Call to mind the words of Horace that he must have had "a soul of brass who first ventured to sea".'[3]

In the morning light of Sunday the 29th conditions seemed to have eased a little but those who ventured on deck observed the seas were still rough and the crests were breaking in white foam. The decks were too unsteady for mass. Denis Cashman received a present of a fine sweetloaf which he shared with John Flood, Tom Duggan and Jack O'Reilly, and afterwards they enjoyed a long chat together. The afternoon turned more pleasant on deck; the sky cleared to reveal the deep blue typical of the Indian Ocean. The milder conditions continued on the morning of the 30th, and the *Hougoumont* cut her way smoothly through a gentle swell. She was now three-quarters of the way between South Africa and Australia and the crew predicted they would arrive at the end of their voyage sometime in the following week. But the bad weather was not over yet.

Precisely at 4.00 p.m. the ship gave a violent lurch and another squall bore down on them. There followed instant scurrying and confusion on deck; the mate issued orders and the crew and prisoners rushed to obey. The sea, which a quarter of an hour previously had been moderate, was now lashed into fury. Fourteen men were sent aloft to each topsail yard and the sails were hastily taken in; and yet within the hour, the squall had passed over them, and the wind eased. The sun, taunting them, shone again, spreading warmth and comfort. The crew were sent up the mast again to reset the sails. This constant setting and resetting of the sails according to the slightest variation in the weather, the continual need for climbing up and down the ratlines, and the working of the heavy manual equipment on deck, is what gave life on board a sailing vessel the reputation of being the hardest occupation of all. When evening fell, Cashman and Denis Noonan sang Irish folk songs to their Fenian comrades while resting after the exhausting events of the past few days.

As is the way of life in those southern latitudes, calms and storms follow in quick succession. The weather changed yet again during the night and another squall descended upon them. All hands were piped on deck. So unexpectedly had the squall burst on this occasion that the fore mainsail, the mizzen topsails and two jibs were let fly, unloosed to relieve the wind pressure, there being insufficient hands on board to take in all the sail quickly enough to avert danger. Even so, under greatly reduced canvas, the ship sped along and was continually buffeted by waves which pitched her on her beam ends. The pitching, tossing, rocking and lurching threw passengers and crew about the decks. The Fenians trapped below braced themselves in their bunks, finding themselves on their heads one moment and on their feet the next; they were dashed first against the foreside of the bunks and then against the aft, bruising every bone. Sleep was impossible. It is little wonder that they longed for arrival at their port of destination even though that arrival would herald a new life of penal servitude.

There came an easing of conditions at midnight but by this stage in the voyage they had become inured to the discomfort and were experienced enough to know that a lull was only a prelude to more fury to come. How wise they were: within the hour, the squall returned keeping two men on the wheel and all the crew on deck all night. When daylight came on Tuesday the 31st the prisoners, many of whom were suffering from severe bruising, sore limbs and lack of sleep, agreed that it had been the most uncomfortable night of the entire voyage.

The *Hougoumont* sailed on at a remarkable 10 knots on a direct course for Fremantle. In spite of the huge seas, John Flood and Jack O'Reilly were hard at work copying out the entire Christmas *Wild Goose* for Captain Cozens who, being so impressed by it, wanted a copy for himself. How they managed the intricate work must remain a mystery because the whole day was a miserable one of alternating squalls, sunshine and showers, with the vessel shuddering, rocking, and shipping heavy seas. (The diaries of the men do not record how much ink was spilled in the process!) Neither was there respite that night, New Year's Eve, as the weather worsened after 8.00 p.m. For the Fenians on the *Hougoumont*, 1867 was departing with a vengeance.

The rough conditions did not deter—and possibly even encouraged—a group of the criminal convicts from breaking into the ship's store and taking a quantity of food during the night. One of their number was caught, tried, and sentenced to be flogged the next day.

The weather eased as New Year's Day, 1868 dawned but the ship was not yet steady enough for mass; instead, simple prayers were offered at 11.00 a.m. Dinner, supplemented by provisions saved from the previous day, was enjoyed by all, and they sang 'We'll Meet Again Together'. Denis Cashman and O'Reilly spent much of the day in Father Delaney's cabin writing and decorating the copy of the *Wild Goose* for the captain. That evening, O'Reilly transcribed his poem 'In Memory of the French Prisoners' into Denis Cashman's diary, with an explanation of how it had been written originally in his cell in Dartmoor the previous August. The poem had been inspired by the discovery of the graves of prisoners taken captive in the Napoleonic War and buried without ceremony in Dartmoor. Their bones were discovered in the drains being dug by O'Reilly and his comrades. O'Reilly had sought and obtained permission to place them in a proper grave, and erect a simple memorial.

> A plaintive tale is traced on yonder new-raised stone.
> Though few the words, they seem to have a wailing weary tone,
> That well befits such tale as theirs—of suffering and of pain,
> How brave men sank and died beneath the victor's galling chain.
> Of blighted lives, of blighted hopes, and hearts with anguish seared,
> They plainly speak, and gallant hearts grow sick with hope deferred
> A sadder tale was never told—how that devoted band
> Of soldiers drooped and died far from their sunny land.

The long poem of 120 lines is written in the form of a rhetorical eulogy to the unidentified soldier in Napoleon's armies whose remains O'Reilly had been instrumental in having reburied. The poet imagines the soldier, inspired to bravery by his emperor's leadership, riding out to glory in the various campaigns. The style is similar to other epic battle poems of the period—Tennyson's *Charge of the Light Brigade*, for example, or Macaulay's *Battle of Naseby*. O'Reilly's admiration for Napoleon is unmistakeable, and his sympathy for him in exile under the yoke of his English captors is perhaps too naive, but clearly expressed.

At 10.00 a.m. all hands were piped on deck to be present at the punishment of the convict caught stealing food. He was lashed to a spar suspended from the mast and received thirty-six strokes with stoical indifference. Denis Cashman, John Flood, Joe Noonan and Jack O'Reilly could not bring themselves to watch the flogging and surreptitiously talked and smoked until it was all over. Below deck again, Cashman finished copying the captain's *Wild Goose*, and resolved not to do any more writing.

To the intense frustration of all on board, being now so close to Fremantle, flat calm conditions prevailed and the ship hardly moved through the water. 'Nothing is sufficient to dispel the gloom on board the *Hougoumont* but a cry of "land". That monosyllable would act with magical influence on the hearts of all.'[4] The calm weather continued on 3 January, when they were approximately 500 miles west of their destination.

When the two mates saw the captain's copy of the *Wild Goose* nothing would satisfy them until they too received souvenir copies. Weary of writing, though no doubt flattered, O'Reilly, Flood and Cashman agreed to prepare copies of the first and fourth editions. Their trouble earned them further privileges and much appreciated extra food. On 4 January, for example, the three inseparable friends were on deck in the early morning bathing in fresh water, admiring the sunrise, and breakfasting on preserved salmon, ship's biscuit and coffee which were 'a most welcome change from convict rations'.[5]

The fine conditions, typical of those latitudes in January, continued over the weekend while the ship edged towards the West Australian coast. On Sunday, 5 January not a breath of wind stirred the sails. The choir sang at mass, and shoals of porpoises played around the ship enchanting the onlookers. The *Hougoumont* was then 460 miles off the coast.

On 6 January, the Feast of the Epiphany, mass was celebrated and the choir sang as before. Late in the afternoon a shark was sighted, a huge monster slowly gliding beneath the ship. When a pork bait was thrown overboard he took it on the hook and was quickly hauled aboard, though it required the efforts of a dozen men. The fish was about 14 feet long and of a dark blue colour with a silver belly. The shark fought, raising its head and dashing it violently against the deck, causing blood to flow from its mouth and the deck timbers to shake. Eventually, after a gruesome battering, the giant head was severed, yet the carcass still shook. A small fish was still alive when taken from the shark's stomach. One of the sailors took the backbone with which he intended to make a walking-stick. Several of the Fenians claimed pieces of skin to make cigar cases and tobacco pouches, and O'Reilly secured a piece to make a cover for the bible given to him by Father Delaney. The flesh of the shark was snow-white but the surgeon superintendent gave orders that it was not to be eaten.

On 7 January, 350 miles off the coast, the three friends were hard at work again finishing off the copies of the *Goose* for the ship's mates. The sea remained calm and the winds light. On this day, John Boyle O'Reilly wrote a dedication and moving poem in Cashman's notebook in testimony of their close friendship on board the *Hougoumont*. Of the three eight-line stanzas, the last is quoted:

> Let not frowning misfortune appal you,
> Nor shrink with Calamity's rod.
> Remember whatever befalls you
> Is willed by an unseeing God.
> Act yourself, and ne'er trust to another.
> When duty awaits, never rest.
> Look onward and upward, my brother,
> And forget not, what is, is the best.

On Wednesday, 8 January, their last full day at sea, a splendid breeze sprang up and the *Hougoumont* forged ahead under a deep blue West Australian sky. They were greatly cheered by the preparations on board for arrival the next day. The sailors were at work dragging the cable up from the chain locker and placing the anchors in the bows. That night the Fenians held their last concert.

The following morning the convicts were on deck early straining their eyes for a first glimpse of land. The sea was smooth and the summer heat strong. As the dawn lifted they saw only a few miles distant on the lee bow a long, low range surmounted by a lighthouse. This was Rottnest Island. The pilot boat appeared with seven men aboard and by noon they had passed within a stone's throw of Rottnest and witnessed their first sight of Aborigines working in the sand, the island then being used as a place of punishment for natives. O'Reilly was touched and remembered the sight years later when writing his novel: 'Every eye witnessed the strange sight of gangs of naked black men working like beavers in the sand'.[6] The scene would also have impressed itself on the convicts as a reminder of the direction their lives were about to take.

An hour later the *Hougoumont* approached within a mile of the Fremantle pier:

> The surrounding sea and land were very strange and beautiful. The green shoal-water, the soft air, with a yellowish warmth, the pure white sand of the beach,

and the dark green of the broken forest beyond, made a scene almost like fairyland.[7]

There was much commotion and bustle on deck, and orders were given in a commanding voice to release the anchor. The cable roared out through the hawsehole and plunged into the sea. The bell on the forecastle rang the depths as the chain clattered over the side. When the din ceased, the bell signalled to the poop deck that the anchor was holding; and then there was silence—a silence that the weary convicts had not experienced since they boarded the ship at anchor off Portland. After a non-stop voyage of ninety-six days, and covering a distance of 14,000 nautical miles, the *Hougoumont* had finally arrived with the last cargo of convicts for Western Australia. The Fenians lined the gunwales craving a sight of their new home; they were anxious, excited even, and certainly relieved to have come to the end of their uncomfortable voyage.

Ashore, crowds of silent Fremantle citizens had assembled, desirous of watching the ship's approach; they were no less inquisitive and anxious than those on board. For most of them, however, the cargo of the *Hougoumont* was not welcome, and the more belligerent among them waited nervously for the first sign of trouble.

Part Two

THE UNWILLING IMMIGRANT

1868–1869

CHAPTER 11

'THE ESTABLISHMENT'

The presence of convicts was accepted as an ordinary part of life, and the new ones arriving were unremarked. A few children on an occasional verandah might stop their play to stare for a moment at the dingy figures filing by, but the inhabitants as a whole had lost interest in a sight that had been frequent for the best part of seventeen years.

Alexandra Hasluck

THE town of Fremantle which O'Reilly and his fellow convicts gazed at across the water from the deck of the *Hougoumont* on the morning of Thursday, 9 January 1868, differed greatly from the modern port that is the commercial, fishing, industrial and tourist city of today.

True he would have seen some features which are still there, but these for the most part could only have impressed upon him the predominantly penal life of the settlement. There was, for example, the Round House, the original twelve-sided limestone prison which still looks like a fort standing high on Arthur Head; the stately Gothic-styled asylum with its two wings and steeply pitched roofs built for deranged prisoners and which is now the Arts Centre; the Fremantle Boys School, now the Film and Television Institute; the commissariat buildings and stores in Cliff Street and the warders' cottages in Henderson Street, all of which survive today; and the largest, most imposing structure, the new prison, commonly known as 'the Establishment'. Dominating the town on high ground to the east it was to gain the distinction of being the longest-serving State prison in Australia, only being decommissioned as recently as November 1991.

When O'Reilly first saw Fremantle the town was larger, in terms of population and development, than Perth located 10 miles upriver. There was considerable opinion at the time—at least among Fremantle residents—that Fremantle, rather than Perth, should be the capital of the colony.

The town itself, though small in extent, is compact and regular in its arrangement, and as the allotments were originally laid out on a smaller scale than those in Perth, the buildings are not so scattered as in the city, and the place has assumed much more of a town-like appearance. There are few buildings with any great claims to architectural beauty, though the houses are, generally speaking, substantially constructed.[1]

The High Street was aligned as it is today, and on either side were limestone business houses, hotels, and cottages—some with verandahs—all bounded by the Round House at the ocean end, and the new prison at the other. The deepwater harbour of today was over thirty years in the future; the waterfront that O'Reilly saw would be far beyond recognition by a contemporary visitor. In 1868 the Swan River estuary was a different shape, being wide and shallow, and protected from the ocean by sandbanks which precluded shipping from moving upstream. Therefore goods for transport inland had to be unloaded from the long, deepwater jetty and transferred to barges beyond the shallows, which then conveyed the freight upriver.

It is a small unpretending little town, and one which makes but a slight impression upon a newcomer. In the main street and in the three or four short thorough-fares that connect the sea jetty with the river pier and wharf there are a few handsome and substantial houses belonging either to the Government or to some of the principal inhabitants. In these streets, too, are situated some of the larger and more important shops, or rather, 'stores' of the chief traders of the town.[2]

The dominant impressions on O'Reilly, the poet, on that first morning would undoubtedly have been the dazzling brightness of everything in the summer sun and the intense, dry heat. At that time Fremantle would have presented an impermanent, camp-like appearance, with roads and open spaces of compacted white sand and the almost colourless dune herbage trodden bare. The common building material was wood, but the more substantial buildings were made of the locally quarried marine limestone which presented a face as white as the sand on which they rested. The whiteness tended to reflect the dazzling light and increase the heat. We can safely guess that the temperature at that time would have been between thirty and thirty-seven degrees Celsius (the mean maximum for January is thirty degrees Celsius), but the afternoon westerly breeze—the blessed 'Fremantle Doctor'—would have brought relief from the heat if it arrived that day, but would have whipped up the water and made the ship's anchorage uncomfortable.

First on board when the *Hougoumont* dropped anchor in the flat calm of the early morning were Constable Michael Jackson of the Water Police and the port doctor. The time was 9.30 a.m. Then in the afternoon came the Comptroller-General, Henry Wakeford, together with the Governor, Dr John Hampton, with all the ceremony due to them. The Governor 'wore a blue tunic, with epaulettes, like a naval officer, white trousers and a cocked hat', O'Reilly observed.[3] Also clambering aboard from the steam tug, without ceremony, was a reporter from the *Fremantle Herald* who was there to cover the Governor's progress, but just as anxious for a story about conditions on the voyage and the behaviour of the Fenians. In the edition of 11 January 1868 the *Herald* briefly reported the arrival of the *Hougoumont* (the report from aboard the vessel was held over until a later edition):

> The town was in a state of great excitement, and pretty equally divided between those who sympathised with them [the Fenians] and those who from fear or principle were determined to find that they had attempted some desperate deeds during the voyage.[4]

Stepping aboard a convict transport was hardly a new experience for Governor Hampton who had previously served in the navy as an assistant surgeon and had sailed as surgeon superintendent on transports to Van Diemen's Land. He was familiar with the routine, the precautions to be taken, and the punishments to be administered, and from what we know of him in later administrations, we can be sure that on board ship he would have been more severe than the surgeon superintendent, Dr Smith, on the *Hougoumont*. Like those watching from a distance on the shore, Hampton's first consideration would have been to enquire of the conduct of the Fenians, and on this matter he could hardly have been better pleased. He received reports from the chaplains that they had been 'most civil, obedient, and religious' and Captain Cozens told him that they were 'exemplary from the beginning to the end' of the voyage.[5]

The *Herald* reporter was not allowed to speak to individual convicts but published the following in the edition of 25 January:

> We learn that they [the Fenian convicts] expressed themselves pleased at being forwarded to Western Australia and generally led Mr Williams [the senior chaplain] to believe that they had determined to conduct themselves so as to merit, what in all probability will be extended to them—Fenianism being stamped out— the royal prerogative of mercy.[6]

In the early hours of the morning of Friday, 10 January when it was yet still dark, the prisoners on board the *Hougoumont* were aroused from their bunks and ordered into barges which then took them the short distance to the

Fremantle town wharf. As dawn was breaking behind 'the Establishment' they were marching towards it in single file up the High Street, keeping to the centre of the road. At that hour there would be few, if any, of the local populace to watch them: perhaps that is how the authorities had planned it.

That first glimpse of their new home was recorded by one of the civilian Fenians, Patrick Walle, who, like O'Reilly, came from near Drogheda, County Louth. In a letter to his parents he wrote:

> The little town of Fremantle presents to the immigrant eye a rather strange appearance—the houses are constructed in an old-fashioned style, of all white sandstone [sic], nothing is seen but white...the streets are covered with white sand, which floats about with the wind most abundantly; prison all white, yards white, people dressed in white...[7]

On they marched, a shuffling line of some 279 convicts, until after climbing a rise in the ground they came to the imposing prison gatehouse, a castle-like entrance comprising two octagonal towers divided by a central gateway reminiscent of a portcullis. Over the gateway was—and still is—a large, black ominous-looking clock face set in a round pediment. Once through the gateway they found themselves in an immense open area, a parade ground of white sand enclosed by a high wall. Rising in front of them was the prison itself, two

Fremantle at the time of O'Reilly's imprisonment. Fremantle Prison can be seen, top left.
(Courtesy of the Battye Library, 21378P)

massive four-storey barrack blocks built of limestone which formed two wings spreading either side of a two-storey, neoclassical portico. On the ground floor of this handsome central structure were administrative offices and stores; and above, illuminated by large Georgian windows, was the commodious Church of England chapel, its exterior above the doorway crowned by a pediment on which was embossed a crown, the letters 'VR', and the date '1855'. Altogether a solid, imperial building built by convicts, redolent of Victorian notions of punishment and rehabilitation; and yet because of the sense of space, the clear blue sky, and the light pink tinge of the stone, it was neither as grim nor depressing as similar institutions in England.

Greeting the prisoners that day in the manner of a formal military parade were Governor Hampton and Henry Wakeford. The long line of men filed passed them, and saluted. Hampton's reputation then, and since, has been sullied by accounts of his cruelty and is surrounded by controversy. He was autocratic and severe, and had been unpopular with prisoners and administrators alike during his unhappy reign as Comptroller-General of Convicts in Van Diemen's Land. There, it was alleged, Hampton had engaged in corrupt practices including the employment of convict labour for personal profit. A warrant had been issued for his arrest, but before the argument concerning its legality could be settled, he applied for, and was granted, two years leave to go to Canada on urgent private affairs. Surprisingly, with this record, he had been appointed Governor of Western Australia in 1862, and conflict soon dogged him to the Swan River Colony. He came into open conflict with the Comptroller-General, Captain Newland, virtually forced Newland's resignation and appointed his own son, George Hampton, to act in the position despite the fact that he held other salaried posts at the time. Hampton was clearly not a sadist as some have depicted him, nor brutal—his policy towards the Fenians proved moderate—but he was certainly imperious, uncompromising, single-minded and a strict disciplinarian. From the colonists' point of view he achieved good results and they were sorry to see him leave in November 1868. They tried to prolong his term of office by sending a monster petition to the Secretary of State for the Colonies in London.

In view of his strong commitment to building works and roadways in the colony, it is safe to assume that when the new batch of prisoners passed before him on that January day in Fremantle, Hampton would have been assessing their physical capabilities. These men were his last batch of convict workers and he had many unfinished projects on hand.

The routine for admitting prisoners to Fremantle Prison was not to change much over the ensuing 120 years. Each man bathed, had his hair cropped and his beard cut, and underwent a medical examination. His height, colour, build, and other physical features were noted; his background and his prison record documented. He was then issued with prison clothing. John Boyle O'Reilly was recorded as being twenty-three years of age with black hair, brown eyes and a dark complexion. He was described as a 'reporter' but this was later changed to 'compositor', perhaps because it was thought to be a more useful occupation in the colony.

O'Reilly, like the others, was issued with summer clothing: a dark grey jacket, a vest, three shirts (two of cotton and one of flannel), two handkerchiefs, two pairs of socks, two pairs of trousers, one pair of boots and a cap. When O'Reilly emerged from the reception block with his bundle of clothes dressed in a new suit of rough Drogheda linen, ornamented with a red stripe and black bands, he was officially termed a 'probationary convict'. Under the system which at that time was thought to be especially enlightened, because his first six months of solitary confinement had been served in British gaols he was now beginning his probationary period, a period which would run to half his remaining sentence. At the end of the probationary period—provided he was judged to have behaved himself and his record was good—he could expect to be given his 'ticket-of-leave'.[8] (Conversely, in the modern system it is the 'ticket-of-leave' period which is termed 'on probation'.) A ticket-of-leave prisoner was allowed to live outside the prison, marry and seek paid employment, but he had to report at regular intervals to the local magistrate. In March, shortly after O'Reilly arrived in Western Australia, the convict population involving both probationary and ticket-of-leave prisoners numbered 3,220, approximately one in six of the entire population of 20,000.[9]

The reception process for 279 convicts stretched on throughout the day and into the next. But at noon on the first day there was a break when the bell sounded for dinner. The men queued up at the kitchen for their rations; the Fenians were in a separate division from the other convicts. They were each given 14 ounces of fresh meat, 12 ounces of potatoes, and 6 ounces of bread: this amount if weighed out on a plate today represents a substantial though perhaps uninteresting meal. Afterwards they were allowed into the exercise yard for a smoke and talk. It was the free issue of tobacco once a week which prompted Anthony Trollope's often quoted, testy complaint on visiting the prison in 1872: 'Why a man who had come from England with a life sentence against him should receive tobacco...I could not understand'.[10]

The cells in Fremantle Prison still occupy four floors, or galleries, in the traditional prison fashion; the length of the barrack block is open from ground floor to ceiling in the centre. The only features of architectural interest are the jarrah roof with its tie beams and rafters, and the jarrah stairways at either end of the block which, together with the limestone walls, slightly soften the overall

*Fremantle Prison, commonly known as 'the Establishment'. Main entrance, c. 1860.
(Courtesy of the Battye Library, 5183P)*

austerity of the design. Originally the individual cells were tiny, 7 feet long by 5 feet wide (they have been enlarged since O'Reilly's time), and lit by a small barred window high up so that unless the prisoner could stand on some item of furniture (which he did not possess) he could not see out. Two large hooks were inserted in the end walls of the cell from which to swing the prisoner's hammock, there being no beds. One advantage of the thick limestone walls was the relative coolness of the building even on the hottest days outside.

O'Reilly was awakened on his first morning in Fremantle by the insistent bells ringing at 4.30 a.m. He washed, stowed his bedding and cleaned his cell, and paraded for breakfast at 5.30 a.m. At 6.00 a.m. he attended chapel with his fellow Catholics where prayers were said by the chaplain, Father Lynch. At 6.30 a.m. all the convicts paraded in the prison yard for inspection and to be counted, after which they assembled informally in the exercise areas until 9.00 a.m. They worked at their allotted tasks until 11.50 a.m. when again they paraded before being dismissed for dinner and a two-hour break. At 2.00 p.m. they returned to work until 5.00 p.m. and they paraded again at 6.00 p.m. At that time tea was served. O'Reilly and his friends then spent a period in 'school' until 9.00 p.m. before being locked in their cells for the night.

On the Monday following their initiation into Fremantle, the Fenians and other convicts commenced the work to which they had been assigned. Most of them were sent to bush camps on the outskirts of Perth and Fremantle, to work on roads. Two groups of twenty civilian Fenians remained separated from the others, under supervision of the warders who had been in charge of them on board the *Hougoumont*. This arrangement was ordered by Hampton himself who, it may be inferred, had been influenced by the advice from Father Matthew Gibney and J.T. Reilly (see page 53). Hampton took a harder line in dealing with the seventeen military Fenians:

> [T]he risk of such men combining together for evil purposes, induced me to disperse them as widely as possible throughout the colony, not sending more than one or two of them to the same station.[11]

Six Fenians were retained at the gaol for special duties. O'Reilly's close friends, John Flood and Denis Cashman, were appointed clerks, one in the superintendent's office, the other in the clerk of works' office. Others were appointed to the prison store. John O'Reilly himself—perhaps at first being overlooked as a military Fenian—was appointed orderly and librarian to Father Lynch. In this capacity he was both sacristan and cleaner of the chapel; he was in charge of members of the choir when practice occurred four times a week; he was a monitor during school periods, responsible for the issuing of paper and writing equipment; and he was responsible for the library and the issuing of books. He was also allowed to pass out of the prison to run errands for the chaplain and to tend and feed his horses. John O'Reilly was ideally suited to all this work and we can only speculate why he was suddenly ordered elsewhere after a period of only three weeks. No evidence exists that the chaplain found him unsatisfactory; it seems highly unlikely that it was Father Lynch's wish to lose him. But on 11 February the superintendent of the prison issued an order that Prisoner 9843, John Boyle O'Reilly, be transferred 115 miles south to Bunbury to join a party of convicts at a nearby bush camp who were engaged in building the Bunbury-Vasse road. A logical explanation could be that the superintendent, on receiving a request from Father Lynch for O'Reilly's services, had overlooked his status at first, and afterwards quickly rectified his mistake once he was aware of the Governor's attitude towards military Fenians; perhaps he was even instructed to do so.

How O'Reilly took the news of his posting we do not know. His work as the chaplain's assistant would have suited him and given him certain favours and privileges. Compared with his experiences in English prisons working in Fremantle, though hardly pleasant, was freer and more humane. And yet, ironically, his sentence to road gang work at a bush camp set in train circumstances for his eventual escape—an escape that could not have been accomplished had he remained in the comparative comfort of the prison chaplaincy.

Escape was a constant dream of all the convicts and many of them attempted to turn the dream into reality, but with no success. According to an official report in 1862, not one convict had successfully escaped from custody during the previous twelve years, despite an average of 500 convicts each year attempting to do so. The reasons for this disheartening lack of success are easy to understand. To escape inland was only inviting starvation, illness, and injury from exposure. Inland, there was simply nowhere to escape to. Escape by sea on one of the visiting trading ships, or preferably on an American whaler, seemed a reasonable alternative, but to do so required not only money to secure a passage but also support from sympathetic friends and a favourable set of circumstances. The result was that although a third of the prison population attempted to escape at some time during their sentences, including nineteen from the *Hougoumont* in the first year of their stay, all were brought back to face the severest penalties: penalties which, in Hampton's reign, included 100 strokes of the lash and six months in solitary confinement. Absconders were also required to wear special clothes and to work in chains for two years, supervised by warders with loaded firearms. The everyday sight of these pitiable men, deliberately made public examples as proof of the futility of escape, was calculated to deter others from following their hopeless path. And yet a large number were not deterred judging by the figures quoted above. A contemporary of O'Reilly's in Fremantle Prison was Western Australia's most notorious escapee, the legendary Joseph Bolitho Jones, popularly known as 'Moondyne Joe'. He may be described as Fremantle's own Houdini and became the scourge of Governor Hampton. He and O'Reilly quite probably met, but it could have been only briefly because from 1866 Moondyne Joe spent his time in prison in a specially constructed reinforced cell—an 'escape proof masterpiece'—which has since become a tourist attraction. Joseph Bolitho Jones's story evidently so impressed O'Reilly that he made Jones a major character in his novel *Moondyne* (1879), albeit the character in the novel was more ennobled and more deserving of sympathy than the known historical figure. In the novel Moondyne, recaptured once more, is befriended and saved by Aborigines:

> The chain-gang of Fremantle is the depth of penal degradation. The convicts wear from thirty to fifty pounds of iron, according to their offence. It is riveted on their bodies in the prison forge, and when they have served their time, the great rings have to be chiselled off their calloused limbs.
>
> The chain-gang works outside the prison walls of Fremantle, in the granite quarries. The neighbourhood, being thickly settled with pardoned men and ticket-of-leave men, had long been deserted by the aborigines; but from the day of Moondyne's sentence they began to build their *myers* and hold their *corroborees* near the quarries.
>
> For two years the chain-gang toiled among the stones, and the black men sat on the great unhewn rocks, and never seemed to tire of the scene. The natives never spoke to a prisoner, but sat there in dumb interest, everyday in the year from sunrise to evening.

One day they disappeared from the quarries and an officer who passed through their village of *myers,* found them deserted. It was quite a subject of interesting conversation among the warders. Where had they gone to? Why had they departed in the night?

The day following an answer came to these queries. When the chain-gang was formed to return to the prison one link was gone—Moondyne was missing.[12]

It is more than likely that O'Reilly gave as much thought to ways of escaping as any other prisoner. But after months of incarceration in English prisons and having had time for contemplation on board ship, he had grown from the impetuous, dashing Hussar into a mature, more reflective young man who was probably hardened by his experiences. At any rate, he was prepared to bide his time. He knew that if he was to have any chance of succeeding in an escape bid he must not rush into it unprepared as he had apparently done in Chatham, Portsmouth and Dartmoor: his first consideration was to establish a reputation for good conduct and dependability.

O'Reilly, the prisoner, maintained his belief in the Fenian cause, and beneath his submissive exterior he was still a passionate republican. When he learned from a newspaper smuggled into the prison of the executions on 27 November 1867 of the three Fenians—Allen, Larkin and O'Brien—following the Manchester incident, he was deeply moved. Overnight in his cell he composed a eulogy to the 'martyrs to the cause' as they appeared to him to be, and as they have since been styled. His sadness and burning anger is evident in his poem 'The Dead Who Died for Ireland':

> The dead who died for Ireland!
> Oh, these are living words
> To nerve the hearts of patriots —
> to steel avenging swords —
> They thrill the soul when spoken,
> and lowly bend the head
> With reverence for the memories
> of all our martyred dead.
>
> The dead who died for Ireland —
> the noble ones — the best,
> Who gave their lives for Motherland,
> Who poured upon her breast,
> In Freedom's cause, the blood she gave —
> Who with their dying breath,
> Sent prayers to God to heal her woes —
> then sealed their love in death.

The dead who died for Ireland,
How hallowed are their graves!
With all the memories fresh and green,
Oh! how could we be slaves?
How could we patient clang the chain?
How could we fawn and bow?
How could we crouch like mongrels
'neath the keeper's frowning brow?

Be proud, ye men of Ireland!
Be proud of those who died;
Never men o'er all the earth
Had greater cause for pride —
Hope and strive, and league for freedom,
And again the souls will rise
Of the dead who died for Ireland
To cheer you to the prize.[13]

As has been noted earlier O'Reilly's stay in Fremantle Prison was of short duration. Scarcely had he been there three weeks when, on 12 February, we find him submissively accepting articles of clothing and personal supplies and packing two days rations in a haversack for a journey. The order had been issued by the superintendent that:

[Prisoner] 9843 John O'Reilly will be transferred hence to Bunbury for the party about to clear the new line of road between Bunbury and the Vasse. The Accountant of stores will make the necessary requisition for transport.[14]

The prisoner relinquished his post as chaplain's orderly and prepared to board a coastal steamer from the deepwater jetty, bound for Bunbury. His friend Denis Cashman, who was to remain in Fremantle, remembered the day of O'Reilly's departure and years later wrote in his obituary in the *Boston Herald* of 24 August 1890:

We waved him an adieu as we were bustled through the gates. Our hearts were heavy: we could not speak. A tear—well, no matter. Flood, whom O'Reilly loved, never saw him again.

CHAPTER 12

THE BUSH CAMP

Western Australia is a vast and unknown country, almost mysterious in its solitude and unlikeness to any other part of the earth. It is the greatest of the Australias in extent, and in many features the richest and the loveliest.

John Boyle O'Reilly

FOR the second time within the space of two months, O'Reilly found himself pacing the deck of a sailing ship; in this case, a small coastal trader on charter to the government. The voyage of two days duration was likely to have been in pleasant conditions in hot summer weather. As the vessel neared the port of Bunbury, O'Reilly may have dreamed of escape. He was not to know that almost exactly a year later he would be in the same vicinity, striving desperately to keep a secret rendezvous with his deliverers.

Bunbury, on the west coast, actually faces north. This is because the little port town sits comfortably in the curve of Koombana Bay which sweeps round in the form of a 'J'. Looking north the upright of the 'J' represents the coast, and the curve at the base is known a Casuarina Point. The bay is therefore well protected from the prevailing south-westerly storms, a fact much appreciated by the American whaling fleet which had made it an important base for its operations in the Indian Ocean in the mid-19th century. Also appreciated by smaller shipping was the Leschenault Inlet, a huge, elongated saltwater lake stretching northwards. After passing through the narrow entrance from Koombana Bay ships of light draught could rest in its waters well protected from sea and weather by a tongue of land comprising high dunes, bush and scrub vegetation. Leschenault Inlet was to prove a critical factor in O'Reilly's escape a year hence.

The original native name of Bunbury was Goomburrup—the 'up' at the end of the word indicating 'place of water'. Governor Stirling bestowed its new name in 1836 in honour of Lieutenant H.W. Bunbury, the surveyor and explorer who first mapped the area. At first the settlement was slow to develop. Most interest and energy in the late 1830s and 1840s was directed a short distance up the coast to Australind where the London-based Western Australian Company was intent on a grandiose but ill-fated scheme to attract immigrants and develop a modern city on the shores of Leschenault Inlet. But Bunbury had the advantages of port facilities, a river system—the Preston and the Collie—and proximity to agricultural settlements further south in the district known as the Vasse. It was only a question of time before Bunbury became a more important agricultural and trading centre.

By the time of O'Reilly's arrival in mid-February 1868 Bunbury was a busy export centre for timber and sandalwood cut from the hinterland. Jarrah, then known as Swan River mahogany, was in demand as a building material, and for making pit props and furniture. The railway sleepers for London's new underground railway system and the cobbles for the roads were also made of jarrah from forests in the vicinity. Will Sheridan, O'Reilly's hero in his novel *Moondyne*, works as an agent for a timber export business and eventually makes his fortune. The timber cutters in the novel—and in fact—were invariably ticket-of-leave men, some of whom had been granted their parole before arriving in the colony.

In the town itself a large trading store, several warehouses, a hotel, a convict hospital, a courthouse, and police and pensioners' quarters served a growing agricultural population scattered throughout the surrounding bushland. Archdeacon Wollaston had built his first timber Anglican church at Picton on the outskirts of the town, and Father Patrick McCabe was building a more substantial brick-constructed Catholic church on a lime cement foundation. A steady supply of convicts was required for work on the government buildings—a customs house and bonded stores—and the roadways. For this purpose a convict depot had been built overlooking the port. Here were housed a principal warder, a medical officer and a Church of England chaplain. The depot acted as headquarters for up to a hundred convicts supervised by twelve warders, most of whom were split into working parties stationed at nearby bush camps. The warder in charge of each camp was required to report to Bunbury and draw stores at regular intervals. Prior to O'Reilly's arrival thirty-eight convicts from the *Hougoumont* had been sent to Bunbury, one of whom was a military Fenian called John Lynch, also of O'Reilly's regiment but, unlike O'Reilly, serving a comparatively short sentence of five years.

A new road—now known as the Vasse Highway—had been planned to link Bunbury with settlements in the region of the Vasse which lay to the south-west, on the shores of Geographe Bay. The district took its name from the River Vasse which flows into the bay at modern-day Busselton. Geographe Bay, Cape Naturaliste and Vasse are French names; the first two locations were named after

French exploration ships, and Vasse was named after the unfortunate French sailor who was drowned at the entrance to the river in 1801.

We do not know how O'Reilly was employed during the first month of his stay in Bunbury but it was certainly not on the new Vasse road because a start on construction was delayed until the end of the month. It seems that officials in Perth were unaware of the delay. The principal warder in Bunbury was asked in a memorandum of 11 March to explain why work had not begun. O'Reilly may have been rushed down to Bunbury prematurely. However, by 29 March all stores, tools and equipment had been moved to a camp 5 miles south, and work was ready to begin. O'Reilly was a member of the party and in the charge of Warder Henry Woodman.

Woodman had come to Western Australia as an assistant warder in 1860, and was promoted to the rank of warder in 1866. He was regarded as 'a most zealous, energetic and valuable officer'.[1] At about the time O'Reilly was being instructed in Fremantle Prison to make ready for his journey, Woodman, accompanied by his wife and two children, was also heading south. He was being transferred the 60 miles from Pinjarra to Bunbury to assume the responsibility of opening up the new road. When the time came to begin work on the road the warder's family remained in town while Woodman himself was posted to the bush camp. The relationship between the two men, warder and felon— and between felon and the warder's family—was to prove of the utmost significance to O'Reilly in the ensuing months and remains, even to the present time, an enigma which can be only partly explained.

From the writings of O'Reilly in his novel *Moondyne*, and the letters home from other Fenian convicts (no letters from O'Reilly exist from that time) we are able to get a fairly accurate picture of what life would have been like for the *Hougoumont* convicts in the road working camps. The men were housed either under canvas or in rudely constructed huts made of logs and dried reeds with roofs of paperbark or blackboy rushes. They slept in hammocks with neither sheets nor pillows and were often tormented by fleas and mosquitoes. Their rations, drawn from the Bunbury depot, were supplemented by savoury kangaroo or cockatoo stew, and they brewed hot pannikins of billy tea.

O'Reilly's first month in the bush, March, was still liable to be very hot although it was the beginning of autumn. It is a month famous for stifling, drying, easterly winds and midday temperatures of forty degrees Celsius. Working a nine-hour day breaking rocks, sawing down trees, digging out obstinate roots with primitive tools and hacking a pathway through lacerating bush under the burning sun—with little or no protection, and no comfort from refrigerated drinks—could have broken the spirit of the strongest of men and seriously damaged their health. O'Reilly has left a vivid description of the scene at his camp in the second chapter of his fictional story *Moondyne*. No one who knows the bush can doubt that such an evocative passage was written from first-hand experience:

> Had there been any moisture in the bush, it would have steamed in the heavy heat. During the midday heat not a bird stirred among the mahogany and gum trees. On the flat tops of the low banksia the round heads of the white cockatoos could be seen in thousands, motionless as the trees themselves. Not a parrot had the vim to scream. The chirping insects were silent. Not a snake had courage to rustle his hard skin against the hot and dead bush-grass. The bright-eyed iguanas were in their holes. The mahogany sawyers had left their logs and were sleeping in the cool sand of their pits. Even the travelling ants had halted on their wonderful roads, and sought the shade of a bramble.
>
> All free things were at rest; but the penetrating click of the axe, heard far through the bush, and now and again a harsh word of command, told that it was a land of bondmen.
>
> From daylight to dark, through the hot noon as steadily as in the cool evening, the convicts were at work on the roads—the weary work that has no wages, no promotion, no incitement, no variation for good or bad, except stripes for the laggard.[2]

While working in the bush O'Reilly suffered many hardships but probably his worst deprivation was being separated from the company of his Irish compatriots: it is not likely that the other Fenian in the district, John Lynch, served in the same working party. O'Reilly was thus thrown into the company of ordinary convicts.

It is tempting for us, at this distance, to suppose that transportees – other than political prisoners – were for the most part gentle, innocent victims of cruel, retributive British justice. Doubtless some were, which gave rise to Dickens's character Magwitch, the infamous case of the six Tolpuddle Martyrs, and the many authenticated stories of starving, unemployed breadwinners convicted for stealing bread for their families out of sheer desperation; but it would be a mistake to believe that the majority of O'Reilly's companions were in this category. Even if we allow that his friend and biographer, Roche, exaggerated O'Reilly's predicament somewhat (the more to emphasize his nobility and his forgiving nature), his descriptions – based on conversations with O'Reilly – were probably somewhat near the mark.

> Among the criminals with whom he was forced to associate were some of the most degraded of human kind—murderers, burglars, sinners of every grade and colour of vice. They were the poisoned flower of civilisation's corruption, more

depraved than the savage...They were the overflow of society's cesspool, the irreclaimable victims of sin—too often the wretched fruits of heredity or environment.[3]

A list of crimes committed by the non-Fenian prisoners aboard the *Hougoumont* includes twelve convicted of murder, twelve of manslaughter, twenty-two of rape, forty-six of burglary, twenty-one of larceny, thirty of robbery and theft, eight of arson and two of incest.[4] Not salubrious company for one of O'Reilly's sensibilities and accomplishments. And yet, according to Roche, O'Reilly looked upon 'his fellow-sufferers with eyes of mercy, seeing how many of them were the victims of cruel, selfish, social conditions'.[5] The following passage from *Moondyne* bears this out:

> Who or what was that man? An escaped convict. What had he been? Perhaps a robber and a mutineer—or maybe he had killed a man in the white heat of passion. No one knew—no one cared to know...they have found bottom, where all stand equal.[6]

O'Reilly had undergone a gradual change as a result of his experiences on board ship; and more particularly as a result of his friendship with John Flood and Denis Cashman. He had matured. He was still a convinced patriot, smarting under the injustices inflicted on his country—carrying them from his mother's womb, to paraphrase Yeats—but the two older, wiser and deeply spiritual men with whom he had spent long hours in conversation undoubtedly reined in some of that earlier, youthful impetuosity, and helped him to see Ireland's suffering in the context of the wider suffering of all subject peoples. This is reflected in the untitled poem he wrote about Western Australia, showing extraordinary insight and a degree of reconciliation:

> Nation of sun and sin
> Thy flowers and crimes are red,
> And thy heart is sore within
> While thy glory crowns thy head.
> Land of the songless birds,
> What was thy ancient crime
> Burning through lapse of time
> Like a prophet's cursing words?
>
> Aloes and myrrh and tears
> Mix in thy bitter wine;
> Drink while the cup is thine,
> Drink, for the draft is sign
> Of thy reign in the coming years.[7]

While our impulse may be to direct our sympathies towards the luckless convicts in the then inhuman penal system—especially when those convicts are epitomized by so attractive a figure as O'Reilly—we should also remember that there were other less obvious victims of the system. The position of a warder in charge of a convict road gang in the bush in 1868, for example, would not have been an enviable one. He was isolated from his family and friends. He had to camp out in all weathers some 10 to 15 miles from headquarters, and in the company of a group of men who at best were grudgingly subservient, at worst openly hostile. The warder would have been answerable to higher authority for every movement and decision, day and night. He could never be off duty. He would have been required to strictly supervise a program of work determined by others far removed from the site and ignorant of local difficulties; and he would be judged efficient or incompetent according to how closely the program was followed. Charged with such a responsibility he could never relax his guard, and if he were ever tempted to apply leniency, or bypass regulations, he risked being found out, censured, and inevitably demoted. The warder in charge of a convict road gang could be said to be as much a prisoner of the system as the convicts themselves.

Because warders were expected to be at one and the same time armed guards, works supervisors, administrative clerks, camp supervisors and stores managers, they were allowed to choose a promising convict from the gang to be their assistant. Inevitably, in Woodman's road gang the choice fell on O'Reilly: he was appointed probationary convict constable.

The system at that time was to appoint some of the best behaved probationer prisoners as convict constables to lighten the work of the regular warders, not only in road gangs but at the various convict establishments. It may be considered ironical that the orderly functioning of the prison system was dependent to a great extent on the cooperation and help of some of those who were its victims. Convict constables were rewarded with a remission of sentence, extra cash gratuities, and status. They wore a red stripe on their sleeve, and upon release could be recommended for service in the colonial police force. According to the records O'Reilly was never a fully-fledged convict constable—as erroneously stated by Roche—but was clearly in line for such a promotion. It is reasonable to suppose that he would have had to serve a probationary year: but at the end of that year he chose a different path.

O'Reilly's duties as assistant to Woodman would have been primarily clerical such as keeping records, ordering stores, keeping the accounts, and generally supervising the management of the group's activities. It is clear from subsequent events that he was also used frequently as a messenger and was required to travel the distance between the road camp and the district convict establishment in Bunbury. In a practical way he became freer than the warder himself.

It has been an intense disappointment to all those who have researched O'Reilly's life, and attempted a biography, to discover that penal records from the Bunbury depot, faithfully kept all those years ago, now no longer exist. The detailed daily workings of O'Reilly's road gang and even its exact position, its personnel, and O'Reilly's written records, remain a secret from us. And so for a picture of those months in the bush we have to rely on Roche's biography of 1901, on O'Reilly's own writings, on scraps of information in the official records where they are found to exist, on local hearsay evidence collected by the scholar and historian, Martin Carroll, and finally on carefully formed guesses.

It is one such guess to suppose that Warder Woodman used the occasion of O'Reilly's journeys to Bunbury not only for official messages, but also to keep in touch with his family; to take them money perhaps, and letters, and to receive in return messages and gifts. It is probable that Woodman came to rely on this means of contact with his family, and that his family, in turn, welcomed the visits of O'Reilly. It is further possible to deduce that O'Reilly's charm, good manners, and civility endeared him to the members of Woodman's family. It was not uncommon at the time for women to espouse a more sympathetic attitude towards convicts and Aborigines than their husbands in positions of authority. The man was frequently paid to uphold and maintain the law; the wife was free to judge on her instincts. (A good example of this had arisen some years earlier when Louisa Clifton had pleaded with her lover, the local magistrate, to deal lightly with an Aboriginal offender.)[8]

That O'Reilly became a frequent and welcome visitor to the Woodman household cannot be doubted and, in becoming so, it was inevitable that he would attract the attention of Woodman's eldest daughter, Jessie. Michael Davitt's narrative, following his visit to Western Australia twenty-six years after O'Reilly's sojourn,[9] together with Martin Carroll's researches,[10] first brought to light the existence of the strong attachment between John Boyle O'Reilly and Jessie Woodman. That there was an attachment has been hotly contested by some of O'Reilly's admirers, but the affair has since been amply confirmed by the recent discovery of O'Reilly's notebook and shorthand jottings.

But before we pursue further the story of their hopeless love—and its conse-quences—there are other events to be followed, and stories to be told of O'Reilly's adventures in the West Australian bush in the year 1868.

CHAPTER 13

'NO RAMBLING POET'

It may be, I have left the higher gleams
  Of skies and flowers unheeded or forgot;
It may be so, — but, looking back, it seems
  When I was with them I beheld them not.
I was no rambling poet, but a man
  Hard pressed to dig and delve, with naught of ease
The hot day through, save when the evening's fan
  Of sea-winds rustled through the kindly trees.

How can I show you all the silent birds
  With strange metallic glintings on the wing?
Or half tell all their sadness in cold words, —
  The poor dumb lutes, the birds that never sing?
Of wondrous parrot-greens and iris hue
  Of sensuous flower and of gleaming snake, —
Ah! what I see I long that so might you,
  But of these things what pictures can I make?

John Boyle O'Reilly

AT the time of the year when O'Reilly arrived in the bush south of Bunbury and joined a working party there, his first experience of bush heat and the resultant discomforts would have been of short duration. The hot, dry conditions of March usually give way to milder April; a month in which the sun loses its bite, the mornings and evenings are cool, the average midday temperatures are some five degrees Celsius lower, and an occasional shower lays the dust. April is a month of transition, mellow and invigorating after the debilitating summer; a month not unlike those rare but ideal warm Septembers O'Reilly would have remembered from his boyhood in Ireland. If one is going to camp out in the bush in Western Australia, April is an ideal month to do so, and it

111

is likely that the fit, athletic O'Reilly would have welcomed the extraordinary change in his living conditions.

Welcome or not, the pain and humiliation that O'Reilly suffered as a result of his servitude, his loss of freedom, and his oppression by an unforgiving penal system cannot, and should not, be passed over lightly. Pictures in our minds of parties camping around the fire cooking their own food and living in exotic bush settings free from chains and prison restrictions certainly seem more humane and more healthy, and in dramatic contrast to the solitary confinement of Millbank and the cells of Fremantle. But to a man of O'Reilly's sensitivities and intellectual gifts, being a member of a convict work party in the Australian bush was nothing but enforced exile: a humiliating imprisonment unjustly earned, and fraught with dire penalties for even small, technical misdemeanours.

To some extent O'Reilly, the novelist, like many another storyteller, was not above exaggerating his condition and adding colour and drama to his fictional account of convict life in the bush so that we cannot wholly rely on *Moondyne* for an accurate picture of his own experiences. But only a writer who was scarred by the sense of a deep injustice could write, for example, of the ticket-of-leave convicts in *Moondyne* eleven years later:

> The crying evil of the code was the power it gave these settlers to take from the prisons as many men as they chose, and work them as slaves on their clearings. While so employed the very lives of these convicts were at the mercy of their taskmasters who possessed over them all the power of prison officers. A report made by an employer against a convict insured a flogging or a number of years in the chain gang at Fremantle. The system reeked of cruelty and the blood of men. It would startle our commonplace serenity to see the record of the lives that were sacrificed to have it repealed.[1]

And yet, just as when he was confined in Millbank and elsewhere O'Reilly's spirit was able to transcend the oppression of his immediate condition, so too in the bush he was quick to take an interest in his surroundings; he delighted in its strangeness and its beauty. The poet O'Reilly is more forgiving than O'Reilly the novelist. His poet's eye noted everything, every detail, and for one who did not have the benefit of guidebooks, he surprises us with his knowledge of local vegetation and wildlife. He delighted in what he saw and compared the native flora and fauna—sometimes unfavourably—with what he knew and loved in Ireland. In his poem 'Western Australia', for example, he personifies the bush, praising its beauty, but suggests that God was interrupted in the act of creation, meaning to return to His work later. The poet gives this as a reason why the flowers do not have the rich perfumes of the northern flowers, and why the birds do not sing as sweetly:

O Beauteous Southland! Land of yellow air
That hangeth o'er thee slumbering, and doth hold
The moveless foliage of thy valleys fair,
And wooded hills, like aureole of gold.

Oh thou, discovered ere the fitting time,
Ere Nature in completion turned thee forth!
Ere aught was finished but thy peerless clime,
Thy virgin breath allured the amorous North.

O Land, God made thee wondrous to the eye!
But His sweet singers thou hast never heard;
He left thee, meaning to come bye-and-bye,
And give rich voice to every bright-winged bird.

He painted with fresh hues thy myriad flowers,
But left them scentless; ah! their woeful dole,
Like sad reproach of their creator's powers,
To make so sweet fair bodies, void of soul.

He gave thee trees of odorous precious wood;
But, midst them all, bloomed not one tree of fruit.
He looked, but said not that His work was good,
When leaving thee all perfumeless and mute.

He blessed thy flowers with honey; every bell
Looks earthward, sunward, with a yearning wist,
But no bee-lover ever notes the swell
Of hearts, like lips, a-hungering to be kist.

O Strange Land, thou art virgin! Thou art more
Than fig-tree barren! Would that I could paint
For other's eyes the glory of the shore
Where last I saw thee; but the senses faint.

In soft delicious dreaming when they drain
Thy wine of colour. Virgin fair thou art,
All sweetly fruitful, waiting with soft pain
The spouse that comes to wake thy sleeping heart.[2]

O'Reilly's road party, like others posted around the colony, would have consisted of between twenty and forty men, depending on how many could have been made available at the time. Because of the extensive public works in the vicinity of Perth and Guildford and the road building elsewhere (all planned with enthusiasm and single-mindedness by Governor Hampton) there were scarcely enough convict workers to go round. To administer this program convict depots had been built at Bunbury, York, Guildford, Toodyay and Albany. Convicts with appropriate trades such as carpenters, plumbers, brick-layers and blacksmiths (when available) found themselves sent to gangs engaged on building bridges and government offices; the less skilled were sent to work on the roads.

Attached to each convict depot was a serving officer from the Royal Engineers who had responsibility for planning and overseeing building oper-ations in his district. He may have had several different constructions under his wing at any one time with many sites to visit and check. Having to rely on a force of amateur and often unsuitable workmen to carry out his instructions, the Royal Engineer in charge had an additional burden over and above the normal difficulties of his profession. For example, Lieutenant Edward F. DuCane, Superintendent of Convict Works in the York and Toodyay districts (1852–1855), wryly noted in a report:

> The efficiency of these road parties has at times been questioned. The construc-tion of roads is of course the principal work to be done, and at this employment clerks, tradesmen, and labourers are alike kept. They often make a queer mess of affairs and none of them seem to exert themselves.[3]

While most of his Fenian colleagues were set to work on the road between Perth and Guildford on the north side of the river—known at the time as the 'Fenian Road'—O'Reilly and his gang were starting to clear a path through the bush for the new Bunbury-Vasse road. The main work entailed sawing down trees on the route, digging out the stumps with pickaxes, and clearing, levelling and compacting the soil. The tools were few and simple. They had a horse-drawn plough for digging drainage ditches on each side of the road, a crude grader (also horse-drawn) and rollers for compacting the surface. On some roads of the period wooden blocks were cut from tree trunks and laid as a base; the base was then surfaced with crushed limestone. Because of the blocks' round shape and their origin—they were said to have been suggested by Hampton—they became known as 'Governor Hampton's cheeses'.[4]

Such work, as can be readily appreciated, called for unremitting hard, physical toil. No help could be obtained from the mechanized instruments we take for granted in modern times. All day, every day and in all weathers the bush rang out with the sounds of clearing: there were cracks like pistol shots as multiple axes cut into tree trunks, and the splitting of wood and ripping of branches as the canopies crashed to the ground through a bed of dense undergrowth. And men in pairs, stripped to the waist and bent to the cross saw, pushed and pulled in never-ending rhythm, hands sore and calloused. Some swung axes, broke rock and tore at stubborn roots while others loaded rubble and spread it on the new surface. If, as Lieutenant DuCane observed, they did not exert themselves it is of little wonder.

Some might see such an existence as a healthy life. But surely only healthy when moderated by periods of rest with close attention being paid to physical wellbeing. The power to alleviate the convicts' daily drudgery with a kind word or encouragement rested solely on the character of the warder in charge. In this regard, some road parties were better off than others. For example, Assistant Warder McGarry, who was in charge of a Fenian work party at West Guildford, was disciplined for allowing convicts 'to ramble about the bush and do as they liked' after two had been spotted by policemen and arrested while picking wild mushrooms in a field half a mile from their camp. (Perhaps McGarry had sent them in search of the mushrooms to add to their communal evening meal.) But in another instance, Fenian Martin Hogan had abused and threatened his warder, Munday, and then left his work site at a quarry by the Swan River. Hogan alleged at his trial that his warder had spoken insultingly of Ireland and because of this he demanded to be transferred to another site. As was the custom, the magistrate preferred the warder's evidence to the prisoner's and Hogan was sentenced to six months solitary confinement. However he was released after three months and transferred to Champion Bay—a victory of sorts.[5]

We have no record of how Warder Henry Woodman treated the members of his work gang, only that he was an 'energetic, zealous, and valuable officer'. He could have earned this official reputation, and yet at the same time worked his men with humane consideration. It is probable that he and his clerk, O'Reilly, respected each other and remained on friendly terms.

Soft, verdant April in the bush gave way to approaching winter. By mid-May it had become unpleasantly cold at night, and the rain-bearing depressions of winter were making an appearance from across the ocean and increasing in frequency. In that area of the south-west, day and night skies throughout June and July can be thick with cloud and cold winds bring driving rain. 'It rains fearful...every drop as large as a musket ball and falls with the rapidity of lightning.'[6] The flimsy camps could not give adequate protection against such an onslaught. Rain and wind penetrated the wicker walls, or came in through splits and gaps in the canvas. Floors oozed with mud and water; bedding became damp, impossible to dry, and was insufficient to keep out the cold. Fires for cooking were difficult to light. Without proper clothing and protection, the daily tasks of road building in the grey gloom and the wet cold became relentlessly depressing. It is more than likely that the men, caught in these winter conditions, looked back approvingly to the hot sun and dryness of the summer: 'the peerless clime' of O'Reilly's poem.

O'Reilly himself, at some time soon after joining the work camp, was excused from all manual labour and devoted his time to clerical duties which included the necessity of travelling between the road camp and Bunbury. The first Vasse road camp was some 5 miles from town but as the work progressed it was moved further south, and later in the year it was situated at Koagulup—now Cokelup—15 miles from Bunbury. The new acting constable probably made his journeys on foot, although on some occasions he would surely have taken a horse and cart for stores. In the winter this duty would not always have been easy. Nevertheless he tasted the rare privileges of freedom of movement, independence and being alone. As a probationary constable he was always bound by strict regulations and was required to make his journeys within a set time while following a prescribed route. But it is likely from what we know of O'Reilly that he interpreted his instructions with Gaelic logic and took risks—risks that were worth taking in such an underpopulated area—surrounded as he was for the most part by sympathetic free settlers and ticket-of-leavers.

One story which illustrates O'Reilly's affinity with nature, his charm, and the respect he must have commanded, has now become part of the folk lore of Western Australia: that of how the poet saved an especially graceful, giant eucalypt from destruction. O'Reilly had noticed that one of the surveyors had judged the tree to be an obstruction in the line of the road and had marked it down for cutting. Roche wrote that it was 'a giant among its fellows, the growth of centuries towering aloft to the sky and spreading enormous arms on every side'.[7] O'Reilly, with the enthusiasm of a modern-day conservationist, determined to save it and first obtained from Warder Woodman a postponement of execution. This allowed him time to plead his cause with Principal Warder Woodrow at the Bunbury depot. According to Roche's account:

> He went—this absurd poet in a striped suit—to the commander of the district, and pleaded for the tree. The official was so amused at his astounding audacity that he told his wife, who, being a woman, had a soul above surveys and rights of way. She insisted on visiting the tree, and the result of the visit was a phenomenon. The imperial road was turned from its course, and a grand work of nature stands in the West Australian forests as a monument to the convict poet.[8]

The exact location of the tree was, up until the early 1950s, a matter of local argument. The favoured choice fell on a huge tuart gum overhanging the old Vasse road where the road suddenly angles—now called Spencer Street—just

116

outside Bunbury. Known locally as 'O'Reilly's tree' for nearly a century it had to be felled in 1953 as it was considered dangerous to passers-by. The only mark of its existence afterwards was a 5-foot diameter stump denoting its size and age.[9]

Apart from the charm of the story itself, the details provide us with important additional proof that, (a) O'Reilly was on sufficiently good enough terms with Warder Woodman at the time to receive his cooperation (another warder might have dismissed such a request out of hand), and (b) that he made visits to Bunbury and while there was able to gain access to senior staff on his own account. Roche's story suggests that Principal Warder Woodrow indulged O'Reilly out of amusement, but this may not necessarily have been the case. It could equally have been true that he respected O'Reilly and knew of his work and his integrity.

Another incident recounted by Roche, but which cannot be verified in official records, may be described as the matter of the delayed letter. At one of the stations to which O'Reilly was routinely sent—presumably Bunbury—there was an overseer who took an instant and exceptional dislike to the convict poet. Perhaps O'Reilly's friendliness and good nature did not accord with the overseer's conception of how a convict should behave. Perhaps he was prejudiced against the Irish. (Reports of the attempted assassination in Sydney of Prince Alfred, the Duke of Edinburgh, by an Irishman claiming to be a Fenian were received in Western Australia that April.) Whatever the reason, on their first meeting the overseer threatened O'Reilly: 'Young man, you know what you are here for...I will help you to know it'. And from that time forward the overseer watched his victim and determined to trap him.

The opportunity occurred soon afterwards when O'Reilly arrived at the station a few minutes later than he had been expected. The overseer was triumphant: he had reason then to report O'Reilly for a breach of the regulations, one of the penalties being that the offender was not allowed to send or receive letters for six months. When O'Reilly was making another trip to the station, the overseer called him into his office and showed the prisoner a letter heavily bordered in black and clearly addressed to him. O'Reilly feared that it contained news of his mother's death for he knew she had been ill for some time. But when O'Reilly prepared to receive the letter, the overseer (having first read it) tossed it into his desk drawer saying, 'you will get it in six months'.

At the end of the six-month period O'Reilly was given the letter, and it did indeed contain news of his mother's death. The effect of that news on O'Reilly, and the weeks of waiting for it, must have deeply grieved him. That O'Reilly was influenced by his mother, and held her in high regard, can be seen from his little poem entitled 'My Mother's Memory':

There is one bright star in heaven
   Ever shining in my night;
God to me one guide has given,
   Like the sailor's beacon light,
Set on every shoal of danger,
   Sending out its warning ray
To the home-bound weary stranger
   Looking for the land-locked bay.

In my farthest, wildest wand'rings
   I have turned me to that love,
As a diver, neath the water,
   Turns to watch the light above.[10]

It is perhaps difficult for us, so long after the event, to accept the existence of such sadistic cruelty on the part of an official; we want it not to be true. And yet we know from other evidence from the convict era that wanton cruelty did exist all too frequently, and that the system not only encouraged it but protected those who were responsible for it. Although no record of the incident exists—throwing some doubt on the story—Roche cited a conversation with O'Reilly as his source, and concluded by recording that the victim bore the overseer no malice: '[a] man who could do a deed of that kind must be insane and irresponsible—a being towards whom one could not cherish animosity'.[11]

If the incident of the letter took place early in O'Reilly's period in the bush, and his reading of the letter was delayed for six months, he would have learnt of his mother's death at the end of winter, probably in the September or October of 1868. At that time the worst of the weather had passed. Although short periods of rain occur well into the month of October, and equinoctial gales can occasionally remind one of the worst excesses of July, the spring months in the bush are predominantly fine and warm. Vegetation is green and lush after the winter rains, birds are nesting, the earth—and even the air itself—exudes a freshness and new life. O'Reilly, the poet, on his constant journeyings along bush paths and tracks could not have failed to be stirred and inspired by the beauty around him.

In spring the bush is alive with sound and new life. And as the warmth increases in November the traveller on foot has to keep on the alert for slow-moving snakes, such as dugites, awakening after their hibernation. O'Reilly and his companions in the bush would have been familiar with these unwelcome creatures, and no doubt shared stories—mostly exaggerated—of their danger to man. His long poem, 'The Dukite Snake',[12] is set in the form of a campfire yarn

repeating the legendary belief that when a snake is killed its mate close by will
seek revenge on the killer:

> Now mark you, these Dukites don't go alone:
> There's another near when you see but one;
> And beware you of killing that one that you see
> Without finding the other; for you may be
> More than twenty miles from the spot that night
> When camped, but you're tracked by the lone Dukite;
> That will follow your trail like Death or Fate,
> And kill you as sure as you killed its mate!

The poet's story goes on to tell of poor Dave Sloane, who lives in bush
isolation with his young wife and baby child. One day, homeward bound, Dave
jumps off his wagon and kills a snake on the road. Having no love for snakes
he is proud of his deed and ties the carcass to the cart, not realizing that the
snake's blood is marking a trail to his house. The next day he leaves for work
unconcerned; he will spend the day hunting up his cattle. On his return in
the evening

> ...he gazed at his home with pride
> And joy in his heart; he jumped from his horse
> And entered—to look on his young wife's corse,
> And his dead child clutching his mother's clothes
> As in fright; and there, as he gazed, arose
> From her breast, where t'was resting, the gleaming head
> Of the terrible Dukite, as if it said,
> 'I've had vengeance, my foe: you took all I had'.

Two other consequences of the awakening spring affected O'Reilly at that
time. The first was a renewed restlessness and longing for freedom. Escape, never
far from his thoughts, now became a determination. In this matter he turned for
advice to someone who had become his friend and confidant: the local Catholic
priest, Father Patrick McCabe. McCabe's parish extended across a wide area of
Bunbury and the Vasse and O'Reilly would have seen him frequently, not only
on his many visits to Bunbury, but also because McCabe, being a zealous priest,
constantly visited his scattered flock in the bush on horseback.

The priest was a respected citizen, a man known for his charity and
compassion. Inevitably the two men, who had similar backgrounds, education
and beliefs, would have been drawn together. Officially the Irish clergy at that
time were forbidden by their bishops to support Fenianism (in fact some Fenians
believed the attitude of the Irish hierarchy in Ireland contributed towards the

collapse of Fenianism) but many priests, as private individuals, supported the republican cause as zealously as their flock. In view of McCabe's subsequent activities on behalf of O'Reilly we can assume he was of that number.

When O'Reilly discussed his own crude plans for escape with Father McCabe, the priest was openly sceptical. 'It is an excellent way to commit suicide', he said. But O'Reilly had touched his heart, and although the priest advised him to think no more about escaping at that time, Father McCabe promised as he rode away on his horse that he himself would devise a plan and would contact O'Reilly later.[13]

Another consequence of the glorious spring weather, the promise of new life, optimism, and the fecundity of the bush, was a story as old and as inevitable as new life itself—that of the growth of human sexual love. Occurring as if to confound and complicate his quest for freedom, O'Reilly found himself in the throes of a love affair with the daughter of the man who was his gaoler. And it is now time to consider that extraordinary turn of events in as much detail as is available to us.

Chapter 14

The Warder's Daughter

'Do you love me?' she said, when the skies were blue,
  And we walked where the stream through the branches glistened;
And I told and retold her my love was true,
  While she listened and smiled, and smiled and listened.

'Do you love me?' she whispered, when the days were drear,
  And her eyes searched mine with a patient yearning;
And I kissed her, renewing the words so dear,
  While she listened and smiled, as if slowly learning.

John Boyle O'Reilly

WHEN O'Reilly is describing in *Moondyne* the details of convict life, or the atmosphere and wildlife in the bush, or the sound of axes rebounding in the forests, or the conditions on board the *Hougoumont*, we know that he is writing truth born out of experience. On the other hand, the contrived plots and events and the assumptions such as goldmines in the Vasse, all stand out as clearly fictional. It is as if he were writing on two different levels: one level is the canvas on which he paints the landscape and his personal experiences—a form of documentary; the other is the fictional story, superimposed on the documentary canvas and always clearly visible to the reader.

Towards the end of O'Reilly's novel *Moondyne*, in the fifth part subtitled 'The Valley of the Vasse', the hero Will Sheridan, arriving on horseback, calls at the house in the bush where the heroine, Alice Walmsley, is staying. He is told by the farmer's wife, Mrs Little, that Alice has already gone out, 'away on her favourite lonely walk'. The author describes the scene as having a glorious richness of light, colour, and life.

> Every inch of ground sent up its jet of colour, exquisite, though scentless; and all the earth hummed with insect life, while the trees flashed with their splendid colours of countless bright-necked birds.[1]

121

Will Sheridan is directed by the sympathetic Mrs Little to where Alice might be returning, and he walks along the path by the river, breaking off a branch here and there, but at first not seeing her. Then after a few minutes he does see her—before she sees him—coming towards him beneath the trees; and he watches her. Suddenly, she turns and sees him, and his hands reach out towards her:

> He came forward, his eyes on hers, and the eyes of both were brimming. Without a word they met. Alice put out both her hands, and he took them, and held them, and after a while he raised them, one after the other, to his lips, and kissed them. Then they turned towards the house and walked on together in silence. Their hearts were too full for words. They understood without speech. Their sympathy was so deep and unutterable that it verged on the bounds of pain.[2]

It is difficult not to see in Alice the figure of Jessie Woodman, and in Will Sheridan the character of O'Reilly himself. Jessie was the elder of Woodman's two children, and of marriageable age. The meeting on the bush path of the two figures was clearly drawn from life, and in all probability occurred frequently in the spring of 1868 when O'Reilly was making his regular, routine visits to Bunbury and at the same time calling at the home of the Woodmans. Mrs Woodman, like the fictional Mrs Little, probably welcomed O'Reilly for his friendliness and honesty. Michael Davitt left no doubt as to his attractive personality:

> His handsome face and dark and laughing eyes, his manly bearing and his sunny disposition, with good feeling running from every pore of his nature like refreshing water from a perennial spring, set prison rules and warders' frowns at defiance.[3]

And Davitt also wrote, 'It would be impossible for O'Reilly to be anywhere on earth where human beings congregated without making friends'.[4]

Mrs Woodman and her children would have led a lonely existence, relying on O'Reilly for news of her husband. She may even, unwisely, have encouraged O'Reilly in his friendship with her daughter.

Was Jessie's head turned by this handsome, cultured Irishman who wrote poetry and talked to her about his experiences in the army, about his country, and about his voyage on the *Hougoumont*? Clearly he was in love with her, and she with him if we accept the evidence of the manuscript book of poems which was recently discovered and presented to the Battye Library in Perth in 1989. The slim volume, bound in vellum, contains about twenty poems and intimate notes in an old, obscure shorthand as well as a dedication to Father McCabe, and includes the appendage: 'By John Boyle O'Reilly, 13 March sixty eight, in the bush near Bunbury'. Exhaustive tests by library staff in the years following its discovery leave little doubt about its authenticity.[5]

Although translating the shorthand at first proved almost impossible, the code was eventually broken by a Perth historian, Gillian O'Mara, and what she found confirms what was, until that time, merely speculation. 'I wish she was not so fond of kissing', O'Reilly complains mildly; then his shorthand continues: 'I am in love up to my ears', and adds, 'it would take a saint to give her up'.[6] Were these words—written for his eyes only—a kind of prayer, evidence of a struggle within himself, an argument for more self-control in the interests of wisdom? He would have known the futility of their liaison, he a convict with eight more years to serve before he was even eligible for ticket-of-leave status; and she, the daughter of his gaoler. Even by associating with him she may have been endangering her father and jeopardizing the chances of his advancement. And yet O'Reilly, at that age virile and unnaturally segregated from women, would have struggled to put these negative thoughts aside—at least at first—and grasped at the comfort that such love would have brought him: a love and tenderness beyond all possibility in the lives of the majority of convicts. Had O'Reilly's situation been known to his fellow convicts, he would indeed have been envied by them.

It is frustrating for us that the true story of the love between John Boyle O'Reilly and Jessie Woodman may never be fully known. The episode remains, in detail, an intriguing mystery. Some of the evidence—the pieces in the puzzle—fits together neatly, but we are left with large gaps and we can only guess how the completed picture might have appeared.

But is that not exactly how O'Reilly would have wanted it to be with the story known only to himself, unrecorded by others, and impossible for others to reconstruct? He himself took care never to mention it after his escape; there are no poems referring to it, at least not in the collected poems which he edited; and Mary O'Reilly, his wife, who edited the poems after her husband's death as an addendum to the Roche biography, did not include any. Roche, his trusted Boswell, made no mention of the affair in his biography. Some of O'Reilly's admirers have wanted it that way too and believe that the story of Jessie Woodman is purely an invention, a wish on the part of some of those who have written about him to inject into O'Reilly's sojourn in Western Australia a colourful, prurient episode in keeping with his known romantic temperament. Love in the bush between a convict and the daughter of the convict's warder is, after all, a wildly attractive, if tragic, story: the stuff of grand opera. Fidelio and Tosca, no less, have been that way before.

But no responsible biographer can ignore the scraps of evidence which are available. These point clearly to a brief but passionate affair. And then there remain those intriguing hints provided by O'Reilly himself in his novel *Moondyne*, written, one might almost suppose, under some inner compulsion to reveal the truth in spite of his better, private judgement. There is also Michael Davitt's account, the first mention in print of the affair:

> No man or woman could resist the magnetic charms of O'Reilly's personality. He succeeded in winning the confidence of the warder in charge of the road-making gang at Bunbury, and was placed in a position of trust. He helped the officer to write his reports, regulated the business of the convict stores, and was privileged to become the bearer of reports from one depot to another. In those journeys he attracted the ardent attentions of a young girl, daughter of a warder, who conceived a strong attachment for the young rebel, whose convict dress could not disfigure the fine physique and manly bearing of the prisoner. I was assured when in Fremantle that the girl to whom I refer had shown great devotion to O'Reilly...[7]

In his account published in 1898, Michael Davitt quoted—sometimes inaccurately—from Roche's biography published seven years previously, but when writing of Jessie Woodman he was relying on the testimony of friends of O'Reilly whom he had met and talked to in Western Australia. Further proof of the affair can be found in the hearsay evidence quoted by both Martin Carroll and Keith Amos; and there is an amount of circumstantial evidence too.

How often O'Reilly was able to meet with Jessie cannot be known but he would have made his journeys to Bunbury at least once a week. Sometime in the early spring of 1868 the bush camp was moved further south to Koagulup which would have entailed a longer bushwalk into the town (doubtless along the new road that his gang had made), a distance of about 15 miles. O'Reilly described the place somewhat exaggeratedly in *Moondyne* as

> one of the greatest and dismallest of the wooded lakes of the country, its black water deep enough to float a man-of-war. The lakes thereabouts are shallow, swampy, and of less than a mile in circumference.[8]

Some insight into the dilemma and the mental anguish experienced by O'Reilly in the face of his hopeless love affair may be gained from his recently discovered manuscript poems. Supposedly written at some time towards the end of 1868 (it is difficult to date most of O'Reilly's poetry), they were not subsequently included in his published verse. Perhaps the poet feared that they might have revealed too much to his American readers of an episode in his life best forgotten. The two poems under the frankly suggestive title, 'Night Thoughts', are an impassioned cry of despair; and there is a strong hint that some recent and unwelcome event has occurred, though whether arising from the clandestine nature of their meetings or a change of heart by Jessie Woodman, is not clear.

> Have I no future left me?
> Is there no struggling ray
> From the sun of my life outshining
> Down on my darksome way?
>
> Will there no gleam of sunshine
> Cast o'er my path its light?
> Will there no star of hope rise
> Out of this gloom of night?
>
> Have I 'gainst heaven's warnings
> Sinfully, madly rushed?
> Else why thus were my heart strings severed?
> Why was my love-light crushed?
>
> Oh! I have hopes and yearnings —
> Hopes that I know are vain
> And knowledge robs life of pleasure —
> And death of its only pain.[9]

If only the first two verses were recorded we could interpret the poet's despair as arising from his imprisonment and exile, but the third and fourth verses show clearly that O'Reilly is writing about some other sorrow, a wrongdoing which has resulted in a penalty. What was this wrongdoing, real or imagined? Could he have been referring to his love, his sexual knowledge, of Jessie Woodman? Because of O'Reilly's strict Catholic beliefs—''gainst heaven's warnings'—his affair with Jessie is likely to have troubled his conscience. In *Moondyne* he describes the loss of sexual innocence of Alice Walmsley with extraordinary perception, and it is tempting to think that this kind of experience might also have been true of Jessie Woodman:

The moment of communion was reached at last, when her girlish life plunged with delicious expectation into the deep—and in one hideous instant she knew that for ever she had parted from the pure and beautiful, and was buried in an ocean of corruption and disappointment, rolled over by waves of unimaginable suffering and wrong.

From the first deep plunge, stifled, agonised, appalled, she rose to the surface, only to behold the land receding from her view—the sweet fields of her innocent joyous girlhood fading in the distance.

She raised her eyes, and saw heaven calm and beautiful above her...and she cried.[10]

125

Was it a real-life sexual union which troubled the conscience of O'Reilly and caused him to write 'Night Thoughts'? And we are led to ask a further intriguing question: did Jessie become pregnant?

There is a popular belief—local rumour unearthed by Martin Carroll—indicating that this may have been the case; but there is no firm evidence. Official records do not reveal the birth of a child under the name of Woodman or O'Reilly to coincide with that time. That, however, is no proof that a birth did not occur. It may have been that Jessie miscarried, or a child was stillborn: all is conjecture. What is known is that on 1 March 1869, two weeks after O'Reilly had absconded (but was still at large in the bush), Jessie married a local farmer, George Pickersgill, in the Congregational Church, Bunbury.[11] She probably stayed in the district with him because she is not included in the official records as moving to Guildford with her father the following April. Did she marry Pickersgill in haste, having come to see that her liaison with O'Reilly was hopeless? Or was Pickersgill a suitor in the background, a preferred rival to O'Reilly all along? The second poem in 'Night Thoughts' gives considerable support to this latter view:

> Oh! no! I would not love again
> E'en had I still the power given;
> I would not risk its pain and fears
> E'en though its joys were taste of heaven.
> A breath may blight the heart we prize;
> A whisper weave deceit around it:
> And then our heart's most tender chord
> Is wounded by the chain that bound it.
>
> 'Tis hard to see death's chilling hand
> The life-strings of our treasure sever:
> But harder still when loving hearts
> Are rudely rent apart for ever.
> But ah! such griefs are naught to those
> That fill the heart where passion burned
> Till falsehood burst the mask and showed
> That love by heartless scorn returned.

That John Boyle O'Reilly was deeply troubled at this time is clearly demonstrated by these poems; and knowing what we do of his tragic situation, we cannot wonder at the causes. Previous writers on O'Reilly have opined that the poet was torn between his love for Jessie on the one hand, and the desire to escape on the other; and that this grievous dilemma was responsible for the next extraordinary turn in the story. But with the discovery of 'Night Thoughts', it would seem that O'Reilly, in addition to the humiliating sufferings imposed by his imprisonment and exile, suffered at that time from none other than that well-known serious disease of youth—a broken heart.

And it may well have been this last event that led him to take the extraordinary step of walking out into the bush two days after Christmas, where, in loneliness and despair so uncharacteristic up to this point, he attempted to take his own life.

CHAPTER 15

FACING THE ABYSS

———

There is a shadow on my heart today,
A cloudy grief condensing to a tear:
Alas, I cannot drive its gloom away —
Some sin or sorrow casts the shapeless fear.

John Boyle O'Reilly

WHEN O'Reilly met his friend Father McCabe in the bush sometime in the West Australian spring and told him of his plan to escape, the priest had responded by saying that he thought it was 'suicide' but that he, McCabe, would devise a better plan. No doubt O'Reilly was greatly heartened as McCabe was a man to trust, 'he was kind to all men, whatever their creed, and a sincere Christian worker'.[1] But then as the weeks and months dragged by without the subject being broached again, O'Reilly may have thought it best to put it out of his mind. And in any case, Jessie Woodman was firmly occupying his mind at that time.

And then, apparently without warning, in early December the possibility of escape confronted O'Reilly again in the form of a stranger who accosted him in the bush while he was travelling to Bunbury. He was on a routine errand for Warder Woodman. O'Reilly, long accustomed to suspect the probity of chance acquaintances, was wary of this man who called himself James Maguire and spoke with an Irish accent. But when Maguire produced a note for O'Reilly in Father McCabe's handwriting, all suspicion vanished.

Maguire told O'Reilly not to lose heart because Father McCabe and his friends were working on a plan that would see the Fenian prisoner secreted aboard one of the two American whalers due in Bunbury in February. Arrangements were not then complete, but Maguire would be in touch with him nearer the date. Maguire then rode off to resume his work clearing open level ground which was shortly to become—as it still is to this day—the Bunbury Racecourse.

Did O'Reilly call on Jessie Woodman that day? He probably did if we accept that he included a visit to the Woodman home as part of his routine errand.

And if he did we can only guess at the anguish in his mind caused by the conflict between the prospect of freedom which had been dangled in front of him earlier that day in the bush, and the price that he would have to pay for it: giving up his love for Jessie Woodman even to the point of denying to himself that it had ever existed.

Whether he discussed escape with her then, or kept it to himself, we do not know. But either way the conduct of their relationship must have changed from that time forward. And we know that O'Reilly's agony of mind—whether over this matter or over a noticeable change in their affections is not easy to say—was too great for him to bear in the weeks ahead, and drove him to do what arrest, humiliation, exile, solitary confinement and transportation had not been able to do: he cut the veins in his arm. His words in the poem already quoted (on page 125), '...knowledge robs life of pleasure—and death of its only pain', now have particular poignancy when read in the light of this event.

There are three pieces of written evidence, substantial and convincing in themselves, which confirm O'Reilly's suicide attempt. The first is an entry in the diary of Sub-Inspector William Timperley of Bunbury Police Station, dated 27 December:

> Started for the Vasse at 4.00 p.m. Overtook Dr. Lovegrove as far as Woodman's camp where the probationary constable Riley [sic] one of the late head centres of Fenianism had attempted suicide by cutting the veins of his left arm and being accidentally discovered by a brother prisoner when in a faint from loss of blood... was saved.[2]

William Timperley was to be charged with the responsibility of attempting to recapture O'Reilly after his escape two months hence. He also gives us our second piece of evidence which is almost in the form of an addendum to his official report on O'Reilly's escape: 'I may also state that this prisoner attempted suicide on 27th December last (by cutting the veins in his arm)'.[3]

Those who have questioned the veracity of the suicide story point to the wrong spelling of O'Reilly's name in the diary, claiming that Timperley was referring to a different prisoner altogether. But, as Keith Amos has shown, the prisoner named Riley was 120 miles away at Guildford.[4] And Timperley's linking of the suicide with the escapee in his later report, leaves no doubt that they were one and the same person. All other details point to John Boyle O'Reilly, and we can be confident that Timperley either made an all too common spelling error when writing in his diary, or, as sometimes was the case, he showed his casual disregard for the convict by being deliberately careless with the name.

The third piece of written evidence can be found in O'Reilly's file of newspaper cuttings and is an interview with the second mate of the whaler, the

Gazelle, reported in New Bedford some years later. When O'Reilly feared he was about to be discovered on board the ship in Roderiquez harbour, according to the mate he threatened to kill himself rather than be taken: 'I knew he meant what he said; for the priest [Father McCabe] had told me he had tried to commit suicide...'.[5]

There are other more puzzling questions to be asked concerning the incident: what were the exact reasons why it took place when it did (when in one sense O'Reilly's prospects never seemed brighter), and why was it never reported by Warder Woodman to the Fremantle authorities? Had it been reported, O'Reilly would surely have been transferred back to 'the Establishment' for special observation. In such a serious case it was clearly Woodman's duty to make that report. He has already been described as a 'most energetic, zealous and valuable officer', and yet Woodman failed to carry out that duty. The only explanation must be that he had a special relationship with O'Reilly and he understood the reasons for O'Reilly's action; in short, he probably knew of O'Reilly's association with his daughter. But the mystery deepens when we realize that the event was known to Sub-Inspector Timperley, Dr Lovegrove and, presumably, to the men in Woodman's work gang. It was therefore hardly a secret.

In attempting to unravel this tangle there are two factors for consideration. The first is the high esteem in which O'Reilly was held by most people who knew him (if we discount the actions of the warder who withheld O'Reilly's letter). Some of the warders and policemen (though not Timperley) were Irish themselves and obviously warmed to O'Reilly's charm. Privately they may even have been sympathetic. In a letter which O'Reilly wrote to the Police Superintendent of Western Australia from Boston in 1876 he added these words: '...please tell your officers, especially Sergeant Kelly, once of Bunbury, that I send them my respects'.[6] 'Respects' may not seem an especially warm greeting, but it was as far as O'Reilly dared go in his effort to save his friends in Australia from embarrassment. The second factor governing why the police knew of the suicide attempt, but the prison authorities did not, probably rests on bureaucratic lines of communication. It was not the duty of the Bunbury police to report internal convict matters to Fremantle prison authorities. Prison warders had their own departmental lines of communication, but as we know Woodman, for his own reasons, chose not to observe them.

Another question might be asked concerning O'Reilly's suicide attempt, given the almost universal praise of his character, his hitherto positive attitude to life, his humour, and his religious beliefs: was not such an action totally out of character and simply unbelievable? The answer to this must be that suicide *is very often* out of character. The dark forces of despair active within the human mind lie concealed from general view. In so many cases of suicide, of both ordinary people and public figures, surprise and disbelief is often expressed afterwards; the simplistic epitaph is uttered, 'one would never have thought it possible, he/she was such a happy/lucky person'.

We know a great deal about O'Reilly derived from written evidence, his own poetry and writings, and official records, but we cannot fully understand the hidden, mental agony he must have suffered. We cannot get inside his mind. He was a poet blessed—or cursed perhaps—with acute sensitivities and insight: he would not be the first artist to stare into the abyss and see only blackness.

But O'Reilly recovered physically due to the prompt action of a fellow convict, and perhaps also because of the care and understanding of Woodman himself. The degree to which he recovered mentally—and whether this was a long, slow process which left a scar—is hard to say. Presumably he carried the physical scars of his action on his arm for the rest of his comparatively short life. But how he explained these away to his wife and children in the years to come is yet another interesting question which must remain unanswered.

CHAPTER 16

'TAKEN AT THE FLOOD'

And we must take the current when it serves,
Or lose our ventures.

William Shakespeare

IN the weeks leading up to Christmas and in the first days of the New Year, 1869, the faithful Father Patrick McCabe had not been idle on O'Reilly's behalf. It is likely that he would have heard all about O'Reilly's suicide attempt, probably from O'Reilly himself, for Roche stated that Father McCabe was a warm friend to O'Reilly and the best influence he had. Perhaps O'Reilly owed his recovery, in part, to the priest, and in some measure showed his gratitude by dedicating to McCabe his most personal and secret notebook of poems: 'the only means by which the writer at present can evince his deep and heartfelt gratitude to him for all his kindness'.[1]

McCabe's plan for O'Reilly's escape was founded on two equally important, pivotal requirements. The first was the presence in Bunbury of American whalers, and the expectation that one of the captains would be persuaded to take O'Reilly aboard for monetary consideration; and the second was the provision of a group of sympathetic, reliable friends in the Bunbury region to conduct O'Reilly on board.

With regard to the first requirement, whalers from New Bedford and other ports on the coasts of Massachusetts and Connecticut had hunted in the Indian Ocean off Western Australia since the 1840s. Herman Melville, in the introduction to *Moby Dick*, quoted Pliny the Elder's observation:

The Indian Ocean breedeth the most and the biggest fishes that are, among which are the whales and whirlpools called Baleen, take up as much in length as four acres of land.[2]

Early settlers on the shores of Geographe Bay looked forward each summer to the arrival of these sturdy but sleek three-masted vessels of around 90 feet in length and with a 25-foot beam. They were instantly recognizable by their 27-foot longboats, used for chasing the whales, which were prominently slung on davits on either side of the hulls; they were welcomed for trade and social intercourse alike. In 1840 Georgiana Molloy described how six such ships had visited, and that 'they were charmed with the Bay. They are of the greatest use to us'.[3] The ships traded some of their stock of oil, ship's biscuit, rope and rough clothing for fresh supplies of meat, butter and cheese from the local farmers. An important requirement for whalers of the period, and one that was easily satisfied in the Vasse, was for fresh supplies of timber to feed the furnaces used in the production of the valuable whale oil.

By the time of O'Reilly's sojourn in Western Australia, the whaling industry out of New Bedford which had been at its most prosperous in the 1840s—the period of *Moby Dick*—had begun to decline. Refined petroleum was replacing whale oil for most applications, such as heating and lighting. But the oil of the whale was still preferred for the running of machinery: the decline, therefore, was slow. New Bedford would continue to be the centre of a whaling industry up until the end of the century, and in 1876 (the year of the *Catalpa* rescue) over 100 ships were still operating out of the port. They sailed south for the hunting grounds off the Cape of Good Hope, and so into the south Indian Ocean on much the same track that the *Hougoumont* had followed. The establishment of Bunbury as a port, with its natural advantage of shelter and its increasing population, all contributed to it becoming a home from home for the whalers. When the fleet was in, in February, the excited interest among the local people would seem strangely familiar to those of us who observe from time to time the welcome given to American warships in Fremantle today:

> It is really amazing to witness the doing of the people. No sooner does a Yankee whaler drop anchor than the news is immediately telegraphed throughout the district. Then all are in bustle and confusion; dowager dames are anxious to go on board to see what can be got, while the younger ladies are equally eager to form fresh acquaintances. Visitors are always made welcome on board these vessels, and pleasant parties are sometimes formed. The good people here return the compliment by making the officers and men welcome in their houses—the acme of their enjoyment consisting in a dance in a room about 10ft square, with the glass at 84°.[4]

Keith Amos points out in his book, *The Fenians in Australia*, that anti-British feeling ran strong in the northern states of America during and after the Civil War and so the whaling captains tended to pity the convicts transported to

Australia, reserving special sympathy for the Irish.[5] Ireland, they believed, had not been as fortunate as the United States in achieving independence from the colonial power. It was that sympathy that Father McCabe and his friends counted upon when soliciting a safe passage for O'Reilly.

Although not one probationary convict had managed to escape until O'Reilly's success, forty-two ticket-of-leave holders managed to get away—twenty-one of them on whalers—between the years of 1850 and 1862. They had the advantage of being able to move around more freely, make contacts, and earn money for their passage. The asking price at that time was around £30. The authorities were fully aware that the whalers provided an escape route and for this reason the ships were thoroughly searched before leaving. Rewards were paid to those who helped apprehend absconders and the money was recovered later from the accumulated earnings of the recaptured prisoner.

In February 1869 both the *Vigilant* (215 tons), commanded by Captain Anthony Baker, and the *Gazelle* (263 tons), commanded by Captain David R. Gifford, were among those visiting Bunbury. Father McCabe chose the *Vigilant*, and obtained a promise from Captain Baker to pick up O'Reilly from a rowing boat off the coast at a prearranged rendezvous. Where the passage money came from we do not know; more than likely it was collected from McCabe's parishioners in the time-honoured custom of passing the hat round for a good cause. Martin Carroll suggested that O'Reilly may have had funds of his own, money given to him or sent from abroad perhaps by sympathizers. In Sub-Inspector Timperley's report on O'Reilly's escape to his chief in Fremantle, he stated:

[I have learnt] from several quarters that O'Reilly had plenty of money in his possession to buy and pay his way liberally—I give this for what it is worth—but see no reason why it should not be true.[6]

McCabe may well have been the channel of communication, sending and receiving O'Reilly's letters. (In 1870 the priest was transferred—sacked—from a chaplaincy at Fremantle prison for providing just such a clandestine service to prisoners there.)

Securing a passage for O'Reilly on a whaler was the easy half of the problem; the far more difficult task was getting him aboard. He could not wait around on Bunbury quayside looking for the Blue Peter—the signal that the ship would sail the same day—that was obvious. He would have to be hidden, cared for, and a small boat made available for him at the right moment. Such an operation required the assistance of a group of loyal friends who were independent, brave, and sworn to secrecy. Fortunately, in this regard Father McCabe was well served in the little Catholic parish of Dardanup, 5 miles south-east of Bunbury. The township itself was about equidistant between O'Reilly's camp at Koagulup and the port. In *Moondyne* O'Reilly pays an affectionate tribute to the community, and much of what he wrote then is still true today:

> There is a colony of Irish settlers at Dardanup, free men, who are emigrated there forty years before, when the western colony was free from the criminal taint. The familes were all related to each other by intermarriage, and the men of the whole settlement, who had been born and reared in the bush, were famous throughout the colony for strength, horsemanship, good fellowship, and hard fighting qualities.[7]

The most prominent family in the district (who in a sense masterminded the escape) were the Maguires: James, and his elder brother John. If Father McCabe was the architect in the background, the Maguires were the builders on whom the plan rested. Their descendants still talk proudly of their part in John Boyle O'Reilly's escape, and old photographs of that generation are treasured. Sadly, invaluable family papers belonging to James Maguire, including letters from O'Reilly sent from America, have unaccountably been lost.

James Maguire migrated from Ireland when he was only ten years old, in company with his brother and wife, Catherine. They arrived at Australind on board the *Trusty* which was making its second voyage there in 1844—the year, incidentally, when O'Reilly was born. The Maguires had been recruited by the Western Australian Company to participate in its ill-fated, grandiose settlement scheme for the area. When they arrived they were so disappointed with the land and the general morale of the settlers that they attempted to obtain a return passage on the same ship. Luckily for O'Reilly, as it turned out, the captain refused the Maguires' request because both he and the passengers were under an obligation to the company. The Maguires settled down to hard work in the district, and later became independent, respected citizens owning their own farms in the Dardanup region. James was appointed a justice of the peace and chairman of the Dardanup Roads Board, and John was Dardanup's postmaster. These men and their close friends, 'famous throughout the colony for strength, horsemanship, and good fellowship', protected O'Reilly. And it was their established reputation and position in the district which placed them above suspicion during the police hunt for him.

In mid-February—at a guess, Saturday the 13th—O'Reilly set off for his weekly trip to the convict depot in Bunbury. On his return journey, when nearing the site of the Bunbury Racecourse, he heard the now familiar 'coo-ee' which heralded the appearance of James Maguire.[8]

'Are you ready?' asked Maguire. And of course O'Reilly could only have answered a resounding 'Yes!'. He already knew that whalers had arrived in the port: the news had been brought to his camp by a mahogany sawyer who was working in the district. Therefore, Maguire's visit had been eagerly anticipated. The two men discussed plans and agreed that the following Wednesday would be the day of O'Reilly's bid for freedom. Maguire went back to his contract work and the prisoner returned, elated, to his camp.

But on Wednesday, 17 February O'Reilly was unexpectedly sent to the Bunbury depot on business by Warder Woodman. When he arrived back in the camp in the late afternoon, he reported to Warder Woodman that seven Fenians had arrived in Bunbury on the small coastal cutter, *Wild Wave*. They were confined in the Bunbury lockup because they had refused to be separated from one another when it was learned they would be sent to different road parties.[9] O'Reilly had attempted to make contact with them—perhaps to say his farewells—but had been 'ordered off very smartly'.

That evening O'Reilly sat in his hut writing a letter to his father, telling him of his plan to escape and that he was aiming to settle in the United States. He was interrupted in this work by a convict who came to the hut to borrow tobacco; the visitor overstayed his welcome which made O'Reilly very nervous. Warder Woodman made his rounds at about 7.00 p.m. and checked that the prisoners were all present. O'Reilly himself was night constable on duty and so was able to choose the time of his departure without raising suspicions.

As the minutes ticked by, and O'Reilly listened to the silence of the bush, the enormity and the finality of what he was about to do must have both excited him, and at the same time shaken his nerve. He was about to exchange all the trust, stability and comparative privilege of his position as a probationary constable for an enterprise which, on previous evidence, showed that he had almost no chance of success. O'Reilly would have been well aware that twenty-four convicts had already attempted escape from the Bunbury district but had been recaptured within a short space of time. All these had been sent back to Fremantle—as would happen to him if he failed—to face severe punishment, to work in chains, and then to be marked for the rest of their time as recalcitrant and untrustworthy. Even the primitive comfort of his hut and the glow of the light must have seemed attractive to him in those final minutes. Did he remember, in those last moments, that fifteen months previously he had quoted lofty sentiments in the pages of the *Wild Goose* through the words of Brutus: 'there is a tide in the affairs of men, which, taken at the flood, leads on to fortune'?

If O'Reilly had any doubts about his enterprise, they must surely have been momentary; he was too resolute a character, too brave and unafraid of taking risks, to draw back from action at the last moment. Therefore, just after 8.00 p.m. he changed into a pair of freeman's boots and a suit of clothes which Jessie Woodman had procured for him: evidence that he had discussed his plans with her, and she had cooperated with him.[10] (The boots were especially important because those issued to convicts had a recognizable pattern of spikes which had provided an easy means of tracking previous absconders.) Suitably equipped, O'Reilly took a final glance around his hut and, thinking he was unobserved, slipped silently out into the night.

The forest was dark, but the sky was clear and the stars bright. In any case, he was by that time an experienced bushman who knew the terrain and how to follow the prescribed direction. He headed north-east, leaving the racecourse well to the west. But he had hardly gone more than a few hundred yards when he was startled by the sound of someone following him. Surely he could not have been seen leaving? To be caught now at this early stage was unthinkable. O'Reilly paused. And waited.

The tracker, whoever he was, came closer until he drew level with O'Reilly. Both figures, two dark forms merging with the background, peered uncertainly at each other. Somewhat to O'Reilly's relief he thought he recognized his unwelcome follower: a mahogany sawyer, an Irish ticket-of-leaver named Thomas Kelly.

'Are you off?' whispered Kelly. But O'Reilly did not answer. 'I saw you talking to Maguire a month ago', Kelly went on, 'and I knew it all'.

O'Reilly was dumb with astonishment and alarm. He knew that if Kelly had wished he could put the police on the alert; and he might well do so the next day and claim a reward. But Kelly put out his hand reassuringly and said: 'God speed you! I'll put them on the wrong scent tomorrow if I can'.[11] They shook hands in silence, and then Kelly crept away into the darkness.

John Boyle O'Reilly walked on through the bush for approximately three hours, crossing first the Preston River and then the Ferguson, until he came to the Bunbury-Dardanup road close to Picton. The arrangement was that he would rest there under an old gum tree to await the arrival of the rescue party coming from the direction of Dardanup.

CHAPTER 17

FUGITIVE IN THE DUNES

Our feet on the torrent's brink,
We stray from the roadway here;
We fear the things we think,
Instead of the things that are.

John Boyle O'Reilly

O'REILLY did not have long to wait. In about half an hour two men rode up and then passed by. They may have been farmers or a police patrol, but in either case O'Reilly was well hidden. His party would identify itself with a special signal—the whistling of the tune 'St Patrick's Day'.[1]

Soon afterwards the fugitive heard another sound of horses approaching: two riders and a spare mount. On this occasion they drew up by O'Reilly's hiding place and he heard the unmistakeable low whistling of the password tune. In the darkness O'Reilly recognized Maguire but not the other man who was James Milligan, a friend of Maguire's, also from Dardanup. O'Reilly mounted the spare horse and without a word the three men rode off swiftly in a northerly direction towards the Collie River bridge.

Maguire, Milligan and O'Reilly arrived at the bridge in the early hours of Thursday morning and dismounted; at the sounding of the prearranged signal three other men appeared, two of them cousins of Maguire. One of these three led the horses away after shaking hands with O'Reilly and wishing him well. The remaining five men walked westward along the south bank of the river towards the Leschenault Inlet about a mile distant, keeping to Indian file so as to disguise their number.

After about an hour they arrived at the mouth of the river and halted. Milligan remained with O'Reilly, and the three others went forward to locate the rowing boat which had already been reserved for their purposes. On a signal—the light of a match struck three times—Milligan and O'Reilly went forward to join the others. The boat was waiting for them. Four of them clambered aboard, Milligan declining to join them. He explained that while he had agreed to help in the escape, he had promised his wife that he would not go to sea in the boat. This provoked a scornful jeering from one of the others, but O'Reilly excused him and wrote later that it was not on account of cowardice because Milligan was a brave man.

The remaining four men pulled hard at the oars, rowing the boat 4 miles down the inlet to Bunbury, and eventually out through the estuary entrance into the ocean. The two other men in the boat, apart from O'Reilly and Maguire, were either John McKree, a Bunbury shoemaker known as 'Mickie-Mackie', or Mark Lyons (both Irishmen); and an Englishman, a former convict turned fisherman named Joseph Buswell. Buswell owned the boat and lived on the shore of the inlet. He would have been the navigator with local knowledge of the waters, so necessary to the expedition. Those first few hours of the escape plan were critical: the boat had to pass silently down the estuary towards Bunbury before passing under the eye of the town, and so out into Koombana Bay. There was a danger that at this point they would be spotted by the harbour police, or a small craft, or even by a witness ashore. But luck was with them as well as good planning, and no one would have known at that time that O'Reilly was missing.

Their destination lay some 12 miles up the coast: the deserted beach at the northern end of Leschenault Inlet near Australind. Here they would wait, watching for the departure of the *Vigilant* from Bunbury which was expected within the next couple of days. The party could have travelled to their hiding place overland but wisely chose the more strenuous, if initially more dangerous, sea route. The only tracks they had made terminated at the Collie River bridge leaving no clue as to their later whereabouts.

They pulled strongly and when the sun rose they were well north of the town, some distance out at sea to avoid the reefs, and heading up the coast. Probably at that time, before the sea breeze arrived, the water was calm with a gentle swell, but the day became very hot and there was neither food nor water in the boat. It seems odd that neither Maguire, otherwise so competent in his planning, nor any of the other men had thought to bring provisions in a knapsack. O'Reilly had eaten nothing since noon the previous day and as a result began to suffer acutely from thirst and loss of strength; his reserves of strength, weakened by a night on the run, were sorely tested. But he managed to hold on until, just before noon, they reached the deserted part of the coast selected for their hide-out. While beaching the boat in the strong surf they were drenched by a wave but as a result seemed somewhat refreshed. Then they began looking for water.

The little group searched through the dried-up swamps for some hours, testing at the bases of paperbark trees, but without success. Their situation now appeared to be serious: they were without food or water and faced the prospect

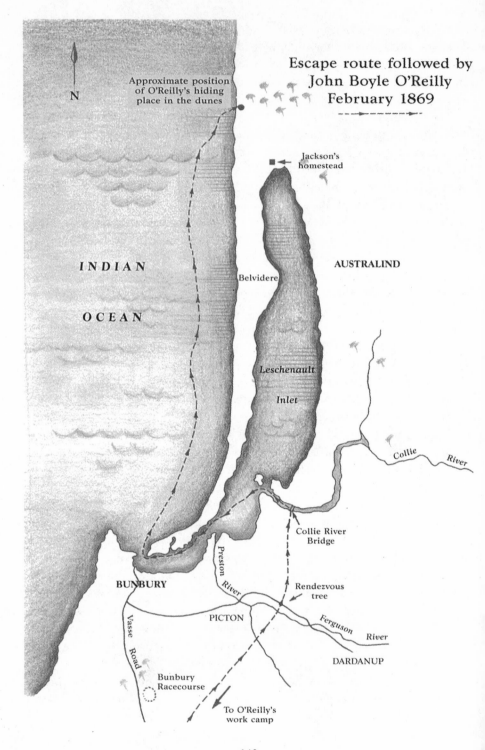

N

Approximate position
of O'Reilly's hiding
place in the dunes

Escape route followed by
John Boyle O'Reilly
February 1869

Jackson's
homestead

INDIAN

AUSTRALIND

Belvidere

OCEAN

Leschenault

Inlet

Collie   River

Collie River
Bridge

BUNBURY

Preston
River

Rendezvous
tree

Vasse

PICTON

Ferguson
River

Road

DARDANUP

Bunbury
Racecourse

To O'Reilly's
work camp

of waiting one or perhaps two days before the *Vigilant* appeared on the horizon. The pain in O'Reilly's chest alarmed him; it burned, as if a blister were forming internally over the whole of the inside of the breast. Incredible as it may seem, no one in the rescue party had planned for survival during the long wait in the dunes. After much scrabbling about in the thick undergrowth, late in the afternoon they were cheered to find a cattle track leading to a muddy pool, but were again instantly disappointed because the water was too foul to drink.

Then one of the men remembered that Mark Lyons's brother-in-law, Thomas Jackson, lived with his wife and son, Matthew, in a humble slab homestead nearby. Jackson was an Englishman, a former convict, who was the hired keeper of an immense herd of water buffalo on 'Buffalo' property which bordered the coast. The others spoke well of him, and although they were loath to bring a stranger into their confidence, they agreed that in the particular circumstances, they would have to take a chance; there was simply no alternative. Leaving O'Reilly hidden in the bush, his three companions went off promising to return with food and water as soon as possible.

O'Reilly watched them go, and then lay down in the sand to try to sleep. But the blistering pain in his chest became unendurable: he could not sleep. He was so parched by lack of water, so dehydrated by the heat of the day, so exhausted, that he was driven almost to madness by his condition. The time went by slowly and the others did not return when expected. His position was then wretched. 'That time of suffering', he was to write later, 'was the worst in my life'.

Driven by that indomitable spirit for survival that had served him so well in the past, he dragged himself up from the sand and resolved to find food for himself. He remembered that the Aborigines lived on freshly killed, uncooked meat when they could get no water and so he set about looking for a tree with possum marks. It speaks well of his acquired bush knowledge that he soon found one, and climbed up to pull the timid animal from its nest. It was a large specimen. He killed it, skinned it, and then ate the raw flesh. O'Reilly found to his satisfaction that the Aborigines were right: the possum meat was indeed a good substitute for water and he felt much restored.

It was well into the night when Maguire returned to O'Reilly with food and a bottle of water, and he stayed talking with him for a short while. The others had not told the Jackson family of their true reason for being in the vicinity, and Maguire left again to avoid raising suspicions. O'Reilly, much strengthened as a result of his own hunting and by the provisions Maguire had brought, broke off branches of peppermint trees and made himself a bed in the low scrub on the eastern slope of the dunes. In his crude nest the exhausted fugitive felt safe and well hidden, and with the promise of freedom the next day he fell into a deep sleep. By then he had been on the run for a little over twenty-four hours.

141

The next morning, 19 February, Maguire and the others returned and woke the still sleeping O'Reilly. The small group of men, tense but hopeful, struggled their way through the low, prickly bush, and up over the tops of the dunes which were some 30 to 40 feet high; then down again on the steep western side through the sparse tufts of spiky salt grass to the beach. In exploring the area today one is struck by the wide belt of the deserted golden strand stretching north and south as far as the eye can see; and the illimitable ocean, deep blue on the horizon, lightening in hue closer to the coast, until nearest the shoreline it subtly changes to translucent green sparkling in the intense sunlight. The beach is deserted and difficult to access which creates a sense of isolation. Over a hundred years ago it would have seemed even more desolate as there were no roads or tracks, and it was too far away from Bunbury town for picnics and outings. The beach was seldom stumbled upon, even by the few local farmers in the area of Leschenault Inlet.

Today's visitor looking south towards Koombana Bay can see gleaming white structures on the horizon which are the grain silos and the tall office blocks of Bunbury. On that February morning in 1869, O'Reilly and his rescuers—one with a telescope—searched anxiously in the same direction for the first sight of a sailing ship leaving the harbour. They were rewarded for their patience at 1.00 p.m. with the sight of the *Vigilant*, all sails set and bearing north as Captain Baker had promised.

Sand dunes at Australind where O'Reilly lay hidden for two weeks in 1869.
(Courtesy of Peter Okely)

Their rowing boat, which had been hidden among the tufted grass near the beach, was quickly run out into the surf; they clambered aboard and pulled away with light hearts. They were confident they could get far enough out to sea to meet the *Vigilant* beyond Australian jurisdiction and out of range of inquisitive eyes ashore. The four men, nearing the culmination of their brave escapade, rowed strongly through the swell. The shoreline receded and O'Reilly looked back, believing that he had left Western Australia for ever.

After two hours, to their great relief, the ship appeared to have seen them: she altered course and sailed directly for the little boat. Grateful for the chance of a rest they stopped pulling and waited, O'Reilly preparing for his departure. He had little to take with him, only his clothes and boots which had been given to him, and a small amount of money. Perhaps he had a notebook, some poetry, we do not know. He was leaving behind some brave friends and sixty-one other Fenians who had accompanied him on the *Hougoumont*. He was also leaving behind someone he had loved passionately, and who had loved him, and had helped him to abscond. He must have made a conscious effort to eradicate that painful memory from his mind. He had chosen escape and had broken with Jessie: he could not have both.

Suddenly, a startled cry from one of his companions aroused him from his thoughts. O'Reilly looked up and saw to his astonishment that the *Vigilant*, scarcely 2 miles off, had veered away as if to avoid them. It seemed impossible. The exhausted rowers, so sure a moment ago of success, were stunned. They began to signal desperately, believing that those on board had not yet seen them. Maguire stood up in the rowing boat waving and shouting. 'Captain Baker had given his word', he kept repeating, 'he accepted the passage money from Father McCabe'; and none of them could believe that he would desert them. Their renewed shouting, they all agreed, must have been heard on board.

Slowly and painfully it began to dawn on them that the *Vigilant* was avoiding them on purpose. At first Maguire would not accept it, and hoisted a white shirt on the end of an oar and waved even more frantically while shouting all the more; but to no avail. The captain of the *Vigilant*, for his own private, inexplicable reasons, refused to acknowledge their proximity and sailed onward, ever increasing the distance between them.

As the barque disappeared from view northwards, the bitter reality of their situation was now quite plain. The escape route had failed. True, O'Reilly was still free, but obviously at great risk of being discovered and recaptured like all the rest before him: there was nowhere for him to go. Defeated and bitter, the four men pulled towards the shore, to the place where they had so recently embarked in high spirits. The questions in all their minds were why had it happened and what was to be done now?

Maguire, the leader, proposed that they should beach the boat as before and leave O'Reilly in hiding. It was the best chance he had of remaining undetected. The other three would have to take a risk and tell Jackson of the situation. They would need his help in caring for O'Reilly while they returned to their homes; they must not be absent for too long otherwise it would raise suspicions in the neighbourhood. Maguire knew that the one ray of hope was the presence of other whalers in the harbour. He would contact Father McCabe and try and arrange a passage for O'Reilly on another ship. This was agreed to by all as the best thing to be done under the circumstances.

It was evening when they reached the shore. The sun was going down over the sea at the end of a cruelly disappointing day. O'Reilly's three friends—for they must have become very dear to him by this time—saw him safely hidden in his nest beneath the trees. In a week at most, they promised, someone would come from Bunbury with news of another ship, and in the meantime they would send food and water. A week in hiding while troopers and police scoured the neighbourhood—was it possible to survive? None in the group could have been optimistic about their chances of success but they all shook hands and dispersed. O'Reilly felt lonely when they had gone, but there was nothing to be done but wait. He had a little water left in a jar and the remains of his food from the previous night. He settled down to a lonely vigil.

At about midnight he was startled by a man's voice calling, cautiously hallooing through the trees, and by the crackle of footsteps approaching. He was afraid to answer. But then he heard his name and guessed it must be Jackson coming in answer to Maguire's plea for help. O'Reilly emerged from his hiding place and found that it was indeed Thomas Jackson, 'a fine old fellow' he recalled years later, and he had brought the fugitive some food. He had brought news, too, that Maguire and the others had started for home on horses borrowed from him. He urged O'Reilly not to be foolhardy, but to remain hidden because the police often combed the area when convicts had absconded. He promised that he would come to see him as often as was wise. Jackson evidently liked to chat and stayed with O'Reilly for a while longer.

When Jackson parted from O'Reilly later that same night, he renewed his warning about the police. The generosity of the 'fine old fellow' and his disinterested kindness—punishable if discovered—could only be explained by the wondrous camaraderie of early bush life born out of the sharing of hardship and the understanding between those who had suffered alike. O'Reilly thanked his new friend and settled down to a long, lonely, dangerous sentence. He was in an uncomfortable situation, but he was far from defeated.

CHAPTER **18**

'The Utmost Vigilance'

When constabulary duty's to be done,
The policeman's lot is not a happy one.

W.S. Gilbert

IF O'Reilly and his companions had been aware of other events occurring in Bunbury during the very night chosen for his escape bid, they would have had good cause to be pessimistic about their chances of success. That these events— and the unusual police activity they provoked—served in the long run to confuse the police hunt for the Fenian, would not have been appreciated at the time by his supporters. It may be said, with only a touch of exaggeration, that the township of Bunbury on the night of 17 February 1869 was alive with the sounds of sleuthing and investigation.

It happened as one of those maddening coincidences that two other prisoners had chosen that same night to abscond: a probationary prisoner named Thompson, and a ticket-of-leaver attached to the Bunbury town party, George Corton. The wife of Principal Warder Woodrow raised the alarm when she told her husband that she was sure she had seen a convict walking through the town after curfew. Woodrow enlisted the immediate aid of Sub-Inspector Timperley who in turn instituted a search which continued unsuccessfully until 2.00 a.m. Incredibly, this would have happened about the time that O'Reilly— whose escape at that time was still unknown to the police—was in Joseph Buswell's rowing boat with his companions, creeping down the estuary under the very noses of the search party. Mrs Woodrow's suspicions may have been greeted with a deal of sceptical muttering among the police who returned to barracks in the early hours without having seen anything suspicious. The comedy of the situation is obvious, but the comedy did not last long. At 3.00 a.m. a report was received that the two above-mentioned prisoners had indeed

145

absconded, and therefore a more thorough search was put into operation. The party on this second occasion included native trackers.

Suspicion centred on the *Vigilant* which was due to sail that day. Timperley's officers combed the ship as well as they could, the decks being loaded with casks, firewood for the boilers, and provisions. Timperley reported later that his officers had a job squeezing in and out of the small spaces and frequently used long steel spikes to thrust into corners and inaccessible areas, in order to cause anyone hiding there to cry out. No cries were heard.[1]

Other police and trackers scoured the sandhills around the town and within a short time both Thompson and Corton were apprehended. (Two weeks later they were sentenced to three months solitary confinement in irons and thirty-six lashes.) After such a night of police activity and broken sleep one can only wonder at the reaction of Timperley when, the next morning, the news was brought from Woodman's camp at Koagulup at about 8.00 a.m. that the trusted and popular probationary constable John Boyle O'Reilly was missing.

Could O'Reilly have been the man that Mrs Woodrow had seen in Bunbury the previous night? No, because Warder Woodman had stated in his report that the prisoner was in camp between 10.00 and 11.00 p.m. when he had checked. He knew this, Woodman wrote, because he had spoken to the prisoner. It was his opinion, added the warder, that O'Reilly had left sometime later, and had probably boarded the *Vigilant* which was by then under sail and leaving the harbour.[2] Obviously if O'Reilly was in camp at 10.30 p.m., he could not have been seen by Mrs Woodrow in Bunbury 15 miles away at the same time. But we know from O'Reilly's own account, and from other evidence, that he was not in camp being checked by Woodman at that late hour: he was already two hours on his way. So why did Woodman lie? Could it have been that Woodman, having some secret, personal association with the prisoner, was actually covering for O'Reilly?

Sub-Inspector Timperley was deeply puzzled and wondered whether Woodman had been mistaken. He rode down to Koagulup to hear the details for himself. When he arrived Woodman stuck to his story; he insisted that he had spoken to O'Reilly at about 10.30 p.m. But the observant police officer noticed that there was no mention of this in Woodman's occurrence book. Meanwhile, Mrs Woodrow insisted that the convict she had seen at about 10.00 p.m. *was* O'Reilly; she knew him well by sight and recognized his distinctive walk. Clearly Mrs Woodrow and Warder Woodman could not both be correct; the evidence conflicted. Timperley was even more puzzled, and in one of his later reports to the superintendent in Perth, F.C. Hare, he broached what he termed a 'matter of delicacy' by suggesting that Warder Woodman had attempted to mislead the police in this matter.[3]

Sub-Inspector William Timperley was the head policeman in the Bunbury-Vasse district and reported to his inspector in Fremantle. Aged thirty-eight in the year O'Reilly escaped, he was tall and dark with receding hair combed back, a large moustache, and a trimmed beard. He had a strong face and kindly eyes and was a decent and conscientious man who went to church twice on Sundays. He played an active part in the affairs of the district and, in the week prior to O'Reilly's escape, was preoccupied with two charity concerts at the Mechanics' Institute. He sang 'The Camp Town Races' dressed in a borrowed jockey costume and his performance was applauded so heartily that the item had to be repeated. He was gratified to learn that the concerts raised the sum of £15. After milking his cow early each morning, he spent much of his time in the office writing reports, directing his staff, appearing in court, and riding back and forth between Bunbury and Busselton.[4]

With the escape of a Fenian prisoner—an exceptionally serious matter—William Timperley assumed the role of the archetypical hardworking, tenacious detective. He organized search parties, interviewed those who might provide clues, offered a reward of £5 to tempt someone to come forward with information, pondered the evidence, took statements, and wrote reports to his superintendent. No probationary prisoner—still less a Fenian—had successfully escaped from custody until that time. From past experience it could not happen and surely it was impossible now. And yet, as the days passed, even Timperley came to believe that those who insisted that O'Reilly had got away on the *Vigilant* may have been correct. The native trackers were unsuccessful in locating footprints; Maguire had seen to that by driving a herd of cattle through the bush on the day after their trek in the dark. Enquiries at Dardanup, that enclave of suspect Catholic sympathizers, had failed to provide a lead. It would have taken more than £5 to have broken their loyalty. James Maguire, they said, was away in Pinjarra at a Roads Board meeting and uncontactable, so he could not be involved, could he? And his brother John? Well, he was the postmaster at Dardanup and therefore beyond reproach. Timperley wrote in his report:

> That O'Reilly has friends, I can have no doubt, having had constant and frequent opportunity for communicating with different persons while travelling about as a constable and I am equally certain that many would assist a Fenian who would not offer a hand or foot for an ordinary prisoner of the Crown.[5]

The search continued relentlessly. The dunes, the hills and the bush around Bunbury were combed for traces of the fugitive; but all the efforts of the police patrols were of no avail. As the days went by and no one came forward with any fresh evidence—apart from the redoubtable Mrs Woodrow—the assiduous sub-inspector was under increasing pressure to bring the hunt to a successful conclusion. In one of his reports, dated and dispatched on 20 February while O'Reilly was still hiding anxiously in the dunes about 12 miles away, one senses Timperley's desperation when he admitted that the escape of O'Reilly

> involves more mystery than any other that has ever come to my notice, I simply wish to point out that I have constantly and carefully considered the matter and acted under the circumstances to the best of my ability with the means at my disposal.[6]

At first, Timperley rejected the general opinion that the fugitive had boarded the *Vigilant* and maintained that it was merely a question of time before O'Reilly was apprehended. But he gradually altered his opinion and reported—reluctantly—that escape on the *Vigilant* seemed the most likely explanation.

Timperley's superior in Perth, Superintendent Hare, an Irish Protestant from Galway and therefore likely to have been openly hostile to O'Reilly's politics, would not accept Timperley's reasoning. There is a clear admonishment in his reply which must have hurt his conscientious subordinate:

> It is of no use folding your arms and saying that you are satisfied he got on board and was stowed away—Is any horse missing in the neighbourhood, for O'Reilly was a cavalry soldier? Could he swim? I expect the utmost vigilance and if you want help you must have somebody sent down who will undertake the necessary enquiries.[7]

The threat of sending someone else to take over the case must have been particularly humiliating. And so for the time being Timperley put aside his interests in fishing and concerts, and ordered that the hunt for O'Reilly be continued with renewed vigour.

CHAPTER 19

COURAGE REWARDED

Then here's to brave John Boyle O'Reilly,
Who first blazed a trail o'er the sea,
By escaping from Bunbury to Boston,
And vowing his comrades to free.

From 'The Catalpa Ballad' (trad.)

THE twisted trees and bushes, stunted by the winds and the hungry soil, which carpet the east side of the dunes north of Bunbury are almost impenetrable and provide excellent cover for anyone wishing to hide there. From the air, the foliage of the various paperbark, peppermint, and banksia families looks like an undulating green forest; an army could be moving about underneath albeit with difficulty, but without detection. Again, from the air, one would be struck by the tongue of land forming a spit some 19 kilometres in length and between 2 to 3 kilometres wide which divides the Indian Ocean from the serene Leschenault Inlet. At the head of the inlet, in an area which is now prized farmland, Thomas Jackson had his homestead; a little to the south of the homestead, John Boyle O'Reilly lay hidden under the trees.

Maguire and the others had departed late on Friday night, the 19th, leaving O'Reilly to wrestle with his forced inactivity over the next three days. He wrote later that he was in no physical discomfort, but full of suspense. He was visited by Jackson bearing food, and on the second day Jackson's son, Matthew, came in his stead, 'a rough lad of twelve or thirteen'. Matthew had been kept in ignorance of O'Reilly's presence by his father to begin with, but had then discovered him for himself when out riding. His horse had nearly trodden on the poet who was deep in a book. A friendship developed between them during the remainder of O'Reilly's stay there.

In the lonesome hours while hiding under the trees, O'Reilly's thoughts returned continually to the strange behaviour of the *Vigilant*. It obsessed him. Turning over in his mind the details of the episode he tried to reconstruct what had happened, and come up with some form of a satisfactory explanation. Why should the ship have turned away when it was evident that someone aboard must have seen them? Why had Captain Baker accepted the money from Father McCabe and then broken his contract? The more he thought about it, the more certain O'Reilly became that the captain had not intended to avoid them but that the *Vigilant* was still out there, somewhere on the ocean, looking for him. If this was so, then surely he should be out there too, looking for his rescuers!

What was forming in his mind was an extraordinary and foolhardy plan which was born of his frustration and inactivity. Quite contrary to the instructions of Maguire he would borrow a boat from Jackson (Buswell's boat was too heavy for one man), leave the safety of his hiding place, and attempt a rendezvous with the *Vigilant* on his own. Matthew had told him of an old dory (a small flat-bottomed boat) half-buried in the sand some distance up the coast.

On the third day (probably Monday, 22 February) O'Reilly went in search of it. This necessitated a trudge through the sand for 6 or 7 miles before finding what he was looking for. And what he found must have presented a forlorn appearance. In a poor state of repair, the dory's seams had opened up due to the heat and months of neglect: it was scarcely seaworthy. But irrepressible O'Reilly set about reclaiming it by caulking the planks with paperbark and making it serviceable. The work took him longer than expected. When it was finished he returned to his hiding place and resolved to go back to the dory the next morning.

On Tuesday, 23 February he walked once again up the deserted coast to find the dory in the sand where he had left it. On this occasion he was armed with a length of rope made from paperbark, and some possum which he had trapped the previous night. Lashing his meat supply to the stern to keep it cool he pushed the boat out into the surf. She was light and easy to row. Once he had negotiated the surf, he directed the little craft well out to sea on a northerly course.

O'Reilly remained at sea all that day and throughout the night. The dory bobbed about in the water, an insignificant speck on the ocean; the thin line of coast on the horizon was O'Reilly's only navigation aid. His survival must have been due, in part, to a spell of calm weather. A strong westerly breeze on that coast can whip the water up into a dangerous broth for a small open boat.

The next morning he watched and waited, straining his eyes for a sight of the ship he so desperately sought. The sun became scorching hot as the morning progressed and the reflection of light on the water dazzled him. Only those who have been at sea in small craft, and without any cover for protection in the middle of Western Australia's February heat, will fully appreciate the discomfort he would have suffered. To add to his troubles the meat he was towing had become putrid, and during the night the best part of it had been taken by a shark.

Towards noon on the second day he was rewarded with the sight of a sail that he recognized as the *Vigilant*. She drew so near him that he was able to hear voices on the deck. This surely was to be the moment of deliverance, he thought. His spirits soared.

But to his horror, the ship veered away once again, the distance between them lengthened and the sails, which had given so much hope at noon, were below the horizon by nightfall. Depressed and disappointed he had little choice but to pull away in the direction from which he had come, rowing all through the night; his second at sea. The dew and the cooler air refreshed him. In the early hours of the morning as the sun came up, he recognized the dunes off Australind and headed for the point where he had originally found the dory. Exhausted and disheartened, he climbed ashore, put the boat back where he had found it, and trudged back to his hiding place. 'After that', he says in his account of those days, 'I left the sand-valley no more'. He admitted that he was so tired he needed the next five days to sleep and recover.

What Maguire, the leader and careful strategist, said about the episode when he heard of it, we do not know. He made at least two visits to O'Reilly during the fourteen days of hiding to bring him food from Dardanup and news and encouragement from Father McCabe. In 1952, Maguire's last surviving daughter, Annie Stokes, who was then over ninety years of age, recalled those days when her father was engaged on some mysterious business not wholly divulged to the children. She remembered how her mother frequently prepared food for O'Reilly and on one occasion, while at the open range, she was so tense that an accident happened with the fire. Annie received a burn on her forehead which she carried for the rest of her life. 'I can still remember', she said, 'my father talking of how Boyle, poor Boyle, cried and cried in desperation for help'.[1] Annie also believed that O'Reilly was hidden at Dardanup for a short time while he was on the run, but it seems highly unlikely that Maguire would have risked such a course. O'Reilly's own account is more plausible. The notion that he came to Dardanup may be attributed to a little girl's half-remembered fancy.

All this time in the township of Bunbury, Father McCabe was hard at work supervising the building of his new Catholic church. In January he had taken delivery of 400 bushels of lime from William Brown, and a little later had paid £26 to Charles Zeddi, a carpenter, for laying the floor and making the altar rails. The business of the church must go on, whoever might lay secretly hidden in the bush dependent on his help. That Sub-Inspector William Timperley did not think to include the priest among those questioned in regard to the escaped Fenian was due, no doubt, to the general high standing the priest enjoyed in the neighbourhood. McCabe, by reason of his office like Maguire in his, was above suspicion. Looking at it purely from Timperley's point of view it was a critical mistake, an omission which probably cost Timperley the successful outcome of his detective work. If he had taken a keener interest in the priest's business deals at that time—at any rate those deals that were unconnected with church building—O'Reilly's future might have been very different. The priest had not been long in arranging a meeting with another captain of a whaler in Bunbury harbour; and he was at pains to see that a hitch would not occur again. Money changed hands between the priest and the captain (£10) and an undertaking was received that the Fenian would be conveyed as far as Java. The captain's name was David Gifford and the ship was the *Gazelle*.

On Tuesday, 2 March (if the estimated lapse of time is correct) Maguire, accompanied by James Milligan and another man, arrived at O'Reilly's hide-out with a letter from Father McCabe. So that there would be no confusion the priest explained the arrangement he had come to with Gifford, namely that a sum of money had been paid, and an important condition agreed upon in that the rendezvous should be more than 3 miles out at sea to be outside Australian waters. The letter concluded by asking O'Reilly to remember his friend in his prayers. Whether the presence of the third man was explained in the letter, or whether the introduction was left to Maguire, we do not know.

The third man was, potentially, a dangerous blow to their plans. He was Thomas Henderson, alias Martin Bowman, who had been transported in 1856 at the age of twenty-five on the *Runnymede*; his crime had been wounding with intent to murder. His conduct both in Millbank and on the transport ship had been noted as 'very bad', but apparently he reformed in the colony and was granted a ticket-of-leave in August 1860. But during his period of comparative freedom he gained a bad reputation for stirring up trouble among both prisoners and warders, and his application for a conditional pardon was refused on these grounds. He became hated by convicts and warders alike. Henry Wakeford, the Comptroller-General, in rejecting Bowman's request for a pardon noted that he was an 'incorrigible scoundrel'. Rebellious now, Bowman decided to escape, and by chance found out about Maguire's activities on behalf of O'Reilly. He threatened to expose them to the authorities unless he was taken on board the *Gazelle* along with O'Reilly. The blackmailed Maguire had no alternative but to agree. When Maguire arrived with the unwelcome guest, Bowman only stared at O'Reilly coolly, saying nothing. He knew that he was in a strong position. That night O'Reilly confessed they slept little, 'someone always keeping an eye on Bowman'.

O'Reilly brings Bowman into his novel, *Moondyne*, and paints an unflattering picture of him:

> [He was] all evil, envious, and cruel; detested by the basest, yet self-contained, full of jibe and derision, satisfied with his own depravity, and convinced that everyone was just as vile as he.[2]

In the story Bowman betrays Moondyne Joe and, as we shall see, the real Bowman very nearly succeeded in betraying O'Reilly.

The next morning at daybreak, Jackson and his son Matthew came down to the shore to help them launch Buswell's rowing boat. On this occasion James Milligan consented to accompany them, and so together with Bowman they had the necessary four oarsmen. O'Reilly must have been deeply moved as he waved goodbye to the faithful Jackson and his young friend Matthew, both of whom had had no particular reason for aiding him other than comradely sympathy. In doing so, they had placed themselves in grave danger of being punished if the truth were ever discovered.

By noon, when over 3 miles from shore, they were able to see two ships in full sail leaving Bunbury Harbour and heading north. The next few hours were as tense as before. Would the captain of the *Gazelle* look out for them? And even with the best of intentions, would the ship be able to locate them? Surely this time, after so much planning and disappointment, O'Reilly would get away. He had been on the run fourteen days.

Towards evening the four men in the rowing boat were cheered to see the *Gazelle* alter course and bear down on them. As it came closer, O'Reilly thrilled to hear his name called. And when he answered, he heard another cry in a broad Yankee accent calling, 'Come aboard!'.

They pulled alongside the barque, and John Boyle O'Reilly clambered up onto the deck and into the strong arms of Henry Hathaway, the second mate. Captain Gifford was there to greet him too and make him welcome. Then Bowman came aboard—but did not receive a similar welcome—and was taken down into the crew's quarters. It may be assumed that Father McCabe had explained Bowman's blackmail before the *Gazelle* left port and Captain Gifford had agreed, for the sake of O'Reilly, to take the other man along with them too. But he was never to have the support and friendship on board that O'Reilly had, and his future turned out very differently indeed.

The rowing boat, safely delivered of its cargo, drifted away from the hull of the larger ship. O'Reilly, high up now, looked down over the gunwales to wave to his friends for the last time. Maguire stood up and shouted at him: 'God Bless You! Don't forget us; and don't mention our names until it is all over'.[3] And O'Reilly recalled that James Milligan shouted a farewell also, but he could only wave and answer them both with tears of gratitude in his eyes. And so, as he looked upon his friends and the distant shore of Western Australia in the dying of the light, the *Gazelle* slowly pulled away leaving his brave rescuers to return to their homes.

A simple memorial stone and plaque (unveiled on 13 March 1988) marks the place near where John Boyle O'Reilly escaped from Australind in Western Australia. (Photograph by the author)

CHAPTER 20

HUNTING THE WHALE

___

'I will have no man in my boat', said Starbruck, 'who is not afraid of the whale'. By this he seemed to mean, not only that the most reliable and useful courage is that which arises from the fair estimation of the encountered peril, but that an utterly fearless man is a far more dangerous comrade than a coward.

Herman Melville

STANDING on the deck of the *Gazelle* that late, but still hot, early March afternoon in 1869, after being welcomed aboard by friendly Yankees whose grandfathers had won their independence from the same British who had imprisoned him, John Boyle O'Reilly must have experienced a euphoric sense of triumph and exhilaration. With his erstwhile prison reduced to a thin line of sand and scrub on the eastern horizon and his exact whereabouts unknown to his pursuers, the chance of his immediate recapture must have seemed remote. O'Reilly knew that the local police had no vessel capable of giving chase, even if they had been sure of their quarry which, of course, they were not. His early patience and fortitude, and his daring escape against all the odds, seemed to have paid off.

Yet in reality the freedom he experienced on the deck of the *Gazelle* was of a fragile kind. The power and influence of the British Empire, even by the middle of the 19th century, had already extended worldwide so that one-quarter of the earth's surface was estimated to be British territory through treaty, settlement or conquest. This included a large number of islands in the Indian and Atlantic Oceans which American whalers were in the habit of visiting for necessary stores and trading. The *Gazelle* was on a long, routine whaling expedition two and a half years out from its home port. The presence of O'Reilly on board, although welcomed, would not be allowed to divert the ship from its main purpose. It is of special significance, in view of what was to happen, that while whalers cruised back and forth across selected hunting grounds for long periods, ships on general business made the quickest possible passages. Thus the authorities in Western Australia had ample time to send dispatches to their colleagues in these imperial outposts alerting them to O'Reilly's escape. His safety, even on board an American vessel, could not be guaranteed.

As we imagine O'Reilly being escorted by Captain David Gifford and the second mate, Henry Hathaway, to the comparative comfort of the officers' cabins in the aft of the ship (and Bowman being escorted, less warmly, into the cramped crews' quarters in the forecastle), we will take the opportunity of looking around the *Gazelle* which was to be O'Reilly's home for close on five months, and consider not only the situation in which he found himself but also the kind of life that he would lead aboard.

The sketch of the ship reproduced on page 158 probably gives a sleeker, more glamorous impression of the vessel than was in fact the case. The sails and the rigging depicted were certainly common to whaling barques of that period: the foremast and mainmast carrying square sails, and the mizzenmast being fore and aft rigged. Staysails would have been set in between the masts in appropriate weather conditions. Whalers out of the east coast ports such as New Bedford, Nantucket, New London, Sag Harbour and others, were generally heavy, beamy ships with blunt, almost flat, bows and square transoms. The whale chasers, or whaleboats, which were slung on davits above the gunwales were the chief distinguishing feature. In the sketch the artist conveniently allows the boat on the davits aft to hide the raised quarterdeck and cabin accommodation for the officers. Also hidden, and thus flattering the ship's general appearance, is the clutter on deck; not only the usual forest of lines, ratlines, cleats and gear common to all sailing vessels, but also the extra paraphernalia of a crude factory ship: the clutter of whale processing tools, barrels, knives, hooks and lines, and the store of firewood for the brick-built tryworks in the centre of the deck.

The tryworks was nothing less than a brick kiln set down in the body of the ship over which rested two great metal trypots rather like old-fashioned domestic laundry coppers. On the *Pequod*, Captain Ahab's ship that searched for Moby Dick, the tryworks were

> planted between the fore mast and the main mast, the most roomy part of the deck. The timbers beneath are of a peculiar strength, fitted to sustain the weight of an almost solid mass of brick and mortar, some ten feet by eight square and five in height. The foundation does not penetrate the deck, but the masonry is firmly secured to the surface by ponderous knees of iron bracing it on all sides, and screwing it down to the timbers. On the flanks it is cased with wood, and on top it is covered by a large sloping hatchway. Removing the hatch we expose the great try-pots, two in number, and each of several barrels capacity. When not

in use they are kept remarkably clean. Sometimes they are polished with soapstone and sand, till they shine within like silver punch bowls.[1]

When a whale was caught by crews in the whale chasers—often a considerable distance from the parent vessel—the vast hulk was towed back to the ship, lashed to the side, and the cutting in, or flensing process, commenced. A number of the crew, wielding an assortment of knives on long poles, went overboard and stood upon the corpse where they set about cutting away the thick blubber. The huge strips unwinding from the carcass like orange peel were then hauled aboard by means of block and tackle, and fed into the tryworks for boiling down. The work continued around the clock until all the blubber was aboard, at which time the corpse of the dead whale was cut free and abandoned.

A large sperm whale yielded about eighty barrels, or approximately 3 tons of oil, and a small female yielded between 1 and 2 tons. A whaler out from New Bedford on a two- to three-year voyage might return with the products of as many as a hundred whales and hundreds of barrels would be stacked in the hold comprising a cargo of between 150 and 200 tons of oil.

At the time that O'Reilly boarded the *Gazelle*, the east coast whaling fleet had declined in number. Its peak had been in the year 1846 when over 700 vessels and 70,000 men were engaged in the industry, but by the year of O'Reilly's escape the number had been reduced to around 260 vessels. While this was partly on account of the disruption of the Civil War years (1861–65), there were far greater changes looming.

For a period after the Civil War whaling activity actually increased and the price of whale oil boomed unrealistically. But in the longer term, progress in discovery and modern manufacturing processes were to prove the saviour of the sperm whale as a species. Oils from the several families of whales had been traditionally used in the manufacture of soaps and lubricants, and for lighting— the street lamps of Boston, New York and Philadelphia were lit with whale oil—as well as in the tanning and textile industries. There seemed no limit to the human need for the whales' bounteous, though cruelly extracted, legacy. But with the discovery and mining of petroleum from 1857 onwards, the demand for the natural product diminished.

The appearance of oil wells in Pennsylvania and New York heralded the gradual decline of the east coast whaling fleets. While this was plainly evident in the boardrooms, the investment houses, and the offices of the fleet owners, the casual visitor walking the wharfs of New Bedford and neighbouring ports would have continued to observe intense whaling activity: the hustle and bustle, the unloading of cargo and the business of victualling ships. Trading in oil products was to continue throughout the remaining years of the 19th century and into the early years of the next.

The Gazelle, the New Bedford whaler which rescued O'Reilly in March 1869.

The *Gazelle* had sailed from New Bedford as early as August 1866, coinciden-tally at the time when O'Reilly was serving his first months in prison, a full year before he was sent to Australia.[2] The whaler's voyage was to last a little over three years. She followed a well-tried whaling route to the south, leaving the coast of Brazil to starboard and crossing the south Atlantic toward the Cape of Good Hope. Her destination, like so many of her sister ships, was the Indian Ocean.

The first of her two visits to Australia on that particular voyage occurred in 1867 when she entered King George Sound, Albany on 14 January. Four days later she was at sea again, working northwards around the coast of Western Australia and arriving off the coast of Java by the end of June. She was following the whales in a great circle through the Indian Ocean, and was repeating the circuit in 1868–69 when O'Reilly made his appearance.

The *Gazelle* had embarked a mixed racial crew in New Bedford totalling thirty-one and comprising fourteen Americans, fourteen Portuguese (one of whom wrote up the log each day), two Dutch (one of them being the cook), and one Brazilian. A whaler carried a blacksmith and a cooper who made barrels from bundles of staves and iron rings in which to hold the precious oil. They also carried the harpooners, those men with special skill and daring who stood in the prows of the whaleboats and thrust their long harpoons into the head and mouth of the whale at the right moment.[3]

The crew did not receive fixed wages. All hands, including the captain, received a share of the profits—called 'lays'—which were apportioned according to the importance of the position held in the ship. It was this method of paying by results that ensured all members of the crew continued working at sea until the ship was incapable of carrying any more cargo:

> ...being a green hand at whaling, my own lay would not be very large; but considering that I was used to the sea, could steer a ship, splice a rope, and all that, I made no doubt that from all I had heard I should be offered at least a 275th lay—that is, the 275th part of the clear net proceeds of the voyage, whatever that eventually might amount to. And although the 275th lay was what they call rather a *long lay*, yet it was better than nothing, and if we had a lucky voyage, might pretty nearly pay for the clothing I would wear out on it.[4]

With O'Reilly aboard and comfortably settled sharing a cabin with one of the mates, the ship continued about its business. The course was northwards and running parallel with the West Australian coast which, O'Reilly would have noted, lay a safe 200 miles over the horizon. Daily life for the new passenger and the mates—if not for the forecastle hands—proved relaxing and uneventful. Hours were spent on deck idling, talking, and basking in the typical fair weather of that time of the year. One of the favourite pastimes was making and rigging model ships which were inserted by the age-old method through the narrow necks of bottles. The second mate Henry Hathaway, who was to became a dear friend of O'Reilly's, described in a letter to him (after O'Reilly had left the ship) the progress on these models:

> The old man has made his schooner for Jimmy, and has got her all rigged and the sails on. Mariano, Mr Joseph, John Vitrene, Bill Malay, and the boy Andrew are each building a vessel: but I have seen none to equal the one the poor Carpenter built and which I have in my possession.[5]

The sympathy expressed in the letter for the carpenter refers to a fatal accident which happened while hunting whales shortly after O'Reilly joined the ship. The date was Sunday, 7 March and whales were sighted in the afternoon. The ship's position at the time was latitude 29°S, longitude 108°E, roughly 200 miles west of Geraldton. While the *Gazelle* hove to in a rough sea, three boats were launched in pursuit. The first mate's boat captured one of the whales and the second mate's caught another. Although the details of the ensuing accident are not clear from the log, it seems that in trying to tow the second whale to the ship's side, a line caught around some freestanding equipment— possibly a barrel of oil—which crashed across the deck, barely missing Captain Gifford and creating panic among the crew. The ship was pitching and tossing violently and as it was then 9.00 p.m. it was 'too dark to see anything'. The whale escaped, wounded. Later, in the darkness and confusion it became apparent that the carpenter, who was also one of the ship's harpooners, was missing. He was an American called William Freeman who was aged twenty-seven, and it was presumed he had been knocked overboard and drowned. His body was never recovered.

Two days later, the ship's log noted dispassionately that the captain promoted a Portuguese, Mariano Joaquim de Costa from the islands of the Azores, to take the carpenter's place. Death by accident on board the whalers was regretted, but a common enough occurrence.

The ship continued northwards making slow progress. The crew, being dependent upon the sea for their livelihoods, were more interested in searching for whales than in covering great distances. According to Melville:

> The three mast-heads are kept manned from sun-rise to sun-set: the seamen taking their regular turns (as at the helm) and relieving each other every two hours. Your most usual point of perch is the head of the t'gallant mast, where you stand upon two thin parallel sticks (almost peculiar to whalemen) called the t'gallant cross-trees. Here, tossed about by the sea, the beginner feels about as cosy as he would standing on a bull's horns.[6]

O'Reilly, known as 'Brown' to the majority of the crew, became a popular figure on board by writing and reciting poetry, singing Irish songs, and insisting upon joining in the work of the vessel. The captain treated him with kindness and generosity and the two men admired one another; but it was O'Reilly's friendship with Henry Hathaway which developed into a special intimacy that deepened beyond all others. The two men often sat together on deck and discussed religion, politics and poetry through the long watches. The experienced sailor also enlivened these occasions by playing his flautina. He was a slow-speaking, gentle, religious man, such as might be found ashore in the bleak Sailors' Chapel on the wharf, as described in *Moby Dick*, when 'each silent worshipper seemed purposely sitting apart from the other, as if each silent grief were insular and incommunicable'.[7] O'Reilly has left us a picture of what life was like aboard the *Gazelle* in the warm latitudes, in the opening stanzas of his poem 'The Amber Whale':

> We were down in the Indian Ocean, after sperm, and three years out;
> The last six months in the tropics, and looking in vain for a spout,
> Five men up on the royal yards, weary of straining their sight;
> And every day like its brother—just morning and noon and night—
> Nothing to break the sameness; water and wind and sun
> Motionless, gentle and blazing—never a change in one.

160

Rough seas aboard a whaler.

Everyday like its brother: when the noonday eight bells came,
'Twas like yesterday; and we seemed to know that tomorrow would be the same.
The foremast hands had a lazy time: there was never a thing to do;
The ship was painted, tarred down, and scraped; and the mates had nothing new.
We worked at sinnet and ratline till there wasn't a yarn to use,
And all we could do was watch and pray for a sperm whale's spout—or news.
It was whaler's luck of the vilest sort; and, though many a volunteer
Spent his watch below on the look-out, never a whale came near.
At least of the kind we wanted; there were lots of whales of a sort,
Killers and finbacks, and such like, as if they enjoyed the sport
Of seeing a whale-ship idle; but we never lowered a boat
For less than a blackfish—there's no oil in a killer's or finback's coat.
There was rich reward for the look-out men—tobacco for even a sail,
And a barrel of oil for the lucky dog who'd be first to 'raise' a whale.[8]

Relieving the boredom of inactive days aboard the whalers were the sightings and frequent meetings at sea with other whalers, defined amusingly as 'gams' in *Moby Dick*:

[T]he Gam is a social meeting of two or more whale-ships, generally on a cruising ground; when after exchanging hails, they exchange visits by boats' crews; the two captains remaining, for the time, on board one ship, and the chief mates on the other.[9]

There was no shortage of meetings with fellow whaling vessels on the voyage of the *Gazelle*. The most frequent entries in the ship's log, apart from the sightings of whales which were always noted along with the positions at sea, are entries about the gams.

If two strangers crossing the Pine Barrens in New York State, or the equally desolate Salisbury Plain in England cannot mutually avoid a mutual salutation; stopping for a moment to exchange the news; then how much more natural than upon the Pine Barrens and Salisbury Plains of the sea, two whaling vessels descrying each other at the ends of the earth should not only exchange hails, but come into still closer and more friendly contact. And especially would it seem to be a matter of course, in the case of vessels owned in one seaport, and whose captains, officers, and not a few of the men are personally known to each other; and consequently have all sorts of dear domestic things to talk about.[10]

On 28 March the *Gazelle* had a meeting with the barque *Clarice*, and they seem to have kept company because another gam is noted in the log for 15 April. On 16 April they met and talked with the ship *Governor Troup* on latitude 26°S and 200 miles west of the North West Cape. On 28 April the familiar cry went up from the yards in the afternoon: 'There she blows!'. But the whales were too far away and disappeared before the boats could reach them.

The next day, Thursday, whales were sighted in the forenoon which left plenty of light to give chase. Two whaleboats were lowered; the first mate, Frederick Hussey, in command of one and Henry Hathaway of the other. O'Reilly had begged on several occasions to be allowed to accompany Hathaway on a whale hunt but up until that time he had been dissuaded from doing so. It is easy to understand why. By far the most dangerous part of the whaling operation was the chase in the small boats and the kill itself. It was at those times that the majority of accidents, sometimes fatal ones, were apt to occur.

According to the invariable usage of the fishery, the whale-boat pushes off from the ship, with the headsman or whale-killer as temporary steersman, and the harpooneer or whale-fastener pulling the foremost oar, the one known as the harpooneer-oar. Now it needs a strong nervous arm to strike the first iron into the fish; for often, in what is called a long dart, the heavy implement has to be flung to the distance of twenty or thirty feet. But however prolonged and exhausting the chase, the harpooneer is expected to pull his oar meanwhile to the utmost. With his back to the fish the exhausted harpooneer when he hears the exciting cry—'Stand up, and give it to him!' has to drop and secure his oar, turn round, seize his harpoon from the crotch, and with what little strength may remain, he essays to pitch it somehow into the whale. No wonder, taking the whole fleet of whalemen in a body, that out of fifty fair chances for a dart, not five are successful: no wonder that so many hapless harpooneers are madly cursed and disrated'.[11]

'I finally consented', Hathaway wrote later, and O'Reilly was allowed into Hathaway's boat. When they reached the whales Mr Hussey's crew harpooned the creature first and when the second boat came up to give assistance, Hathaway ordered his steerer to harpoon the whale again in the back. The great whale, now in pain, raised his flukes in a rage and struck Hathaway's boat four successive times, splitting her to atoms. The crew jumped into the sea and swam away from the seething confusion, wildly clinging to their oars. Hathaway recounted that he clung to the stern part of the boat, that being the only piece left that was large enough to provide buoyancy. Hathaway could not see O'Reilly and thought his friend must have drowned as he knew O'Reilly had been hurt:

Boulter, who was close by my side, said, 'There he is, on the other side, under water'. I looked, and sure enough, there he was about two feet from the surface of the water, bobbing up and down like a cork. I threw myself over, and by clinging to the broken keel with my left hand, reached him by the hair of the

The hazards of hunting the whale. An imaginative watercolour by an unknown artist whaleman, c. 1840. (Courtesy of the New Bedford Whaling Museum)

head with my right hand, and hauled him on the stoven boat. I thought then he was dead, as the froth was running from his nostrils and mouth; but a thought struck me, if he were dead he would have sunk; so I raised him up on my shoulder. As I lay on the side of the boat with his stomach across my shoulder, I kept punching him as much as possible to get the salt water out of him.[12]

Through Hathaway's prompt action O'Reilly lay unconscious but alive. He and his rescuer, together with the other shipwrecked crew, were ferried twelve weary miles windward to where the *Gazelle* was hove to and awaiting them.

O'Reilly lay confined to his bunk for several days, nursing injuries to his head which had resulted from blows aimed by the whale. For the second time within weeks O'Reilly had come close to death and was lucky to have survived. But these experiences were not enough to cool his enthusiasm. When he was up and about again he convinced Hathaway to let him join the chase a second time. On that occasion O'Reilly had his revenge; a whale was caught and towed back to the *Gazelle*. In O'Reilly's poem the chase for the amber whale was not resolved so happily. Somewhat in the style of the *Rime of the Ancient Mariner*, O'Reilly's narrator of the poem breaks the law of the sea and he tries to cheat his fellow crew members from their fair share of the spoils. He pays dearly for it as he is the only member of the crew to survive the voyage and is overcome with remorse.

That night fell dark on the starving crew, and a hurricane blew next day;
Then we cut the line, and we cursed the prize as it drifted fast away,
As if some power under the waves were towing it out of sight;
And there we were, without help or hope, dreading the coming night.
Three days that hurricane lasted. When it passed, two men were dead;
And the strongest one of the living had not strength to raise his head,
When his dreaming swoon was broken by the sound of a bark's sail!
And when he heard their kindly words, you'd think he should have smiled
With joy at his deliverance; but he cried like a little child,
And hid his face in his poor weak hands,—for he thought of the selfish plan,—
And he prayed to God to forgive them all. And shipmates, I am that man!

The *Gazelle* continued its way northward and by 23 June was off the coast of Java approaching the Straits of Sunda. This narrow waterway patterned with small islands (including the temperamental, volcanic Krakatoa) is notoriously hazardous, and on this occasion the ship was unable to pass through to reach her destination, Batavia (now Jakarta). She turned tail and sailed west. Denied a port at which to purchase the necessary stores and conduct trade, the *Gazelle* sought another at Roderiquez, an island in part of the Mauritius group which was, at that time, a British colony. Danger from drowning and injury were not the only threats to freedom that O'Reilly faced aboard the *Gazelle*.

CHAPTER 21

THE POLITICAL REFUGEE

---

*I have profound reason for gratitude. These experiences
prove how much solid kindness and unselfishness there are
in the world. I am happy to say that the men who then
helped me on my way are my dear friends still; and no act
of mine, I trust, will ever cause them to lose the friendship
which began under such remarkable circumstances.*

John Boyle O'Reilly

IN mid-Indian Ocean, on 28 June 1869, John Boyle O'Reilly celebrated his
twenty-fifth birthday. Two weeks later the *Gazelle* negotiated the reefs surrounding the island of Rodriquez and anchored off the chief settlement, Port
Mathurin. Once again the ex-convict was placed within the shadow of British law
and was seriously at risk of being recaptured.

Had the *Gazelle* not abandoned its planned visit to Java, O'Reilly would have
disembarked there under the terms of the agreement between Captain Gifford
and Father McCabe. But weather conditions prevented this, and the ship's need
for water and fresh vegetables left the captain no choice other than to make for
Rodriquez. It must have been an anxious O'Reilly who waited on board for the
first sign of an official enquiry.

He did not have long to wait. On the evening of the day of their arrival,
10 July, a launch drew alongside and the resident magistrate—the Governor of
Mauritius's local deputy—came aboard accompanied by a police guard. Both
O'Reilly and Hathaway were on deck. The magistrate told Hathaway he had
information that an escaped convict from Western Australia was being hidden
on the ship, and demanded that he be identified and given up. Hathaway denied
that there was such a person aboard. Not satisfied, the magistrate then demanded
that the crew be mustered for inspection.

The authorities had been notified about three other ex-convicts, in addition
to O'Reilly, who were believed to have absconded on whalers: Henderson (alias

Bowman)—whom we know was on the *Gazelle*—Connor, and McGuiness. The log confirms that Bowman was taken ashore but it is not clear from the near illegible script whether the latter two were actually on the *Gazelle* or on another whaler in the harbour, only that they were quickly identified and detained. According to Roche, the crew so detested Bowman that one of them gave him away 'with a jerk of his thumb and a knowing look'. O'Reilly himself was not recognized.

For a while the magistrate seemed satisfied and departed for the shore with his prisoners, but O'Reilly and Hathaway feared that Bowman, now in irons and with nothing to lose, might bargain with the police by informing on him.

> As soon as they were gone [O'Reilly] half crazy says to me: 'My God! it's all up with me! What can I do? They'll come back for me, but I'll never be taken alive'. I knew he meant what he said; for the priest had told me he'd tried to commit suicide, and if he shouldn't escape had determined to kill himself. I calmed him down and told him to go below and keep out of sight and I'd try to think up something.[1]

Hathaway was as good as his word and formed a plan. While two of the crew were on anchor watch, he secreted O'Reilly inside a small, little-known locker under the cabin companionway. Earlier, Hathaway had ordered the watch to keep a good lookout for 'Brown' who might try to jump overboard and swim for safety. At the appointed moment, when the watch was looking the other way, Hathaway tossed a grindstone and O'Reilly's hat overboard, and then quickly retreated.

The loud splash in the water confirmed Hathaway's warning in the minds of the simple crewmen, and immediately the cry went up, 'Man overboard!'. Those off watch rushed on deck, boats were lowered and the water searched for an hour. Only O'Reilly's hat was recovered. The crew—some of whom were sincerely fond of 'Brown'—were convinced that he had drowned.

Next morning there was general grief aboard the *Gazelle*. Captain Gifford, who had not been told of the plan, was greatly upset and Hathaway himself appeared to be in tears. Flags were flown at half-mast.

It was still early when the police boat returned with the magistrate. Bowman was also with them ready to identify his victim. What they witnessed was the unmistakeable distress of everyone born out of an unshakeable belief that the wanted man had indeed been drowned. Fortunately this was enough to convince the officials and the search was called off.

But was the magistrate himself convinced? Roche wrote that the magistrate's wife was a loyal Irish woman, and that her sympathy for O'Reilly may have influenced her husband. When Bowman was arraigned in court the magistrate, now presiding, ordered him to keep silent when he attempted to tell the story of O'Reilly. And moreover, the search for O'Reilly's body in the harbour was called off on the magistrate's orders.[2]

The *Gazelle* sailed from Rodriquez on 13 July, bound for the Cape of Good Hope. But the log does not describe the amazement of the crew when O'Reilly emerged, safe, from the cramped locker. Neither does it note the joy of Captain Gifford when he saw him; according to Roche he 'wrung his hand and burst out crying like a baby'.[3]

The experience of O'Reilly's near discovery, and the fact that all the crew now knew his true identity, decided Captain Gifford to transfer him to another ship as soon as was conveniently possible. The *Gazelle's* next port of call was to be St Helena, another British colony, and he guessed that the Irishman would not be so lucky there. By keeping him aboard he was risking O'Reilly's safety and, perhaps more importantly, that of his ship and crew.

On its journey south the *Gazelle* made one more call, at the French island of Bourbon (now known as Réunion). On 29 July, at latitude 30°S and longitude 33°E (about 400 miles east of Durban), they met the American cargo vessel, *Sapphire*. She was forty-one days out of Bombay, loaded with cotton, and bound for Liverpool.

The ships hove to for the traditional gam. Captain Gifford had given O'Reilly the identity papers of John Soule, a seaman who had previously deserted from the *Gazelle*, and arranged with Captain Seiders of the *Sapphire* to take 'Soule' aboard. Gifford accompanied O'Reilly in the longboat which was commanded by Hathaway, and they boarded the *Sapphire* together. O'Reilly recalled:

> When we saw what kind of a man the Captain was, Captain Gifford told him the whole story; and Captain Seiders at once gave me a state-room in the cabin, and treated me as a passenger with all kindness.[4]

On leaving, Gifford pressed 20 guineas into O'Reilly's hand, saying that he was sure his friend would repay the sum when he had settled successfully in America. O'Reilly never forgot the generosity and friendship of Captain David Gifford, and did indeed repay the money. He also publicly acknowledged his debt by dedicating his first book of poems to him, a dedication Gifford never saw because he died before the book reached him.[5]

O'Reilly found it hardest to part from his close companion, Henry Hathaway. Theirs had been an extraordinary union of shipmates. Hathaway pined for his friend after he had left the ship, as evidenced by his private diary in which he 'talks' to the absent O'Reilly, describing his feelings of loss and the detailed events of the days without him.

I am now seated at the old donkey, where we've sat side by side for the last five months, more or less, and have been reading over some of your pieces of poetry, and it makes me lonesome, although we have not parted as yet hardly three hours, and thank God we have lived and parted as friends. Most everybody on board is talking about you, and they all wish you good luck in your undertaking, and all that I have got to say is, 'God speed and God Bless you!'.[6]

The two ships continued to sail south and round the Cape of Good Hope. For a time they were in sight of each other; but then the *Sapphire* drew ahead and disappeared over the horizon.

O'Reilly, surprisingly, made friends with an English passenger from Bombay named Bailey, and he was also told the truth about the Fenian's identity and history. 'He was a true man', wrote O'Reilly later, as he had reason to thank Bailey for his assistance when they arrived in Liverpool.

The *Sapphire* docked on 13 October and O'Reilly, under the name of John Soule, stepped ashore in the country that had imprisoned and condemned him. With his new identity and his seaman's papers he was reasonably safe: his only danger perhaps was falling victim to an informant. But who would know him? Only Mr Bailey and two of the ship's officers. The authorities, who by this time believed that Prisoner 9843 had escaped on a whaler, would not have expected him to have returned to Britain.

O'Reilly had returned to a part of Britain that he knew well from his time in Preston ten years previously. Though tempted to make the short journey to his old town to visit his Aunt Chrissy he decided against it, preferring to lie low in Liverpool. 'I dare not go to Preston', he wrote later to his aunt, but he assured her that he was thinking of her so close to him at that time.[7]

In the event it was Bailey and the ship's mate, John Bursley, who looked after O'Reilly for the duration of his short stay in Liverpool; and it was they who saw him safely embarked for America as third mate on the Yankee vessel, *Bombay*, which was bound for Philadelphia. The captain, who knew O'Reilly's true identity, welcomed him aboard.

As the *Bombay* sailed westward, close to the southern coast of Ireland, John Boyle O'Reilly looked out towards the distant coast under the rays of the setting sun. It was the closest he would ever get to his beloved native country, and the image moved him deeply, remaining with him for the rest of his life.

Ireland was there under the sun, but under the dark clouds also. The rays of golden glory fell down from behind the dark cloud—fell down like God's pity on the beautiful, tear-stained face of Ireland. Fell down on the dear familiar faces of my old home on the hill, the wood, the river. Lighting them all once more with the same heaven-tint that I loved to watch long ago.[8]

O'Reilly must have been very happy on the *Bombay* because he presented Captain F.C. Jordan with thirty lines of doggerel verse in praise of the ship and its crew: 'This little piece is worthless', he wrote in the introduction, '[but] was written with every feeling that one man can possess who addresses and esteems another'. O'Reilly wisely never published it and so it remains in a Boston archive, hastily scribbled in his handwriting on old, lined notebook paper, a heartfelt tribute from one seaman to another at the end of a voyage.

> May the great waves never 'whelm you: may the howling squall pass over,
> And still leave you riding proudly, good and trusty as before.
> May you bear your master always as though perils pass away:
> And whatever sea you sail upon—God speed you old Bombay.

After a safe and uneventful voyage across the Atlantic, the *Bombay* sailed up the Delaware River to dock at Philadelphia on 23 November 1869. It was two years and one month since O'Reilly, the prisoner, had sailed on board the *Hougoumont* to face penal servitude in Australia. At long last John Boyle O'Reilly was on American soil. He was, in his own words, 'a political refugee', but a free man and beyond the reach of the British authorities.

> I am Liberty! Fame of nation or praise of statue is naught to me;
> Freedom is growth and not creation, one man suffers, one man is free.
> One brain forges a constitution; but how shall the million souls be one?
> Freedom is more than a resolution—he is not free who is free alone.[9]

Part Three

THE EXILE OF THE GAEL

1870–1890

CHAPTER 22

WAR CORRESPONDENT

Not the noblest acts can be true solutions;
The soul must be sated before the eye,
Else the passionate glory of revolutions
Shall pass like the flames that flash and die.

John Boyle O'Reilly

WHEN O'Reilly was on the *Sapphire* bound for Liverpool he wrote a letter, dated 27 August 1869, to the editor of the *Irishman* in Dublin in which he briefly described his escape while carefully hiding the names of those who had helped him in Western Australia. He explained that he had received money from the captain of the ship which had rescued him, gave Gifford's name and address, and asked that 'should anything happen to me, that gentleman who assisted me shall not lose his money'. (In the event he paid all the money back himself.) But he added a postscript to the letter asking for an introduction to his fellow countrymen in America. It was that letter which broke the news of his escape to the people of Ireland, and ensured that he would have a welcoming committee on arrival in Philadelphia.

Word quickly spread among his compatriots in America. But when a Fenian delegation came to find O'Reilly aboard the *Bombay* on 23 November 1869, they seriously doubted the identity of the wiry, tanned youth with a sailor's appearance who stood before them. He was described at that time as having jet black eyebrows and hair, a small black moustache and deep hazel eyes, and being of slight though erect build. The eyes were 'very expressive, whether flashing with some sudden fancy, or glowing with a deeper, burning thought, or sparkling with pure, boyish fun'. After doubts were expressed and he was closely questioned by the visitors, O'Reilly's patience gave way and it was only when he threatened to make off independently that the delegation accepted him as the man they were seeking.[1] He stayed only a few days in Philadelphia and then departed by train for New York.

The New York Irish-born, who amounted at that time to over one-quarter of the population, were proud of their daring countryman who had escaped from the clutches of the imperial power and miraculously returned from the dead after 'drowning' at Rodriquez. He was acclaimed and feted as a hero and accorded an official reception in the Cooper Institute on 16 December. That evening several prominent Irish republican activists were present on the platform with their guest of honour, including John Savage, John Burke, and John O'Mahony. An audience of over 2,000 listened enraptured as O'Reilly described for the first time in public his penal sufferings and his momentous escape. He admitted that he and his fellow military Fenians had taken the British Army oath but, he said, 'it is the lips and not the heart of these men that performed the act'.[2] He wrote later that he had an 'overwhelming ovation'.

The meeting was reported in the New York Times and Herald, and in the Boston Pilot, and O'Reilly's initial impact and undoubted oratorical power brought him countless other speaking engagements in the months to follow. He had become a public figure, ready for action; he wanted to use his recent experiences and his passionately held political convictions for the service of his country. He had landed in America an idealist, believing that only by military action could Ireland achieve freedom. In short, he was ready to continue the fight which had engaged him as a Fenian in the 10th Hussars. These views were to change dramatically within a short time, but for the present he became a soldier again.

He joined the Savage wing of the Fenian Brotherhood (the American based society dedicated to the overthrow of British rule in the home country) and the secret society, Clan na Gael. He was appointed adjutant in the first battalion of the Legion of St Patrick—'a very splendid body of men'.[3] The members pledged to be

> faithful to Ireland and obey their officers. The object of every man who joins the organisation is...to be ready, not only drilled, but organised, when the time comes when he may be wanted.[4]

Like most migrants in a new land O'Reilly did not have as easy a time in the first months of arrival as his public reception might lead us to believe. He was soon disappointed to find that Irish patriotic movements in the United States were hopelessly divided by internal wrangling, jealousies and bitter disagreements. Also, he was distracted by, and much concerned about, the plight of his family in Ireland. His father, now a widower, and two of his sisters were living in near poverty in Grenville Street, Dublin. William O'Reilly had retired from teaching at Dowth in 1860 at the age of fifty-three and in the official records a written note stated that he was not to receive superannuation. No reason was given but the decision must have been contested because a later note, dated 1 March 1861, stated that he was awarded a gratuity of thirty-two months salary and the words 'retiring allowance' were added in brackets by way of explanation. This would have been a welcome reversal but obviously far from sufficient to ensure a comfortable old age. If O'Reilly senior had not received occasional financial assistance from supporting friends his situation would have been graver still. In a letter from New York, dated 30 December 1869, John Boyle thanked A.M. Sullivan, the Irish MP and editor of *Nation*, for his generosity towards his father and said he hoped to be able to assist his family before long.[5] He wanted to arrange for his sisters to emigrate, but to Canada rather than America: 'I hate New York and Boston, which are all corruption and misery for poor girls', he wrote. But although he was to contribute to his family's welfare when he became established, and he repaid other friends who had helped them, nothing came of the plan to send his sisters to Canada.

O'Reilly never felt at ease in New York and so, after only a month's stay, took the advice of his friends and left for Boston on Monday, 3 January 1870. He carried with him two letters of introduction: one to Thomas Manning with whom he stayed, and the other to the poet, Dr Robert Dwyer Joyce.

Boston would be O'Reilly's home for the next twenty years and it is where he would become an important, much respected and influential figure. However, for

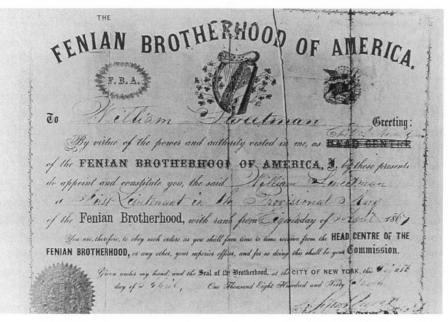

'You are therefore to obey such orders as you shall from time to time receive from the HEAD CENTRE OF THE FENIAN BROTHERHOOD...'. *A certificate of Fenian membership in America, 1867.*

a proper understanding of the social, political and religious society into which O'Reilly was then entering it is necessary to outline briefly the historical events which had shaped Boston and made it, in some respects, unique among older American cities.

Over one million Irish men, women and children fled their country at the time of the Great Famine (1845–49), and it is estimated that a total of over 1,700,000 arrived in America during the twenty years before the start of the Civil War in 1861. By 1850, 26 per cent of the population of New York had been born in Ireland, and by 1855 Boston had an Irish-born population of 20 per cent, which was equal to half the number of those who were native-born Bostonians.[6]

The majority of Irish immigrants who arrived at the port of Boston stayed there. Penniless and half-starved, homesick, and often cruelly exploited by unscrupulous shipowners, most of them could not afford to move far from the overcrowded, disease-ridden tenements of the waterfront. Traditionally a rural people they now had to adjust to an unfamiliar city existence, and they sought what comfort they could find in their shared experiences, their music and dancing, their religion, and their sometimes violent interfamily squabbling. Mostly unskilled, the men took labouring jobs on the wharfs and in the building trade, and the women worked in clothing and shoe factories and in domestic service. The seemingly endless supply of cheap labour was exploited by the clothing and manufacturing industries; the Irish women in Boston sewed at home, making shirts and dresses for companies who paid wages of less than $3 a week. Hundreds of Irish women toiled under miserable conditions for a pittance and wondered whether they had been foolish in leaving their native country.[7]

Economic hardship was not the only burden the Irish immigrant had to bear. The United States was a Protestant nation, inheriting many English anti-Catholic prejudices of the time. The native-born Bostonians who were from the professional class and successful business people—the 'Brahmins' as they were dubbed—looked upon the Irish with disdain. 'They were appalled at the insanitary living conditions of the newcomers and complained that they were turning Massachusetts into a "moral cesspool".'[8] The Brahmins equated the Irish with Catholicism, the two being inseparable. Also, because the Irish continued to love and publicly defend their native land and curse England for all the evils that had befallen it, the Brahmins believed that the Irish immigrants' loyalty to America was questionable and not to be trusted. Newspaper advertisements for the better jobs often carried the warning, 'Positively no Irish need apply'.

In the decade preceding John Boyle O'Reilly's arrival in Boston the intense anti-Irish feeling had abated to some extent. At its height in the 1830s and 1840s it had resulted in violence and bloody riots which had included the notorious burning of the Ursuline convent in Charlestown (just across the Charles River from downtown Boston) in 1834. The Civil War, which concluded in 1865, altered the social and economic status of the Irish, and native Americans noticed that Irish regiments had fought heroically for the Union. Irish civilians had shown their loyalty to their new country by doing war work in the munitions factories and shipyards. And by the 1860s, the Irish population was beginning to assert a political influence; politicians recognized the Irish population as an electoral force to be wooed and won. In 1861, Harvard University conferred the degree of Honorary Doctor of Divinity on Irish Bishop John Fitzpatrick, which would have been an unthinkable gesture of tolerance ten years earlier.

Boston may have become a less hostile environment for Irish people by the time O'Reilly stepped off the train on 3 January 1870, but the populace was still divided economically and culturally into two classes. On the one side were ranged the native-born Yankee Brahmins, Protestant in religion and Republican in politics, who dominated the city's financial and mercantile institutions, and who were guardians of the rich cultural tradition so acutely observed in the novels of Henry James. And on the other side were the immigrants who were mainly Irish, Catholic and generally supporters of the Democratic Party. The conflict between the two sides would take generations to subside completely:

> Other major American cities, to be sure, shared many of Boston's social, cultural, and religious characteristics, but few to the same extent and none to the same degree. Yankee Boston was unique in the depth and intensity of its convictions. The generations of bitter and unyielding conflict between the natives of Boston and the newcomers from Ireland would forever mould the social and political character of the Boston Irish in ways not found elsewhere.[9]

It was John Boyle O'Reilly's destiny in Boston to construct a bridge between these two worlds and ease the tensions. He would achieve this in part by cajoling his fellow immigrants and reminding them of their duties and obligations to their new country. And through his literary work and the sheer force of his character, he would raise the status of the Irish population and break down much traditional hostility between the two factions. But this was in the years ahead. In the winter of 1870 O'Reilly was himself a poor immigrant seeking suitable work.

With his letters of introduction he was received into the home of Thomas Manning and through him met several prominent Irish-Americans in the city. One of these was Patrick A. Collins with whom he formed a lifelong friendship.

Collins was born in 1844, the same year as O'Reilly, near Fermoy in County Cork, and emigrated to America with thousands of others at a young age. He was accompanied by his mother, his father having died of pneumonia. As was the lot of many Irish immigrants the young Patrick was forced through poverty to leave school early, but being a spirited boy, he educated himself at the Boston Public Library in the evenings while he worked as an upholsterer's apprentice during the day. When O'Reilly met him at the age of twenty-four, he had risen to become a Democrat in the State House of Representatives and was completing his law studies at Harvard. Within a few weeks of his arrival in Boston O'Reilly left the Manning residence and went to live with Collins, but soon moved again to a small lodging house at the corner of Green and Staniford Streets, close to Bunker Hill in Charlestown.

Through his new-found friends he was introduced to another Irishman, Merrick S. Creagh, the Boston manager of the Inman Line, and O'Reilly was promptly given a job in the office. Most likely it was a job created for him by the sympathetic Creagh because he found himself with plenty of time to write letters: 'I have nothing to do but read the newspaper', he wrote, 'I hope it will last'.[10] But it did not last. The directors of the British-based company in London, when informed that a notorious revolutionary was on their payroll, ordered his dismissal.

Undeterred, O'Reilly quickly found another job, this time in a printing office in State Street in the heart of downtown Boston, close to the site of what is now City Hall. It was there that he met Patrick Donahoe, proprietor of a publishing company which included the Boston newspaper, the *Pilot*. Doubtless the printing works was closely associated with Donahoe's then flourishing company and the newly employed O'Reilly would have impressed the prominent Irish philanthropist with his keen intellect, his gentle manner, athletic figure, and his confident yet sensitive demeanour.

> He was probably as loveable a character as nature in her happiest moods ever moulded out of Celtic material: handsome and brave, gifted in rarest qualities of mind and heart, broad-minded and intensely sympathetic, progressive and independent in thought with an enlightened and tolerant disposition, in religion, politics, more in keeping with a poetic soul than with an ordinary human temperament.[11]

O'Reilly's meeting with Patrick Donahoe was the turning point in his fortunes, and proved propitious for both parties. Donahoe was a native of County Cavan and was an early immigrant to Boston, leaving Ireland in 1825 before the Famine years. Like O'Reilly he had trained as a compositor and graduated to journalism, working as a young man on the *Columbian Sentinel*. Caught up in the intense and frequently violent anti-Catholic feeling at the time he determined to start his own paper to represent the Catholic point of view. His chance came when Bishop Fenwick's ill-named paper the *Jesuit* foundered, and Donahoe and his partner, Devereux, raised sufficient money to buy it. Despite a change in name to the *Literary and Catholic Sentinel*, which was of little improvement on the original, the new enterprise fared no better than its predecessor.

The two partners tried again and in 1836 launched the *Pilot*. Donahoe bent all his energies into making it a success, travelling the country to promote it and building up a national circulation. This time it worked, and the *Pilot* became a handsome eight-page weekly which printed Irish news and, in its editorials, represented the Irish people in America. It soon assumed the status of a household necessity, eagerly read in all Catholic homes not only in New England but in towns and cities further west.

Donahoe's Pilot Publishing Company flourished in a grandiose French Renaissance-style building of four storeys on Franklin Street. Donahoe himself became one of the richest and most influential Catholics in New England, generous to Catholic charities and a keen sponsor of Irish regiments in the Civil War. When O'Reilly addressed the Massachusetts Irish Americans in the Music Hall in Boston on 31 January 1870, it was Patrick Donahoe who presided. Whether it was on that occasion or a later one at the printing office is not known, but the proprietor of the *Pilot* promised O'Reilly a job on the newspaper.

We do not know the exact date when O'Reilly first started work for the *Pilot* but he was certainly on the staff early in April 1870 as evidenced by a letter he wrote to his Aunt Chrissy which discloses that his fortunes had improved considerably: 'I am likely to become a prosperous man in America', he wrote, 'I just manage to live as a gentleman'. He reported with scarcely concealed pride that he had paid his debts and was leading a busy, happy life:

> I write for the magazines and report for the Pilot, drill the Irish Legion, make speeches at public meetings, lecture for charities etc. etc. The course in the old country would soon make me a fortune; and after a time, here it will have the same effect; but at present all this must be done to establish a reputation.[12]

O'Reilly's first major assignment for the newspaper which brought him into prominence and secured his advancement—and incidentally was to change his opinions on military Fenianism—was his coverage of the Fenian convention in New York on 19 April, and the third Fenian invasion of Canada which followed as a result of decisions taken at that meeting. General John O'Neill had presided in New York and represented the faction in the Brotherhood who favoured striking at England by attacking Canada, and this in spite of two earlier abortive attempts four years previously. O'Reilly had supported O'Neill's plans for the invasion and was confident of his success.

O'Neill's raggle-taggle army was encamped near the Canadian border north of St Albans in Vermont when O'Reilly arrived there by train on the morning of 25 May. His first detailed dispatches, printed in the *Pilot* on 4 June, clearly show his disquiet at the poor morale and lack of discipline among the Irish troops. 'There was none of the excitement here which reporters have so graphically pictured', he wrote. And in describing the first foray, the Battle of Richard's Farm, he admitted that although the Fenian troops opened a tremendous fire

> many of the men—the greatest number—were raw boys who were frightened at the whizz of a bullet, and in spite of the efforts of their officers who were as brave as men could be, they could not keep to the front. At last the officers, in despair gave up the attempt.

O'Neill was greatly discouraged and in a fighting speech to his men said he was ashamed of them and that they had acted disgracefully. In a surprise move he appointed John Boyle O'Reilly in command, but neither O'Reilly nor O'Neill were involved in much more fighting. After some desultory skirmishes and a thinning of the ranks through desertion and loss of life, the Fenians were forced to pull back and lost what little ground they had managed to gain. O'Neill was arrested by the American Marshal of Vermont. President Grant had issued a proclamation forbidding the invasion and indicated that those who persisted would forfeit government protection. O'Reilly was himself arrested, along with others, but released within a few hours. The debacle was complete.

O'Reilly was thoroughly disillusioned and in a series of reports in the *Pilot* delivered scathing criticism of the Fenians and the policies which had attempted a hopeless and costly venture.

> Fenianism now stands before the world with all its jagged corners clear and bare as the peak of Teneriffe, and forming as decided a landmark to the people of the Irish race as does the lofty spire to the mariner. Feniansim has lost its mystery, and with that has lost its power...Fenianism, so far as relates to the invasion of Canada, ceases to exist, but it has done all the evil it could do. It has torn thousands of men away from their homes and their employment in a wild and futile enterprise. It has caused the death of several brave men, and the imprisonment, perhaps death, of many others, and it has given occasion to the enemies of the Irish people to renew the slurs which such enterprises have given birth to before.[13]

And in an astonishing turnabout of opinion—considering O'Reilly's support of O'Neill in New York—the young journalist concluded: 'The men who framed and executed this last abortion of war-making have proved themselves to be criminally incompetent'.

It is clear that the ludicrous third and final Fenian attempt at the invasion of Canada was O'Reilly's 'road to Damascus'. As a result of his experiences at the front, and his close observations as a journalist, he saw that the way to achieve independence for Ireland was not through ill-prepared militancy and quixotic postering: his country surely deserved better than that. O'Reilly saw, also, that an improvement in the status of Irish people in America and their acceptance as loyal citizens could only be achieved first, by raising Irish self-esteem; and secondly, while he did not expect the Irish to renounce their love for their native land, O'Reilly believed they should embrace a firm loyalty to their new country and involve themselves in its political life. And henceforth, in the pages of the *Pilot* and in his writings and speeches, O'Reilly assiduously devoted his energies to this cause.

CHAPTER 23

A Man of Influence

He does not die that can bequeath
Some influence to the land he knows.

Hilaire Belloc

IN June 1870, when O'Reilly returned from the ignominious 'battle front' on the Canadian border to the *Pilot* offices in Boston, he was an older and a wiser man—if not in years then certainly in outlook. And although he never repudiated the ideals of Fenianism, he quickly resigned from both the Brotherhood and Clan na Gael. He continued to be a critic of Fenian tactics and petty squabbles in the pages of the *Pilot* and, with less restraint, in his private correspondence. In a letter to O'Donovan Rossa, for example, he wished that Rossa would have nothing to do with Fenianism or Confederation, '[I] can't believe in them...[I] think Fenianism is a humbug'.[1] And in a letter to John Devoy, O'Reilly showed contempt for 'that infernal name Fenianism. It has done us more harm than men can see...with its associations of defeat, dissension, and trickery [it] has been a millstone on the neck of Nationality for years past'.[2]

Naturally, with undisguised views like these O'Reilly was subject to bitter attack from Fenian stalwarts. He was accused of being an enemy of republicanism and a traitor to his country, both of which so hurt him that he defended himself in a letter to the Fenian Brotherhood of Boston in which he explained that as a Fenian he was

> doing no good for Ireland. Had I remained a member of your organisation, when I did not believe in it (when I might, advantageously to myself, have done) I think I would deserve more ill feeling from you and all honest men than I have earned by severing the connection.

He ended his letter by declaring that he was no enemy of Fenianism and 'wished it all the success it ever aimed at'.[3]

182

O'Reilly's patriotism was never in serious question. He was recognized by the majority as a critic only of tactics and attitudes; and his new conservatism found favour with the proprietor of the *Pilot* who saw in him a remarkable talent for journalism and leadership. He was promoted to the editorial department, and within a year was in the editor's chair. At the age of twenty-six he was probably the youngest editor of a large-circulation, influential weekly paper in America. Neither did O'Reilly's outspokenness harm the reputation of the paper. It was soon noticed and quoted beyond the confines of the Irish-Catholic readership. Here was an Irish paper that did not mindlessly extol Irish factionalism and bombast, but put forward rational arguments and counselled, admonished and directed Irish-Americans in their duties and civic responsibilities.

A test of O'Reilly's new approach to Irish nationalism occurred after reports were received in Boston of a bloody battle in the streets of New York (what became known as the 'Orange Riots' of 1870) on 12 July, the anniversary of the Battle of the Boyne.[4] The New York Orangemen, 3,000 strong, paraded the streets chanting provocative slogans and bearing flags attacking the Pope and Irish Catholic onlookers. The form of the demonstration, and its intentions, are utterly familiar to those of us who have witnessed street confrontations between warring factions today, when many of the participants judge success by the amount of violence which follows. In 1870 it was no different; passions were aroused and the Irish—'the Greens'—retaliated. A melee ensued with loss of life and injuries to both parties.

The *Pilot* might have been expected to defend the Irish rioters on the grounds of gross provocation, but O'Reilly was shocked by the events and, in an even-handed editorial, delivered a scathing rebuke addressed to all his fellow countrymen, Protestant and Catholic alike. He called the action a national disgrace.

> What are we today in the eyes of Americans? Aliens from a petty island in the Atlantic, boasting of our patriotism and fraternity, and showing at the same moment the deadly hatred that rankles against our brethren and fellow country-men. Why must we carry, wherever we go, those cursed and contemptible island feuds? Shall we never be shamed into the knowledge of the brazen impudence of allowing our national hatreds to disturb the peace and the safety of the respectable citizens of this country? We cannot, and we care not to analyse this mountain of disgrace to find out to which party the blame is attached. Both parties are to be blamed and condemned; for both have joined in making the name of Irishmen a scoff and a by-word this day in America.[5]

This was the opening salvo in O'Reilly's long crusade for the recognition of the status and dignity of Irish-Americans. And he started by attacking the factional disputes, the bigotry and the clannishness of the Irish themselves. He believed that Ireland had a special social and religious mission in the New World and that the Irish had a great deal to contribute to American political life; but he also believed that their cause was humiliated and destroyed by traditional rabblerousers. 'We must criticise our own people', he once told O'Donovan Rossa, 'if we want to raise them'.

The crusade was a long one and, at times, a despairing one. The following year it was as though his advice had amounted to nothing. A similar parade took place, and again it erupted into a violent and ugly riot. O'Reilly returned to the attack in his own way, castigating both sides and urging restraint.

> If the Orangemen determine to parade, they have a right to parade; that is, they have as much right to parade with orange scarves and banners, as a Fenian regiment has with green scarves and sunbursts. But it may be that *neither* party has a *right* to parade; that they have simply been tolerated by the authorities. There are two ways of getting rid of this apple of discord. The first is, by an agreement between the general Irish population and the Orangemen foregoing all right to parade, and expressing their determination never to hold processions for Irish political objects alone. This we may rest assured will not be easily agreed to. The second one is the best, and the one that must come in the end, when America, tired out and indignant with her squabbling population, puts her foot down with a will and tells them all—Germans, French, Irish, Orangemen—'You have had enough now. There is only ONE flag to be raised in future in this country and that flag is the Stars and Stripes'.[6]

With strong views like these it may be wondered that the newspaper's popularity among Irish-Americans did not suffer. This, however, was far from the case, and although O'Reilly himself lost some popularity and his hero's status among diehard Fenians, his wide support never seemed to weaken.

Within a year of O'Reilly's appointment as editor of the *Pilot*, circulation by weekly subscriptions had risen to an astonishing 103,000, and the paper was earning generous plaudits from its fellow journals: 'There is no better influence with the Irish in America' (*Boston Daily Advertiser*); 'It is a beneficent power in the community, ably representing the Irish Americans' (*Boston Herald*); 'Unquestionably the best of Catholic journals in this country' (*Springfield Advertiser*); 'It is conducted with rare intelligence and taste, and its discussion of public questions is generally characterised by fairness and candour' (*Boston Daily Globe*).[7]

The outward appearance of the *Pilot* changed too. The old ornate masthead, incorporating sailing vessels at sea and an Irish harp entwined in the capital 'P', was replaced by a simple, bold, black Gothic title and underneath the motto:

'Be just, and fear not. Let all the ends thou aim'st at be thy God's, thy Country's, and Truth's'. The front page was divided into five columns, often including poetry alongside the main news of the week. As a weekly published every Saturday, the *Pilot* was predominantly a vehicle of Irish, Catholic, and Irish-American news and opinion, but it also covered national and international events. There among the continuing domestic concerns of the Boston Irish were reminders of the happenings in the world at large. For example, there was a report on the amazing invention by Alexander Bell which resulted in 'the first conversation by word of mouth over a telephone wire'; there was also an announcement that work had commenced on a tunnel under the English Channel, supervised by Suez Canal engineer, Ferdinand de Lessops. Nor were the arts neglected. The opening of Mr Richard Wagner's great opera house at Bayreuth was reported, as was the first performance of Verdi's new opera, *Aida*, in Cairo in 1871.

But undoubtedly the popularity of the *Pilot* rested mainly on its presentation of news for Irish immigrants, which kept them in touch with events at home. The newspaper also advertised local events of special Irish interest; commented on and interpreted events in the Westminster parliament as they related to or affected Ireland; listed job vacancies; and, with a weekly column peculiarly of its own invention, put new immigrants in touch with those who had already settled, and appealed for information on the whereabouts of missing relatives. This was not just a popular feature; since each insertion had to be paid for, it became a valuable source of income for the proprietor.

O'Reilly may have admonished his erring countrymen out of positive motives from time to time, but he reserved his most scathing and implacable criticisms for policies of the British Government. The memory of his own imprisonment burned in him and had marked him for life. He remained unforgiving and wrathful in the editorial pages of the *Pilot*, such as when he denounced what he saw as undue British influence over the Pope's opposition to a testimonial for Parnell. He denounced England's

> bayonets and prisons and savage lawlessness in Ireland, her abrogation of every human right for the Irish people, her ruling submission of men by terror, her policy of starvation, degradation and banishment. She plays her last card like a desperate gambler and cheat, and in doing so her hand has been nailed to the table.[8]

John Boyle O'Reilly's new prominence rested as much on his public lecturing as on his position on the *Pilot*. While he made the *Pilot* very much his own newspaper (long before he became co-owner of it) he commanded similar attention by reason of his appearances at public meetings. The public lecture, with or without recitation, was a form of mass entertainment on both sides of the Atlantic at a time before film, radio and television. (Charles Dickens died from exhaustion brought about by his many public recitations in the same month that O'Reilly made his first lecture appearance in Boston. And O'Reilly's own death may well have been precipitated by an exhausting lecture tour in the last year of his life.) His first Boston lecture was given—appropriately—in Liberty Hall on 20 June when he spoke of his imprisonment and rescue for the benefit of his old friend, Captain Gifford of the *Gazelle*. Henry Hathaway was also on the platform. He spoke again on 20 October in the Boston Music Hall for the benefit of the Engineer Corps of the 9th Regiment, and again on 11 December for the benefit of St Stephen's Church, Boston.

In December 1870 the then British Prime Minister, William Gladstone, bowed to intense and prolonged pressure mounted by the Fenian Amnesty Association in both Ireland and England, and announced a conditional pardon for all non-military Fenians providing they did not return to the United Kingdom before the expiry of their sentences. This included old *Hougoumont* compatriots of O'Reilly's still in Western Australia: John Flood, John Edward Kelly, Michael Cody, George Connolly, Thomas Fennell, Cornelius Keane, Thomas Baines and Daniel Bradley. The partial amnesty also extended to certain Fenian prisoners in Ireland, including John Devoy and O'Donovan Rossa, who were exiled from Ireland under the terms of the pardon. They arrived in America in January 1871.

O'Reilly feared that the arrival of these men—heroes of republican ideals— would be fought over and exploited by opposing factions among militant Fenians in New York, and perhaps used to bolster plans for fresh military escapades. And in this he proved correct. It was then that O'Reilly wrote to O'Donovan Rossa urging him to abandon Fenianism. And in another letter, to John Devoy, he asserted that:

> Fenianism in New York is a power, and interested knaves will defend it and sneer at the quite neutral element...but believe me that Fenianism is a devilish poor representative organisation for Irish Nationalists—or rather no organisation at all.[9]

Although O'Reilly continued with his warnings in the *Pilot*, the exiles allied themselves with the New York Fenians and when they issued a call for all American-Irish to unite into one great organization, he aired his disapproval in his editorials. He believed that this would further segregate them from native America and reduce their political influence; and although he pledged his friendship with the exiles, he remained aloof from them and their activities. For this stand he was criticized and, on one occasion, his life was threatened.[10]

But O'Reilly was not intimidated and continued to believe that a more conservative, moderate approach achieved far more that jingoistic militancy. His own rising position in the community was proof enough of that, as he explained in another letter to John Devoy:

> Every individual Fenian seems to consider the man an enemy who does not believe with him—but I would wish to see you, and the gentlemen who have been released, have as many friends and as much respect as I have in Boston.[11]

And after a year in the editor's chair at the *Pilot*, O'Reilly could be proud of his record. In a letter to his Aunt Chrissy he boasted:

> My position in Boston—which is the chief city in the country for literature and general culture—is good. I am chief editor of the Pilot—which is the most influential Catholic newspaper in America, probably in the world. My salary is $3,000 a year; $4,000 next year. Besides, I write when I please for the leading magazines and literary papers—which also adds to my income.[12]

Within the short space of two years since his arrival O'Reilly had proved that an Irish immigrant, while not in any sense being disloyal to his country or his intensely held patriotic feelings, could overcome Yankee prejudice, be accepted, and make good in Boston public life.

CHAPTER 24

A PHOENIX TOO FREQUENT

Ah! God, was thy wrath without pity,
To tear the strong heart from our city,
And cast it away?

John Boyle O'Reilly

EARLY in 1871 O'Reilly received news from Dublin that his father, William David, had died on 17 February at the age of sixty-three, and was buried beside his mother, Eliza Boyle, at Glasnevin Cemetery. His father's last years were described by O'Reilly as 'poor and friendless'[1] and it must have grieved the son to know that he could not visit him. O'Reilly was still classed as a fugitive by British authorities and there was the certainty of recapture and imprisonment if he set foot on the other side of the Atlantic.

William David O'Reilly's place in Irish history is secure, not as a patriot and friend of Daniel O'Connell, nor as the simple village schoolmaster often harassed by officious government inspectors, but as the father of John Boyle. And it is the latter's name which is given prominence in his epitaph:

> Father of John Boyle O'Reilly, a good Irish Soldier. Convicted by English Court-martial and self-amnestied by escaping from Western Australia to America. May the brave son live long, and may the remains of the noble father rest in peace.

But John Boyle would have found comfort at this time from his new-found friendship with a certain Mary Murphy from Charlestown. He had been drawn to her by reading her stories in a Catholic youth magazine, the *Young Crusader*. When he asked the editor for an introduction to the author he learned that the name he had seen printed in the magazine, Agnes Smiley, was a pseudonym.

Mary Murphy was twenty-one when O'Reilly first met her. She was the daughter of Irish immigrant parents, John Murphy from County Fermanagh and Jane Smiley of County Donegal. According to Roche they courted for two years before marriage, and if this is correct O'Reilly must have noticed Agnes Smiley's work in the summer of 1870 during routine searches for material at the editor's desk of the *Pilot*. In a letter to Mrs O'Donovan Rossa written in February 1872 he accepted the invitation to be godfather to her baby, but apologized for knowing little about babies: 'I'm a bachelor as yet'.[2] The 'as yet' may have referred to his impending marriage which took place later that year on 15 August in St Mary's Church at the bottom of leafy Winthrop Street in Charlestown. The celebrant was Reverend Father George Hamilton.

John and his bride, 'the very nicest girl in New England', spent their honeymoon travelling in New Hampshire and Maine, and on their return made their home at 34 Winthrop Street. The house is still there, a substantial mid-19th-century residence opposite Winthrop Park whose summit is crowned by the Bunker Hill Memorial. Even in those days it would have been an imposing address, indicative that O'Reilly must have been receiving a salary in excess of the $3,000 mentioned in his letter to his Aunt Chrissy. 'Mary is a wonderful manager', he wrote, 'I give her all the money, and we are prepared for a rainy day'.[3]

Winthrop Street, Charlestown. The O'Reillys' town house was No. 34, next door to the modern fire station. In the foreground are the gates of the park which leads up towards the Bunker Hill Memorial. (Photograph by the author)

At that time O'Reilly presented a handsome, almost dashing appearance with his dark eyes and neatly trimmed moustache, beard and sideburns. His full head of wavy hair was stylishly cut and already showed distinguished streaks of grey. His clothes were fashionable and expensive, his frockcoat had high, wide-cut lapels which were set off by a white undershirt and loosely tied cravat. He was a young man of dignity and bearing who was as interested in sport and physical exercise as in literature, politics and poetry. In his marriage year, at the age of twenty-eight, O'Reilly was already a respected and recognized man about Boston, a political moderate and a convinced Democrat, yet a loyal spokesman for his people. A month before his marriage, in a speech on behalf of the press given at a banquet on the occasion of the Peace Jubilee in Boston in July 1872, he expressed pride in the knowledge that seventy-six years previously the first editor of a leading Boston newspaper, the *Daily Advertiser*, had been an Irishman. But, he said:

> although men of our race and of the religious belief of our majority, have lived down many prejudices and many injustices since then, there still remains a mountain to be removed by us and our descendants. But with the help of an enlightened and unprejudiced Press we can succeed where our forerunners failed.[4]

Within three months of the O'Reillys' marriage the first of a series of disasters hit the *Pilot* newspaper which, indirectly, were to have the effect of advancing O'Reilly's fortunes.

From his house on the side of Bunker Hill, which overlooked the city across the Charles River, O'Reilly would have seen the sky over central Boston lit up for miles around with the glow of a fire which raged through the Saturday night and early Sunday morning of 9 and 10 November.

> Every now and then a broad wave of light would suddenly show distant spires, sharp and clear against the dark sky, from which the next instant they would fade like spectres as the thick curling masses of smoke swelled upwards and spread ghastly smears of black across the heavens.[5]

It seemed as though the whole of the centre of Boston was on fire. And, indeed, it very nearly was. With dramatic headlines such as 'A Terrible Conflagration', and 'Loss of Human Life', and 'Rich Men Beggared in a Day', the newspapers on the following Monday morning told the whole terrible story. The fire had started at about 7.30 p.m. in a granite building at the corner of Summer and Kingston Streets, the central business district of the city. By the time fire engines had arrived the whole corner of the street had been consumed in flames. The flames quickly spread to neighbouring buildings and soon whole streets were on fire, and block after block of offices and warehouses crumbled in a mass of burning cinders. The *Boston Daily Globe* described how the fire, 'adding force to its own movement like a tornado', swept along Otis, Federal, Purchase and Broad Streets devouring all the buildings in its path. The *Pilot* offices on Franklin Street did not escape.

During the daylight hours of Monday the affected area was cordoned off and only those with passes could enter and inspect the damage. Doubtless O'Reilly and Patrick Donahoe would have been allowed through to pick over the still smoking debris which had once been their proud newspaper.

Under these circumstances we may wonder how the *Pilot* managed to survive and appear as usual on the following Saturday. This can be partly explained, no doubt, by the fact that the printing operation was contracted out to Rand and Avery, a well-established company unaffected by the fire. It was in their building that the *Pilot*'s editorial office took temporary shelter, and in the edition of 23 November O'Reilly included his special poem, 'The Wail of Two Cities'. The two parts commemorate the great fire of Chicago on 9 October 1871, and the Boston fire a year later. He asks of the Boston fire whether God had struck the city in wrath and muses that perhaps His hand had fallen to hasten a return of the populace to grace. The last verse ends on an optimistic note:

> Let us rise purified from our ashes
>   As sinners have risen who grieved;
> Let us show that twice-sent desolation
>   On every true heart in the nation
> Has conquest achieved.[6]

If O'Reilly's poetic musings had had any validity, then the hand of God was not appeased—or perhaps it was only cruel coincidence—as fire struck again just eleven days after the original conflagration. The flames, coming from the fifth storey of Rand and Avery's building, were spotted by a passer-by at about 7.00 p.m. on 20 November and the alarm was raised. The fire brigade was unable to save the printing presses, newspaper stock, and the current week's issue of the *Pilot* already set up in type. The damage was estimated to be in the region of $200,000, but the distress to the *Pilot*'s editorial staff and proprietor can only be imagined.

On the principle that matters could hardly get any worse, the *Pilot* staff fought back and found another temporary residence at 360 Washington Street. The newspaper was published as usual. But their ordeal by fire was not over yet. After six months, on 30 May 1873, fire struck again doing considerable, though not irreparable, damage. By that time O'Reilly could only look upon the procession of disasters with wry humour, and he described in an editorial of 14 June that when a fire comes to Boston

> it goes round all the corners looking for its old friend the *Pilot*. It is evident that the fire has a rare appreciation of a good newspaper, and a good companion to pass a brilliant hour. Of course we are used to being burnt out, and it doesn't affect *us* much after the first mouthful of smoke and cinders. But when it comes three times in seven months we must protest.[7]

His boast that 'it doesn't affect us much' was an understatement. Although buildings and stock were insured in each case, the disasters resulted in serious financial pressure on the owner, Patrick Donahoe, from which he would not recover. The process of the ruin of his estate was slow but inexorable, and will be told in a later chapter.

In the meantime, let us report and celebrate John Boyle O'Reilly's gradual acceptance into the hitherto exclusive literary establishment in Boston with the publication of his early works.

CHAPTER 25

'A VERY CLUBABLE MAN'

_____

The charm of the Papyrus is that it is essentially an ideal club. Dining, wining, the patronage of millionaires and politicans, the gorgeous service and elaborate style, are as vapour and mud beside the beauty of standing up for our independent, brotherly, anti-shoddy, aesthetic Papyrus.

John Boyle O'Reilly

O'REILLY'S literary ambitions were manifest in Boston even before he joined the staff of the *Pilot*. In fact it is more than likely he was drawn to Boston partly on account of its pre-eminence as a literary centre where the leading authors, artists and others connected with literature and the arts lived and met socially. The richness and tradition of New England literary life must have been awe-inspiring to a fledgling writer of O'Reilly's youth and inexperience. True, Nathaniel Hawthorne and J. R. Lowell, the first editor of the *Atlantic Monthly*, had gone, but men such as Emerson, Longfellow, Oliver Wendell Holmes, Thomas Aldrich, John G. Whittier and W.D. Howells might be seen on the Boston streets and congregating in clubs and coffee houses in the vicinity of Beacon Hill and Boston Common.

It was while O'Reilly was a bachelor in rooms at the corner of Green and Staniford Streets that he started gathering around him a group of like-minded writers and artists intent on making their reputations. The group included Edward King of the *Boston Journal*, Martin Milmore the sculptor, another newspaperman, Edward Mitchell, who later joined the *New York Sun*, and his friend Dr R.D. Joyce, the Irish poet. They met in each other's lodgings and talked and read from their own compositions.

Later, when O'Reilly joined the *Pilot* he became associated with other members of the newspaper profession and joined the Massachusetts Press Club and the Boston Press Club. In December 1872 when Dr Henry Stanley (of Livingstone fame) was guest of honour at a meeting of Boston journalists, it was

Oil painting realized from a photograph of O'Reilly by an unknown artist, Boston.
(Courtesy of Richard O'Reilly Hocking)

O'Reilly who gave the address of welcome. When the formal part of the evening had concluded the journalists, together with Stanley, repaired to a neighbouring chophouse for a convivial feast. They enjoyed themselves so much that they voted to assemble again, and then yet again. The meetings became regular, new writers joined them, and an association was formed calling itself the Papyrus Club. Its object was to bring together socially the leading writers of the daily, weekly and periodical press, and to provide a place where they could meet and entertain 'gentlemen of reputation in literature and the arts' while on visits to Boston. Camaraderie, good humour and mutual support of almost a Masonic character distinguished the club. As one member, George M. Towle, wrote:

> I suppose most of us feel a kindlier interest in a man when we know he is a Papyrus man. I think we are more ready to help him when he is in trouble, to regret his calamities, to rejoice in his good fortune.[1]

The Papyrus became one of O'Reilly's great and abiding enthusiasms. He was on the executive committee and was later elected president. He even wrote a poem on the occasion when a crystal 'Loving Cup' was presented to the club by one of its members.

> For brotherhood, not wine, this cup should pass;
>   Its depths should ne'er reflect the eye of malice;
> Drink toasts to strangers with the social glass,
>   But drink to brother with this loving chalice.[2]

The Papyrus led to the formation of the St Botolph Club, modelled on the famous Century Club of New York. A much more formal institution, and a richer one than the Papyrus, it boasted its own premises. The membership of 260 included O'Reilly and the leading authors and artists of the day.

The importance and popularity of club life at that time in Boston—and in cities elsewhere where professional men gathered—cannot be overestimated. A man's world revolved around his work and his clubs, his family life taking very much third place. Although O'Reilly dearly loved his family and professed on more than one occasion to have been homesick when away from them, he was a man of his time. He was a busy, public figure whose crowded days were, more often than not, occupied with professional and social engagements and when at home in the evenings he would spend time in his study, writing.

O'Reilly's first poem for the *Pilot* was published as early as May 1870 and entitled 'Pondering'. It is identical to the first of the two poems entitled 'Night Thoughts' which was written in his notebook in Western Australia. It is intriguing to wonder why he resurrected what is plainly a heart-searching, gloomy piece for the *Pilot*, and to speculate on whether he was still mindful of the girl he had left behind. 'Pondering' is of interest because it marked the beginning of a stream of poems regularly published thereafter.

O'Reilly's first poem to appear in print in New York, in the *Tribune* in 1871, was 'The Amber Whale' which brought him a tempting offer to work for that paper. Patrick Donahoe countered with a significant rise in salary and so kept his editor in Boston. The young poet also had some success overseas when two poems were published the following year in the Oxford University magazine, *Dark Blue*. He received £20 in payment, and was very proud until the editors learned who he was and refused further contributions.

On 18 May 1873 a daughter was born to John and Mary O'Reilly. She was christened Mary, but was known throughout her life as Mollie. In a sense another birth took place a few months later—John Boyle's first book of poetry appeared under the title, *Songs from the Southern Seas*. Published by Roberts Brothers of Boston it was dedicated to Captain David R. Gifford of the *Gazelle* in acknowledgement of his kindness and his help at the time of the author's escape. Sadly, Gifford was never to see the dedication as he died aboard his ship in the Indian Ocean on 26 August 1873.

Only ten of the twenty-three poems may fit the title description; the others are on more general subjects including 'The Old School Clock', 'My Mother's Memory', 'The Fishermen of Wexford', and 'The Poison Flower'. Many of the poems first appeared in the *Pilot* and other literary magazines.

In 'My Native Land' the poet recounts how he sailed across the Southern Ocean and visited many lands—'thousand-isled Cathay'—but he comes to the conclusion that 'there is no Southern Land that can fill with love the hearts of Northern men'.

> And thus it was: the yearning turned
>   From laden airs of cinnamon,
> And stretched far westward, while the full heart burned
>   With love for Ireland, looking on Cathay!

The volume was noted for several long narrative poems which he wrote in Western Australia: 'The King of The Vasse', 'The Dog Guard', 'The Dukite Snake', 'The Monster Diamond', and the whaling adventure, 'The Amber Whale'. The first-named is a strange imaginative drama in the Arthurian tradition about an unlikely family of Swedish migrants who land in Western Australia, a land O'Reilly describes as: 'Poor Cinderella! she must bide her woe, because an elder sister wills it so', and with remarkable foreknowledge he adds:

> Ah! could that sister see the future day
> When her old wealth and strength are shorn away.

> And she, lone mother then, puts forth her hand
> To rest on kindred blood on that far land.

The poem goes on to tell how Jacob Eibsen, the little six-year-old child of one of the women and 'secretly her best loved', dies in her arms on the beach. The local king of the land, an Aboriginal, appears before them, sees what has happened and lays a precious pearl upon the child's mouth. Miraculously he comes back to life, but to his mother's and his brethren's horror he has an entirely different character and spends his youth roaming as a savage in the bush. The time comes eventually when the old king dies and the young man 'with the pallid face' claims the right of succession because he owns the pearl—the source of power in the land. The tribes reluctantly agree. They are ruled by the youth for a time but after some years their rebelliousness results in one of them aiming a spear at the upraised hand which holds the pearl

> And split the awful centre of their sight,—
> The upraised Pearl! A moment there it shone
> Before the spear-point,—then forever gone!

In true legendary fashion, reminiscent perhaps of Cinderella or Oscar Wilde's Dorian Gray, the young man changes suddenly; the magic has gone. He remains young at heart, but in appearance he is old, feeble and white-haired.

> So Jacob Eibsen lived through years of joy,—
> A patriarch in age, in heart a boy.

Modern tastes recoil from the once popular, melodramatic, narrative poems which tell stories in ringing, forcible tones but which lack much insight and character study. It is doubtful whether 'The King of the Vasse' would hold its place in a volume of poetry today.

Another poem of the same genre, a tale of bestial horror and cruelty which today might justify an 'X' rating, is 'The Dog Guard: An Australian Story'. It tells of a mass grave of bones on the prison island of Rottnest (called Rottenest in the poem for sake of the metre), and goes on to explain how the bones belonged to long-dead natives who had been captured and marooned there, unable to escape:

> But a government boat went out each day
> To fling meat ashore—and then sailed away.

But some of the natives did find a way of escaping, via a reef offshore. The people on the mainland were fearful, but as they were unwilling to mount a guard themselves, they hit on a scheme for placing half-starved mastiffs on lengthy chains along the reef to do the job for them.

> In a line on the face of the shoal the dogs
> Had a dry house each, on some anchored logs;
> And the neck chain from each stretched just half way
> To the next dog's house; right across the Bay
> Ran a line that was hideous with horrible sounds
> From the hungry throats of two hundred hounds.

The scheme worked well to begin with. Enough food was left for the natives and the dogs and there were no more escapes. That is until the settlers on the mainland deserted their homes to trek north in search of pearls which had recently been discovered. In their absence there was no one to deliver the daily rations to Rottnest: 'The dogs and the natives were all forgot'. The prisoners, suffering pangs of hunger and wild despair, were driven to attempt escape once more and at the risk of confronting the dogs on the reef.

> There were short sharp cries, and a line of fleck
> As the long fangs sank in the swimmer's neck;
> There were gurgling growls mixed with human groans
> For the savages drave the sharpened bones
> Through their enemies' ribs, and the bodies sank
> Each dog holding fast with a bone through his flank.

With lines and stories like these *Songs from the Southern Seas* was bound to attract a good deal of attention. Reviews were mixed, ranging from the frankly gushing to the adversely critical and dismissive. The *Hartford Post* complained of the 'horrible themes and absurdities' of the narrative poems and said they were not worthy of O'Reilly's manifest talent. The *Boston Daily Advertiser*'s reviewer thought that 'The King of the Vasse' was 'in many respects the best poem in the book' showing 'far greater care and finish' than in any of the other long poems. The *Boston Post* thought the poems 'uneven in merit', but the *Baltimore Bulletin* thought that Mr O'Reilly was a true poet: '...no one can read his stirring and descriptive passages without at once recognising the true singer, and experiencing the contagion of his spirit'.

Perhaps the most enthusiastic review was that in the New York *Arcadian* which opined:

Not for long have we experienced so fresh and joyous a surprise, so perfect a literary treat, as has been given us by these fresh and glowing songs by this young and hitherto utterly unknown poet. There is something so thoroughly new and natural and life-like, something so buoyant, wholesome and true, so much original power and boldness of touch.

This was a view not shared by Richard H. Stoddart writing in one of the leading New York literary magazines, *Scribner's Monthly*. He maintained that O'Reilly lacked sentiment and grace, and that delicacy escaped him. But the *Chicago Journal* was the most severe and suggested that his first volume 'might terminate his poetical career'.

The *Chicago Journal* was quite wrong: O'Reilly weathered the adverse criticism and proved that *Songs from the Southern Seas* was not the end but the beginning of a long poetical career. He was accepted as a popular bard and, increasingly, was invited to write poems for important and commemorative occasions. His capacity to tell a stirring story in the language of the people ensured him an enthusiastic following.

In these early poems O'Reilly is impulsive and careless of poetic structure and some of his lines are simple doggerel. For example, in writing about native attacks on the settlers he says, 'That so many were killed and cooked and eaten/ There was risk of the whites in the end being beaten'. This can only raise a smile in the modern reader, which was far from the poet's intention.

O'Reilly wrote hastily and at the end of a day crowded with engagements. His method of work, minutely described in a newspaper article of the time, shows that the outline and intentions of a poem were invariably constructed in his mind long before a word was written on paper. 'Little by little from out the mists of mind appears the phantom form, the disembodied spirit of the coming poem.' At home in the evening after dinner, at about 9.00 p.m when his household was quiet, he would sit at his desk and write with feverish speed the poem which had been in his mind for several days. According to the report, a long poem might be finished in this way within an hour and only minor alterations were ever made. O'Reilly is quoted as believing that freshness of image is marred by rewriting; that concept is superior to art and that true feelings are clearer 'in the first cast of the metal than in later burnishing'.[3] Such a belief may be sincerely held, but because the consequence of that belief is so evident in his work, it may account for the neglect that the bulk of O'Reilly's poetry has been accorded in modern times.

A second daughter was born to the O'Reillys on 25 July 1874. Christened Eliza Boyle after her Irish grandmother, she was known within the family circle as Betsy. The birth of two children a year apart (and two more to follow) was evidently a strain on Mrs O'Reilly's health, and from that time forward she became a semi-invalid causing her husband and her friends much concern. Occasionally she was provided with health-seeking trips to other cities, and in one instance took a sea voyage. It is possible that she suffered from a form of severe postnatal depression which was then unrecognized and unnamed. There is also some evidence that she suffered from nothing more serious than hypochondria.[4]

The O'Reilly household reflected the comfort, tranquillity and conservative tastes of the professional middle-class Bostonian. A contemporary description commented on the spacious, panelled, first-floor study with its crimson furnishings, heavy curtains, long desk, busts on pedestals and pictures on the walls, including one of Dowth Castle. On the floor above was to be found Mrs O'Reilly's parlour and the nursery. Nowhere does John Boyle speak of household servants although doubtless Mrs O'Reilly would have had domestic help and we know that O'Reilly himself had a valet.[5]

After only four years since his arrival as a penniless immigrant fugitive, John Boyle O'Reilly could congratulate himself on having become a respectable, well-to-do paterfamilias, the editor of an influential newspaper and a rising literary figure whose work was generally—if not quite universally—admired. He was about his task of building bridges between his own people and the Jamesian Bostonians: bridges which were far from complete yet, but strong enough to bear the first fruits of social and literary intercourse.

CHAPTER 26

TWICE TO THE RESCUE

Come all you screw warders and gaolers,
Remember Perth Regatta Day;
Take care of the rest of your Fenians,
Or the Yankees will steal them away!

From 'The Catalpa Ballad' (trad.)

THE year 1876 was an important one in the Boston life of John Boyle O'Reilly. In that year the rescue of the remaining six military Fenians from Fremantle took place, an event in which O'Reilly played a low-key but significant role, and which was reported triumphantly in the *Pilot*. Coincidentally, at the same time as the rescue he became part-owner of the newspaper which he had edited for the past four years.

Patrick Donahoe, who had interests in banking and a shipping business as well as his publishing company, could not recover from his losses arising from the Boston fires of 1872. He was heavily mortgaged and although he had insurance, some of the insurance companies had collapsed as a result of the fires. The value of his investments steadily shrank and friends who had lent him money to start up again had to recall their loans. Before the fire he had guaranteed bank loans to a friend whom he trusted, but after the fire the friend's business failed and Donahoe was faced with having to repay debts, with interest, amounting to $170,000. The result was that at the beginning of 1876 Patrick Donahoe was declared bankrupt with debts amounting to $300,000 which included $73,000 owed to poor people who had deposited their savings in his bank.[1] The *Pilot* newspaper, as one of Donahoe's interests, faced collapse too.

In a letter to his friend Charles Hurd, dated 27 January 1876, O'Reilly apologized for not going to see him. He explained that there had been 'trouble around the office', and all his time had been taken up trying to solve it.

> Donahoe is bankrupt—in the worst way. Poor old man my heart grieves for him, and I have given all my wits to help him out. I think I have done so—in a way— the only way to save his honour.[2]

In the afternoon of the day that O'Reilly wrote to Hurd, Donahoe's creditors met and the estate was assigned to Charles Kendall, Charles Shepard and Patrick Collins. O'Reilly's plans for the rescue of part of the estate, the *Pilot*, must have found favour with them because O'Reilly was soon placing the petition he had drawn up before the archbishop, John J. Williams. This was a proposition that the two of them should purchase the paper for $28,000 cash, and assume the mortgage of $6,500 to George P. Baldwin and the interest thereof. For this sum the *Pilot* plant, including the property and the goodwill of its name, would be owned three parts by the archbishop and one part by O'Reilly. The terms were accepted and O'Reilly and Archbishop Williams became joint owners of the *Pilot* with effect from the Saturday in Holy Week, 15 April. Unknown to either of them, on that day the *Catalpa* sailed from Bunbury in Western Australia and would complete the rescue of the six Fenians on the following Monday morning.

Archbishop John J. Williams was fifty-four and Bostonian born and educated. He had studied for the priesthood in Montreal and Paris and in seminary days he was known as a skater and champion handball player. He was also an amateur musician and had a fine singing voice. A sound administrator and a gentle and wise pastor, he founded the first diocesan seminary in Boston. He neither sought nor achieved the notoriety that fell to his successors, Cardinals O'Connell and Cushing. His partnership with O'Reilly was an interesting one because Williams had no Irish connections and the *Pilot* was very much an 'Irish' newspaper. But it was also the diocesan paper serving all Catholics of whatever nationality and Williams trusted O'Reilly's editorial judgement completely because there is no hint of disagreement in any of the routine correspondence between them, nor a record of instructions to the editor from on high. O'Reilly seems to have had a free hand, not only in editorial matters, but also in day-to-day management and the hiring of staff.

Under its new proprietors the *Pilot* entered upon a halcyon period of its history.

> Few journals at that time could have surpassed it for literary excellence, for dignity, sincerity, fairness and true liberality, or for the devotion to the highest ideals in religion, civic and social life. O'Reilly interpreted and defended the Church's position and the cause of Ireland before the American public with a skill, a tact, and a success that had rarely been equalled.[3]

The new arrangement proved highly satisfactory for O'Reilly giving him not only added status and power, but a significant rise in salary. In return for 'his time and attention' and devoting 'his best skill and abilities to the editing and publishing of said paper and the management of said business', he was to receive

$5,200 a year in equal weekly payments. In addition to his salary O'Reilly stood to receive a dividend from profits made by the paper. With the cost of a cloth-bound book at that time being about 50c, a good suit of clothes $10–$15, and full board at a college of education around $50–$60 a term, the equivalent value of O'Reilly's salary today would be twenty times as much.

Contained in the agreement to purchase the *Pilot* was an undertaking by the new proprietors to repay the poor who had deposited, and subsequently lost, savings in Donahoe's bank. Until this was achieved the partners agreed 'not to take from the profits of their said business for their own use any money whatsoever other than the seven percent per annum and the salary of the said O'Reilly'.[4] The archbishop's 'Donahoe Fund' appeal was launched in the *Pilot* and thereafter reports on the fund and lists of donors were printed each week. The voluntary obligation was carried out, and the $73,000 was repaid over a period of ten years.[5]

Let us turn now to the other side of the world and the rescue of the Fenians from Fremantle. The news first appeared in Boston three months after the event, in the *Pilot* of 29 July. The front-page report was brief. It quoted letters received in England on 4 July and gave only the bare facts and the added promise that 'those who have born for ten long and weary years the horrors of British convict life shall have a fitting reception on their arrival in America', which was then imminent. A much more detailed report was printed on 12 August, a week before the arrival of the *Catalpa*.

To understand the rescue, and O'Reilly's part in it, we must look back several years to when John Devoy settled in America after his release from imprisonment. Devoy was imbued with a sense of obligation to the military Fenians who had not been included in the general amnesty of 1871. He, with O'Reilly's considerable help, had recruited them and felt responsible for their plight, and maintained a resolve to release them by one method or another. Appeals to the British Government on their behalf had not worked. It has been claimed that the Duke of Cambridge, commander-in-chief of the British Army at the time, refused clemency on the grounds that if it were granted it would undermine discipline throughout the ranks.[6] Devoy saw early on that the only way of releasing the men was to effect a rescue, probably by force of arms. His task was to convince other members of Clan na Gael to give their support to the enterprise.

At the annual convention of the Clan na Gael in Baltimore in 1874, after much debate and some disagreement, the rescue of the Fenians was approved in principle and a small committee with authority to draw up plans was formed under the chairmanship of John Devoy. The first task, and a thankless one, was to raise sufficient funds from the branches of the organization.

The plan first mooted was to send some twelve to fifteen men—a fully armed commando force—to attack Fremantle Prison and conduct the six rescued prisoners to safety on board a waiting ship chartered for the purpose. The difficulties and the dangers of such a course of action were obvious to the committee who remained divided on the issue. Devoy decided therefore, on his own initiative, to journey to Boston and consult O'Reilly whom he knew had local knowledge of Fremantle and the experience of escaping, both of which would be invaluable to the committee. He chose not to tell the local Clan na Gael branch the purpose of his visit when he found they were prejudiced against O'Reilly, largely because he had resigned membership of the organization. But the advice he received from his old friend was pivotal. They met on Monday, 1 February 1875 in O'Reilly's office where Cashman, O'Reilly's old shipmate on the *Hougoumont* and now business manager of the *Pilot*, was also present. They discussed plans and met again in the evening at O'Reilly's residence.

The gist of O'Reilly's advice was that sending an armed party of men to Fremantle and relying on a chartered vessel would not succeed. He suggested that they should consider purchasing a New Bedford whaler which would be seen to be on legitimate business in the Fremantle area, and would be available to pick up the fugitives according to a prearranged plan. He further advised that they should confide in Henry Hathaway and other friends in New Bedford to whom he would address a letter of introduction.

This advice was accepted when relayed to the committee, and it fell mainly to John Devoy to arrange for the purchase of a ship and to raise the necessary money to pay for her over the ensuing months.

The chosen vessel, although originally a whaler, was more recently used as a West Indian trader and was berthed in Charlestown. Thus O'Reilly was on hand to arrange for an inspection of the vessel by one of his friends, Lieutenant Tobin, an officer in the United States Navy. Tobin, at a dinner with Devoy at O'Reilly's house, pronounced her sound and fit to sail anywhere, and when told the price paid for her—$5,250—was astonished at such a bargain.[7] Hathaway had advised that there was much work to be done to prepare her for whaling and a further $15,000 had to be spent before she was ready to sail.

Her name was the *Catalpa* and she was in the command of Captain George Anthony. When she left New Bedford for Western Australia on Thursday, 29 April 1875, she was sailing into history.

Several months before the *Catalpa* reached Bunbury two agents, chosen by the rescue committee, were sent ahead to Fremantle to make contact with the prisoners and lay plans. They were John Breslin, a man of intelligence and quiet courage who had masterminded the rescue of James Stephens from Richmond Prison in Dublin in 1865; and Captain Thomas Desmond, recommended by the

Californian branch of Clan na Gael. Both men travelled under the aliases of Collins and Johnson respectively, and arrived in Fremantle in November 1875.

Breslin stayed in the port town and posed as a wealthy American business-man; Desmond found work in Perth as a carriage builder. They established their alibis while observing the local conditions and working out a plan. Breslin soon found a way of passing messages to the Fenian prisoners who were long-serving, trusted men by this time and invariably worked outside the prison confines.

Meanwhile the *Catalpa*, which had been expected to arrive in Bunbury in January 1876, was much delayed which caused grave concern to Breslin. When she finally berthed on 28 March the conspirators, greatly relieved, communi-cated with Captain Anthony using prearranged codes on the telegraph. Anthony came up to Fremantle and, together with Breslin, selected the rescue sight near Rockingham at the southern tip of Garden Island. They set the day of liberation for Friday, 17 April and then Anthony went back to his ship in Bunbury. Only later was it realized that the 17th was Good Friday and the prisoners' work routine would be altered. Hasty, dramatic telegraph messages passed between Fremantle and Bunbury and the date was changed to Monday the 19th, a holiday for Perth Regatta Day.

By noon on Easter Sunday the *Catalpa* was about 20 miles south of Rottnest and making for the pick-up area. The following morning Breslin and Desmond, having secured horses and carts in readiness, took up their positions a short distance from Fremantle Prison. An hour later three Fenians—Wilson, Cranston and Harrington—were spotted walking down the road; they got into Desmond's cart and made off swiftly. Moments later the three other men—Darragh, Hogan and Hassett—appeared and they were bundled into Breslin's cart which made off towards Rockingham. Two hours hard driving brought them to Rockingham Beach, about 20 miles south of Fremantle, where they found Captain Anthony and five nervous coloured crew awaiting them. One of the *Catalpa*'s whale chasers was moored alongside the Jarrah Timber Cutters' Jetty. An unforeseen hitch was the presence among them of two timber cutters, John Bell and a youth named Fred Rule. It was feared that one or other of them would raise the alarm. And this is what happened, but only after the escapees had got well away from the jetty. From 2 miles out the men in the boat could see mounted police at the jetty, but by then it was too late for them to be immediately apprehended.

The sequel the following day was told in that first report in the *Pilot* of 29 July:

The *Georgette* [a small steam gunboat which had given chase] came up with the *Catalpa* and fired a shot across her bows, but she would not stop. Coming within hailing distance, a parley commenced. Superintendent Stone demanded, in the name of the Government of Western Australia, 'there are six escaped convicts on board your vessel, and if you don't give them up you must take the consequences'.

Captain Anthony: 'I have no prisoners on board.'

Superintendent Stone: 'You have. I see three of them on deck.'

Captain Anthony: 'I have no prisoners; all are seamen belonging to the ship.'

Superintendent Stone: 'I will give you fifteen minutes to consider my request.'

After that interval Superintendent Stone again demanded the convicts, and the captain ruled he had none on board.

Superintendent Stone (pointing to a gun and men ready to fire) said, 'if you do not I will fire into and sink you.'

Captain Anthony: 'I am on the high seas and that flag (pointing to the Stars and Stripes) protects me.'

The *Georgette* steamed back into port after choosing not to fire and with Stone vowing lamely to demand action from the United States Government— action that never eventuated.

The *Catalpa* arrived in New York on 19 August 1876 to hearty cheers and the first in a series of gala receptions which celebrated the triumphant success of the enterprise and boosted Irish national pride. John Devoy presided and Denis Cashman represented the *Pilot* on that occasion. A week later the *Catalpa* sailed into its home port, New Bedford, to the sounds of an artillery salute: one gun for every state in the Union, and one for every county in Ireland. Great crowds had assembled on the wharf, cheering wildly, and an official reception committee made speeches. The next evening, Friday, 26 August, a capacity crowd gathered in Liberty Hall for a grand reception which, in size and enthusiasm, outshone the earlier one in New York. All those who had played a significant part in the rescue were honoured, including the crew of the *Catalpa*. The band played 'See The Conquering Hero Comes' when Captain Anthony took his seat on the stage beside Henry Hathaway, now New Bedford City Marshal, and a crowd of Clan na Gael leaders and office-bearers. It is of particular interest that in spite of John Boyle O'Reilly's sometimes stormy relationship with the Clan, such was his stature among American-Irish at that time that it was he who was invited to give the principal speech. According to the New Bedford *Mercury*, quoted in the *Pilot* of 2 September, he was 'received with great applause', and his oratory clearly fitted the occasion. He said that it was with no ordinary feelings that he was in New Bedford, that he owed much to the town, and that he would have gladly come a thousand miles to do honour to the whalemen. He referred to his seven years of liberty, his happy home in a free country and the debt of gratitude he owed to New Bedford. He praised the bravery of Captain Anthony for his part in the rescue and drew on his own experiences to describe how the kindness and bravery of the entire crew had contributed so much in his own escape.

A *contemporary reconstruction of the* Catalpa *rescue by E.N Russell. (Courtesy of the New Bedford Whaling Museum)*

O'Reilly used the occasion to direct unforgiving criticism of the colonial government:

England said that the rescue was a lawless and disgraceful filibustering raid. Not so; if these men were criminals the rescue would be criminal, but they were political offenders against England, not against law, or order, or religion. They had lain in prison for ten years with millions of their countrymen asking for their release, imploring England, against their will to beg, to set these men at liberty. Had England done so it would have partially disarmed Ireland. A generous act by England would be reciprocated instantly by millions of the warmest hearts in the world. But she is blind as of old; blind and arrogant, and cruel. She would not release the men; she scorned to give Ireland an answer. She called the prisoners cowardly criminals, not political offenders.[8]

A week later in a *Pilot* editorial, he returned to the attack even more vehemently and in a way which seems to anticipate W.B. Yeats's lines, 'Out of Ireland have we come./Great hatred, little room,/Maimed us at the start':

[England] has maltreated, misgoverned, scorned, derided the island and the people of Ireland, until opposition has generated in their hearts the terrible political mania of national hatred. God forbid that we should exalt in such a feeling; but no one who knows Ireland and Irishmen can deny its existence. England, to save herself, to possess the land, has driven the Irish people over the world. But wherever they went they carried with them the bitter memory of their wrongs and hates.[9]

O'Reilly, who in every other respect demonstrated a charitable, forgiving and generous nature (and there are instances of his charity even to those individuals who had wronged him),[10] carried with him to the end of his life a bitter and unforgiving hatred of England. While this may be understandable given his experience of years of imprisonment and exile, and the harsh treatment inflicted on so many of his fellow Fenians with whom he empathized, there is no doubt that this great hatred maimed—to use Yeats's word—his judgement on occasions.[11]

As a sequel to the *Catalpa* rescue a dispatch from the Superintendent of Police in Perth was received, sometime in August, by the officer-in-charge of the Police Department in New Bedford. It was an official communication informing the New Bedford authorities that six convicts had absconded on the *Catalpa*; it listed their names and gravely demanded information about them. As the officer-in-charge of the Police Department in New Bedford was at that time none other than Henry Hathaway who had helped organize the rescue, the request from Perth was politely ignored.

CHAPTER 27

WRITING FOR REFORM

Charity among the rich simply means the propriety of the poor being miserable—that poverty is unfortunate but not wrong. But God never meant to send the majority of mankind into existence to exercise the charity and religion of the minority. He sent them all into the world to be happy and virtuous, if not equal; and men have generated their evils by their own blind and selfish rules.

John Boyle O'Reilly

ON 19 May 1877 a third daughter was born to the O'Reillys and christened Agnes Smiley—her mother's nom de plume.

John Boyle loved the companionship of his daughters and when he was away from them, as he often was, he wrote lovingly to them, using their family names and referring to their mother as 'dear Mamsey'. He read to his daughters too, inculcating in them a love of good literature, especially Shakespeare. When he introduced them to *Othello* they were so affected that they begged him 'never to read to them again, that tale of the gentle lady married to the Moor'. To their father's regret the young O'Reillys never shared their father's great devotion to his native land, 'they considered Ireland a poor, backward, dull place'.[1] They grew up as young Americans.

Towards the end of the year O'Reilly exchanged correspondence with one of his former Fenian prison comrades, Corporal Thomas Chambers, who was still in gaol, and had recently been transferred from Dartmoor to Woking on 26 November 1877. O'Reilly had been alerted to Chambers's situation by a report in the House of Commons the previous June which quoted from a graphic account by Michael Davitt of Chambers's sufferings.

> He has been forced to mop out filthy dens of dirt with a small piece of rag, to carry a portable water-closet on the public road and across the fields for the use of common malefactors. He has often been sick but except on a few occasions

was not taken to hospital. On one occasion he was sent to the dungeons for applying for relief after he had met with a severe hurt by falling from the gangway of a building. Last year, while laid up with rheumatism, they kept him sixteen days on ten ounces of food daily, two months on half diet, and then put him out of hospital far worse than when he was taken in.[2]

O'Reilly, who had experienced the rigours of Dartmoor himself, was deeply affected when he learned of Chambers's plight and this added to the bitterness he already felt towards the British penal system. He wrote a moving letter to the prisoner three days before Christmas in which he spoke of his shared grief with Chambers and pledged his support on his comrade's release, which was imminent: 'Bear up; remember you have a hearty welcome in the home of a friend, I might say of very many—and now, at the eleventh hour do not despond or sink'.[3]

Two months later, in January 1878, Chambers and other political prisoners who had been confined in British gaols for more than twelve years were released. O'Reilly wrote a poem for the occasion which begins:

> Haggard and broken and seared with pain,
>   They seek the remembered friends and places;
> Men shuddering turn, and gaze again
>   At the deep-drawn lines on their altered faces.

Whether O'Reilly turned away shuddering and gazed again when he first greeted Chambers on arrival in Boston in February, we can only guess. Chambers was to live another ten years before dying prematurely aged and worn-out in Carney Hospital, Boston in November 1888. He had been attended daily by his old comrade, O'Reilly.

Out of his own and Chambers's experiences of prison life came O'Reilly's writings advocating reform of the penal system, notably his novel *Moondyne*, and his contribution to the multi-author novel, *The King's Men*.

Moondyne first appeared under the title *Moondyne Joe* in weekly instalments in the *Pilot* from 30 November 1878. The title derives from the nickname of the notorious West Australian bushranger, Joseph Bolitho Jones, gaoled in Fremantle around the same time as O'Reilly. The writing is hurried and careless, a weakness admitted by the writer himself: 'I never get an hour ahead of the printers and that's awful'.[4] But it is a key work in understanding O'Reilly's life because there is so much of himself in it—both in a biographical sense and as an expression of his social philosophy.

The story is divided into five parts. The opening, which might very well stand on its own, is set in the penal colony of Western Australia. Here O'Reilly comes closest to documentary writing, giving a vivid picture of convict life in Fremantle and of road building in the bush near Bunbury. The main character in this section, a convict of heroic stature, escapes from Fremantle with the aid of Aborigines who then lead him to a secret goldmine in the bush. The convict—whose real identity is not revealed but is named Moondyne by the Aborigines—is recaptured by a cruel, devious trooper and ex-convict, Isaac Bowman (modelled on the real Bowman mentioned in Chapter 19). Moondyne bargains his release from Bowman by promising to show the trooper where the goldmine is located, but Bowman breaks his trust and in the ensuing struggle and flight, dies in the desert.

In Book Two of *Moondyne* the action shifts to Walton-le-Dale and the reader may be forgiven for wondering what the connection might be between Moondyne and rural Lancashire. The young hero, Will Sheridan, is tentatively declaring his love for the heroine, Alice Walmsley, but to his sorrow she prefers his evil rival, Sam Draper, to whom she becomes engaged. Sheridan and Draper are merchant navy officers and, nursing their distrust of each other, sail together on the *Canton* for the Far East. During an argument at sea, Will Sheridan learns that Draper is already married to a girl in Calcutta and, in despair, he deserts his ship and sails for Western Australia where he becomes manager of a successful sandalwood export agency.

After nine years absence Sheridan returns to England to find that Alice Walmsley is in prison for murdering the child she bore as a result of her bigamous marriage to Draper. While in London Sheridan is befriended by a respected, influential humanitarian, known as Mr Wyville, who takes a keen interest in Alice Walmsley's case and believes her to be innocent.

The mysterious Wyville assumes a major importance in the story from this point on and the extent of his political power is one of the implausible coincidences which mar the work. He not only arranges for Alice Walmsley to leave Millbank Prison to be sent out to Western Australia in the care of a nun, Sister Cecilia, but also persuades the colonial government authorities to appoint him Comptroller-General of Convicts in the colony with enough authority to reform the penal system. As the understanding governor of Millbank Prison confides in Sheridan: 'He is going to change the whole machinery. He knows more about humanity and reform than a regiment of your K.C.B.s'.

Wyville becomes the author's alter ego, propounding O'Reilly's social theories. 'At present the laws of civilization', says Wyville/O'Reilly, 'especially in England, are based on, and framed by, *property*—a depraved and unjust foundation. Human law should be founded on God's law and human right, and not on the narrow invested interests of land and gold'. And when he is asked how he proposes to bring this about, Wyville answers: 'To raise all men above insecurity which is the hot-bed of lawlessness'. Reading between the author's lines at this point, the Irish land question was obviously uppermost in his mind because Wyville continues: 'by allowing no one to own unproductive land while a single man is hungry'.

Will Sheridan, soon a firm disciple of Wyville's, asks to return with him to Western Australia on the convict ship, the *Hougoumont*. In another of the convenient coincidences for which the book has been severely criticized, all the main characters are found together on board when she sails and they precipitate a crisis. The evil Sam Draper is appointed captain, and sailing with him is his Calcutta wife, Harriet. Alice Walmsley is also on board along with other female convicts (although in reality none sailed on the *Hougoumont*); and there too are Mr Wyville and Sheridan. Even Constable Lodge, the kindly policeman from Walton-le-Dale who helped Wyville in his detective work, manages to be aboard. Before they reach their destination the voyagers face both fire and fever following the dramatic unmasking of Draper, but calming all fears and resolving disputes is the powerful, wise presence of Wyville.

On arrival in Australia—the last part of the book—Wyville puts his penal reforms into practice: 'Remember, you are dealing with *men*, not with brutes—with men who have rights and the protection of law', he tells the Fremantle warders. In the concluding pages of the novel Draper's wife confesses to the murder of Alice's baby; Alice Walmsley, now freed, is united with Will Sheridan who takes over Wyville's large property; and Wyville, in a selfless action, dies heroically while trying to save Sam and Harriet Draper in a bush fire. It is then revealed on the last page that Wyville was none other than the character Moondyne, hero of the opening section of the book.

That O'Reilly saw himself as the crusading Moondyne/Wyville has been argued convincingly by Roche. In addition to Wyville's views, which almost exactly mirror O'Reilly's, the author seems to be describing himself when describing Wyville:

> He was dressed in such a way that one would say that he never could be dressed otherwise. Dress was forgotten in the man...his voice, as he spoke on entering a room, came easily from the lips, yet with a deep resonance that was pleasant to hear, suggesting a possible tenderness or terror that would shake the soul. It was a voice in absolutely perfect accord with the striking face and physique.[5]

Roche also points to the coincidence of the number '406' which was Moondyne's prison number in the novel. It was also believed to be the number of one of the cells which O'Reilly occupied during his imprisonment, and it was the number of his first hotel room when he arrived in America. The number there had a haunting significance for O'Reilly as we learn from an unfinished poem entitled '406':

I do not know the meaning of the sign,
But bend before its power, as a reed bends
When the black tornado fills the valley to the lips.
Three times in twenty years its shape has come
On lines of fire on the black veil of mystery;
At first, tho' strange, it seemed familiar,
And lingered on the mind as if at rest;
The second time it flashed a thrill came, too,
For supernature spoke, or tried to speak;
The third time, like a blow upon the eyes,
It stood before me, as a page might say:
'Read, read,—and do not call for other warning'.[6]

Moondyne was accorded a mixed reception when it was published by George Roberts in 1880. The Boston Post thought, 'Its originality is a special charm. It is full of manliness and virile power, and yet abounding in gentleness and pathos'. The Boston Journal was more cautious believing 'there were faults of construction and a little lack of symmetry', but that these were more than atoned for 'by the virile strength and intensity which hold the reader to the end'. Overseas, the London Saturday Review thought the book a 'really clever and graphic story of Australian life', and the London Bookseller, in an effort to promote it, described it as 'a fascinating tale...no one who begins the story will be able to stop till it is finished'.

The severest criticism was unexpected and appeared in the New York Freeman's Journal. The reviewer J. McMaster, who was also the editor, stated that it was a bad book because its principles were anti-Christian—a view shared by some Catholic writers who rejected it because they believed that Moondyne and Wyville were pagans. O'Reilly was stung into making a lengthy rebuttal in the Pilot and voiced what other more eminent Catholic novelists have argued since in the face of similar criticism: 'To demand of a Catholic author that his chief character shall be a Catholic is absurd. A novelist must study types as they exist'.[7]

Clearly O'Reilly's Moondyne is poorly constructed, relying too heavily on implausible situations and underdeveloped characterization. A modern reader may smile at the melodramatic, preachy dialogue and the lack of subtlety in presenting the author's message. Notwithstanding these objections the book gives a valuable and fascinating picture of aspects of convict life at the time, provided the reader does not demand unvarying accuracy. O'Reilly mixes fact with fiction but the spirit of the book still lives and the tale keeps the reader guessing until the end. It can be classed with other books of the time which were written with crusading intentions. For example, Marcus Clarke's For the Term of

His Natural Life exposed penal cruelties in Tasmania, and Charles Read's *Hard Cash* argued for reform of mental institutions. Marcus Clarke's book, like O'Reilly's, was originally published in weekly instalments, and then in book form in 1874. Like *Moondyne* it exaggerated penal conditions for dramatic effect, but it is unlikely that O'Reilly would have known of its existence.

Penal reform remained one of O'Reilly's concerns to the end of his life, but his views on transportation as a means of imprisonment actually changed from the harsh one expressed in *Moondyne* to one of guarded support for the system. In the year before he died he set out his convictions in a long letter to Alfred Webb, the Quaker reformer, who had asked O'Reilly to compare and evaluate the prison systems in England with those in Siberian Russia. Lacking 20th-century knowledge of Stalin's gulags, O'Reilly expressed his belief that the Russian system of work camps was to be preferred to the then current system in England which confined inmates to lonely cells isolated from human fellowship. He defended his view by referring to the freer, healthier treatment of transportees in the colonies. He cited his own experience as an example:

> The feeling of relief at the open-air associated labour of Western Australia, after the rigours of Pentonville, Chatham, Portland and Dartmoor, was actual enjoyment...the climate was always healthful and delightful. The effect of associated labour and life in the Australian colony was decidedly beneficial. It brought out the characteristics of manliness, truth, and personal honesty in some such way as they are developed among soldiers. In one year I saw extraordinary improvement in a whole party of criminal prisoners. Transportation to a colony where essential freedom and citizenship can be assured will reform almost the entire criminal class that is not abnormally degraded.[8]

O'Reilly believed in the Christian doctrine of the fallen man, in personal accountability for behaviour, and in the opportunity for redemption for all. While he stoutly attacked imprisonment for political reasons—as in his own case—he became, in his mature years, a disciplinarian and a man who strongly supported civic law and order. The letter to Webb is remarkable for clearly showing this development in his thinking.

O'Reilly cried for justice and adherence to God's law, and he campaigned for social reform in the pages of the *Pilot* and in his writings. He identified himself with the underprivileged and working classes, and called for a fairer distribution of private property thereby anticipating the theories of distributism forty years before Hilaire Belloc and G.K. Chesterton devised their Christian response to the same problems. Like Belloc and Chesterton in the 1920s he believed there must be a Christian alternative to capitalism on the one hand and socialism on the other:

214

The word 'socialism' which ought to stand for the noblest philosophy, is a hissing and an abomination in the ears of men, because of such moral and intellectual monsters as Herr Most.[9]

He admitted the existence of fundamental distinctions in society: there had to be leaders and governors as well as artisans and workers. He was suspicious of utopian ideals of social equality 'where everyone is somebody and no one's anybody'. He was critical of the socialist doctrines of Marx and Engels as propounded by the first Socialist International (1864-72) and which were then gaining currency. He considered they were unallied to Christian principles:

> To this world movement there is only one safe guide—the Catholic Church, the spiritual test for the revolution must be spiritual as well as intellectual. Socialism is the hope of the people. How deep the crime of those who have made the word synonymous with Atheism and disorder. The shallow reasoners of Europe who have dissociated Socialism and Religion have committed an almost unpardonable sin.[10]

O'Reilly's childhood experiences among the rural poor of Ireland, and his subsequent association with the Aborigines of Western Australia, both had a marked influence on his idealism in his later years. In the pages of the *Pilot* he constantly took up the cause of oppressed minority groups such as the Jews, the indigenous Indians of America and, most especially, the Negroes.

In replying to questions raised by the editor of *American Hebrew* about prejudice existing among Christians against Jews, O'Reilly argued that the cause of the prejudice was not religious instruction in schools because the most prejudiced are the least religious or Christian:

> Part of the prejudice is inherited from less intelligent times; part comes from the exclusiveness of the Jews as a race, and the largest part from the marvellous success of the Jewish race in business. In this country, I think, the anti-Jewish prejudice is not at all religious. From personal experience I should say it was wholly racial and commercial.
>
> It has been my fortune to know, long and intimately, several Jewish families in Boston and New York, and many individual Jews in my lifetime. Their standard of conduct is the same as Christians, but their standard of home life and all its relations is the highest in the world. I know three men who are my ideals of mercantile honour, integrity, and business character: one is a Christian and two are Jews.[11]

The *Pilot* under O'Reilly became a relentless champion of American Negro rights. The editor attacked New York policemen who threatened to strike if a Negro was appointed to the force. And he attacked the school in Indianapolis which cancelled graduation ceremonies because eight girls had refused to appear on the same platform with a Negro graduate. The same Christian principles that inspired him to work for the Irish in America impelled him to work for the Negro. In yet another instance of O'Reilly's remarkable ability to be ahead of contemporary thinking, he exhorted Negroes to take pride in their race, to gain self-respect and to realize that they had special qualities and accomplishments of great benefit to the nation. He was thus anticipating the cry of the 1960s 'Black is Beautiful' civil rights campaign:

> The negro is the only graceful, musical, colour-loving American. He is the only American who has written new songs and composed new music. He is the most spiritual of Americans, for he worships with his soul and not with his narrow mind. For him religion is to be believed, accepted, like the very voice of God, and not invented, contrived, reasoned about, shaded, altered, and made fashion-ably lucrative and marketable, as it is made by too many white Americans. The negro is a new man, a free man, a spiritual man, a hearty man; and he can be a great man if he will avoid modelling himself on the whites.[12]

In his latter years O'Reilly became more and more outspoken in his speeches and writings. When eight black men were butchered at Barnwell, South Carolina, he seemed to advocate armed retaliation. 'The black race in the South must face the inevitable', he wrote, 'and the inevitable is—DEFEND YOURSELF...the Southern Blacks cannot fight the Anglo-Saxon by lying down under his feet'.[13] Because of this seemingly inflammatory language he was accused of inciting rebellion. O'Reilly defended himself by arguing that he had only appealed to the great Catholic and American principle of resisting wrong and outrage in order to protect life and home, when nothing else remained to be tried. O'Reilly's contribution to the struggle for racial equality cannot be overestimated. As Schofield has observed, the history of the Negro race would be incomplete if it did not 'record his impassioned interest in their welfare'.[14]

O'Reilly strongly espoused a variety of social reforms during his Boston years but he never sought political office. He was more a philosopher and theorist than a practitioner. He was a zealous supporter of the Democratic Party and the Jeffersonian tradition. Whether deliberately or by natural inclination O'Reilly seemed to reflect his hero's characteristics, notably Jefferson's use of the powerful written word to persuade in preference to competing on the hustings.

CHAPTER 28

'AN AMERICAN OR NOTHING'

Not only is patriotism a part of practical politics, but it is more practical than any politics. To neglect it, and ask only for grievances, is like counting the clouds and forgetting the climate. To neglect it, and think only of laws, is like seeing the landmarks and never seeing the landscape.

G.K. Chesterton

AS John Boyle O'Reilly completed his first decade in Boston he could look back on ten years of remarkable achievement. Although internally he still carried the scars of his prison years, outwardly, and certainly materially, he was a different person from the one who had arrived in Philadelphia in November 1869. He was now a moderately wealthy man and owned two homes. In addition to the Winthrop Street town house, he had bought a summer residence at Hull on the tip of the narrow, sandy peninsular that curves around Dorchester Bay.

The original house had been the Hull parsonage, built in 1644, but when the O'Reillys arrived it was only fit for demolition and they set about designing and building a new house on the site. It still stands, an attractive, two-storey building faced in wooden shingles on a sandstone foundation. The east-facing upper storey has three dormer windows in traditional Cape Cod style and the south end is notable for an arcaded two-storey tower giving superb views of the water and the huge sweep of the Nantasket peninsular. Today, the O'Reillys' old summer residence is the Hull Public Library and some of their furniture in the wooden-panelled rooms remains in use. In the 1880s when the family was in residence, O'Reilly would leave his office in Franklin Street and take the short ferry journey across the bay to the Hull jetty where one or other of his daughters would meet him and lead him the short distance up to the house.

But the visits to Hull must have been fewer than he and his family would have wished because from 1880 onwards he commenced a period of mental and physical activity which was so frenetic and so punishing that it eventually led to a deterioration in his health.

The O'Reillys' summer residence (now the Hull Public Library) situated on the tip of the Nantasket peninsular, overlooking Boston harbour from the east. (Photograph by the author)

In addition to his editorial work, his writing, and his passionate involvement in Irish-American affairs, O'Reilly was deeply committed to various groups working for Catholic welfare and social action. He was a foundation member of the Catholic Union which promoted the interests of Catholics and wrestled with the problem of religious education in public schools. *Pilot* editorials supported the contention that state school education should include religious training. He was on the committee of a home for destitute children and in 1883 became closely involved with the Working Boys' Home, attending the boys' picnics and supervising their athletics program. In between times, he travelled to other cities for conferences and meetings, and was always in demand as the guest speaker at public functions.

In Dublin in October 1879 the Irish National Land League had been formed on the initiative of Michael Davitt, the chief purpose of which was to fight for and facilitate the ownership of land by the occupiers, and also to raise money for the purchase of land from absentee landlords. Charles Stewart Parnell was elected president and commenced a fundraising tour of America, arriving in New York on 2 January 1880. O'Reilly, a great admirer of Parnell, was elected to welcome him. 'Unquestionably this man is marked for his age', he wrote in a *Pilot* editorial, 'he is in full harmony with the times'.

Parnell next visited Boston and was given a rousing reception in the Music Hall on 12 January where a subscription amounting to $1,600 was quickly raised. O'Reilly was again present on that occasion. Similar meetings were held in other cities where Parnell received enthusiastic welcomes. Only the pro-English New York *Herald* attacked the tour and its purpose by mounting its own famine relief and emigration fund and pledging $100,000. O'Reilly criticized the *Herald* in his editorials and accused them of duplicity and wishing to undermine Parnell's efforts. He saw that the *Herald*'s undoubted generous offer was likely to be administered by absentee landlords and government officials as opposed to the Land League Committee.[1]

After a triumphant tour, which included a speech before the United States House of Representatives on 2 February, Parnell returned to Ireland leaving behind a resolve among Irish-Americans to form a local Land League to raise funds and support the home organization in Dublin. O'Reilly was one of the prime movers advocating a national organization and once again travelled to New York where, on 18 and 19 May, he chaired a convention for this purpose. He was offered the position of national president but wisely declined in view of his other many commitments.

Early in April O'Reilly's third book of poems, *The Statues in the Block*, was published by Roberts Brothers of Boston. It was dedicated to the memory of his mother and takes its title from the first of the twenty-two poems. In this the poet imagines four men each considering what may be carved from a block of marble. Love is the first statue; Revenge the second; Suffering Mother the third, and Sorrow the last. It ends with the memorable words, 'I know that when God gives us the clearest sight/He does not touch our eyes with Love, but Sorrow'. Among the shorter poems is 'Jacqueminots' which later became a popular sentimental ballad set to music by Max Eliot; it was published by the White Smith Music Company in 1888. The first verse runs:

> I may not speak in words, dear, but let my words be flowers,
> To tell their crimson secret in leaves of fragrant fire;
> They plead for smiles and kisses as summer fields for showers,
> And every purple veinlet thrills with exquisite desire.

Again reviews were mixed. The New York *Herald* critic likened O'Reilly's work to Walt Whitman's. The *Boston Journal* recognized a Whitman likeness too which 'we confess we do not like', but then went on to praise the poet:

> [He is at his] best when his blood is hot and his indignation roused by the thought of human wrongs; and some of his pieces written under this inspiration have a ring like anvil strokes and stir the blood of the reader as by the sound of trumpets.

George Parsons Lathrop in the *Atlantic Monthly* was unenthusiastic and criticized the poems for what he saw as formlessness, believing that it detracted from any other merit the poems might have. *The Statues in the Block* ran to four editions, testifying to the general public's opinion of O'Reilly as a poet which, perhaps, can be best summed up by the review in the *Boston Daily Advertiser*: 'Mr O'Reilly excels in dramatic poetry. When he has an heroic story to tell, he tells it with ardour and vigour; he appreciates all its nobleness of soul'.

It is not altogether surprising that a Catholic university, Notre Dame in Indiana, bestowed on him—a faithful son of the Church—the honorary degree of Doctor of Laws in June 1880. It was an indication of his rising national prominence. Any suspicion that academic recognition was limited to Catholic institutions is dispelled by his election, at the same time, to membership of the Phi Beta Kappa Society at the exclusive non-sectarian Dartmouth College, New Hampshire. At his formal installation he read his poem 'The Three Queens' in which he personifies Liberty, Law and Learning—the 'queens' of the title. He eulogizes Queen Liberty but describes how she is seized by the forces of a rival queen—Law: 'Man's plundered birthright was the new Queen's dower,/The sorrow of the weak ones was her crown'. But she in turn is overpowered by a third queen: 'Her name is Learning! Her domain unbounded;/Of all the fetters she commands the sky'. A suitable and popular message for one of the leading educational institutions in New England which prided itself in its arts and science faculties.

The O'Reillys' fourth and last daughter was born on 18 June and baptized Blanid, the name inspired by one of Robert Dwyer Joyce's poems.[2] Although O'Reilly bestowed great love on each of his daughters, because Blanid was the youngest (and only nine when he died) and suffered from chronic illness throughout her short life, she seems to have been especially dear to him. His poem, 'To My Little Blanid', is one of his most tender and moving works, a bittersweet threnody for lost childhood innocence:

> I told her a story, a fairy story,
>   My little daughter with eyes of blue
> And with clear, wide gaze as the splendours brightened,
>   She always asked me—'Oh, is it true?'
>
> Always that word when the wonder reached her,
>   She pictured beauty so grand and new—
> When the good were paid and the evil punished,
>   Still, with soft insistence—'Is it true?'
>
> Ah, late, drear knowledge from sin and sorrow,
>   How will you answer and answer true,
> Her wistful doubt of the happy ending?—
>   Wise child! I wondered how much she knew.

With a semi-invalid wife and a little daughter with poor health, O'Reilly's domestic life could not always have been easy. He revealed something of his problems in a letter written to Archbishop Williams two years before his death. He explained that his youngest child had been so very ill for over a week, delirious and calling on him constantly, that he dared not leave the house.[3] One is led to wonder why the child's mother did not care for her during the day. Part of the answer lies in Mrs O'Reilly's own poor health which was often alluded to in her husband's letters. In one he wrote to a friend declining an invitation to dinner because 'Mrs O'Reilly cannot go out this winter, so says the tyrant doctor'.[4] In another he wrote to her doctor to thank him for his wife's treatment: 'She is waiting to see the effects of the voyage before she writes to you'.[5]

With domestic worries like these and constant absences from his office on political and welfare business, the *Pilot* could not have continued successfully without a strong team supporting him. His old Fenian convict friend, Denis Cashman, was the business manager and his brother-in-law, John Murphy, was the company's bookkeeper. On the editorial side O'Reilly had appointed two able assistants, James Jeffrey Roche and Katherine E. Conway, both of whom would succeed him in turn in the editor's chair and would stamp the paper with their own particular qualities. Both were published writers and poets. Roche published the first complete biography of his friend and chief a year after O'Reilly's death, and Katherine Conway—who was more prolific than Roche— also wrote a book on O'Reilly, but it was more literary criticism than biography. Katherine Conway came to the *Pilot* when she was thirty; she had already had editorial experience on a Rochester paper and had contributed to the *Pilot* on a freelance basis. Both Conway and Roche idolized their chief and wrote glowingly of his qualities. In a letter to Bishop McQuaid dated 22 January 1890, Conway wrote: 'I have a generous and considerate employer—a man to be thoroughly respected as well as liked by all who are associated with him'.[6] And in another letter, written after O'Reilly's death she confided: 'when he was gone, the earth rocked under me'.[7]

Another who loved him was his faithful office boy of whom he was so fond that he called him 'my outward conscience'. When the boy lay ill with consumption O'Reilly visited him daily and mourned him when he died.

Working alongside such a busy man with his 'continual rushing to and fro', and one who was so distracted by multifarious work, could not have been easy for the staff. O'Reilly wrote his editorials—and numerous other columns in the paper—at great speed, often impetuously, and invariably close to the deadline.

There is little doubt that O'Reilly was proud of his position as editor and he enjoyed the companionship of the Boston literary set. He dined in their company on formal occasions and lunched with them less formally at the

Marliave Restaurant on the corner of Bosworth Street, a short distance from the *Pilot* offices. There the tables were divided by wooden partitions and set around the walls so that small groups of like-minded friends could meet without distraction from neighbours. The restaurant (established in 1876) still exists, and in the far corner is an alcove which is said to have been O'Reilly's and which has his portrait on the wall together with a brass plate commemorating his one-time presence.

Many of the O'Reilly letters that still survive—of which there are regrettably few—are to writers and editors of the day. These include letters to Henry Wadsworth Longfellow one of which thanks him for a copy of his poems; another invites him to a dinner at the Papyrus Club at which Louisa M. Alcott and Nathaniel Hawthorne's widow would be present; and a third invites him to a dinner celebrating Tom Moore's centenary. There are also letters to Oliver Wendell Holmes and W.D. Howells; and one to Robert Aldrich, editor of the *Atlantic Monthly*, requesting that the title of his poem, 'Marcarius the Monk', not be changed when published in the magazine. O'Reilly was conscious of his place and standing among these writers and had a view of his own worth. When he was asked to contribute an article of 1,000-2,000 words to a new magazine, *Literary Life*, at a payment of one cent per word, he not only refused what he considered to be a niggardly offer but also published his reply in the *Pilot*:

> I cannot see why you should appeal to the charity of literary people for the benefit of your magazine. If your letter is not an appeal for charity it is a humiliation and a disgrace to the literary profession.[8]

Niggardly it certainly was to a man who was paid $150 by Joseph Pulitzer for the publication of his poem 'America' in the *World* magazine, but his airing of the correspondence publicly was an intemperate reaction which provoked criticism from several quarters.

When Oscar Wilde made his first visit to America in 1882—telling the customs inspector that he had nothing to declare but his genius—he spent some time in O'Reilly's company in Boston. He signed O'Reilly's visitor's book, and under Walt Whitman's name wrote: 'The spirit who living blamelessly but dared to kiss the smitten mouth of his own century'.[9] He accompanied O'Reilly to a performance of *Oedipus Tyrannus* at the Globe Theatre on 28 January and pressed him to publish some of his mother's poems in the *Pilot*. 'I think my mother's work should make a great success here', he wrote to O'Reilly later, 'it is so unlike the work of her degenerate artist son. I know you think I am thrilled by nothing but a dado. You are quite wrong but I shan't argue'.[10] We do not know whether O'Reilly attended Wilde's lecture on the Aesthetic Movement in

Europe, held two days after their visit to the Globe and the occasion when a group of Harvard students attempted to mock him, but were silenced by the famous wit. O'Reilly probably did attend because 'the two felt at home together'. Fanny Parnell, sister of Charles Stewart Parnell, was certainly in the audience and probably met O'Reilly there. She wrote a note to him afterwards enclosing her manuscript poems (which the *Pilot* was to publish that year) and, commenting on the lecture, complained that although Oscar Wilde was a great poet he really knew nothing about interior decoration.[11] Wilde wrote to O'Reilly again from New York later in the year and described how he had been robbed by a confidence trickster. 'I have fallen into a den of thieves', was his lugubrious comment.[12]

On 24 March 1882 Henry Wadsworth Longfellow died at his home in Concord and O'Reilly, deeply affected, joined in the general mourning for the most famous and popular of American poets and the elder statesman of the New England literary circle. Oscar Wilde had said when he met him a year earlier that he was 'himself a beautiful poem, more beautiful than anything he ever wrote'. O'Reilly used the same metaphor when he wrote:

> Our Longfellow's death, like his life, was a noble and quiet poem...It was and will remain an illustration of the permanent appreciation of mankind for the beautiful, Un-trade-like spiritual work of the poet. When he succeeds in reaching men's hearts all other successes are as naught to the poet's.[13]

A story recounted by Roche, and published in the *Boston Post*, illustrates O'Reilly's great admiration for Longfellow. A visitor to Westminster Abbey in London some years later noticed that the bust of Longfellow was ornamented with a wreath. On closer inspection she noticed a card attached with an inscription. The donor was none other than Boyle O'Reilly who had deputed a friend to place it there on his behalf.[14]

Less than two months after Longellow's tranquil death a calamitous event was enacted on the other side of the Atlantic which plunged O'Reilly once more into political controversy, accompanied by considerable personal anguish.

In Phoenix Park, Dublin on the evening of 6 May 1882 Lord Cavendish, the Chief Secretary for Ireland, and Thomas Henry Burke, the Permanent Under-Secretary, had chosen to walk to their residences rather than ride in a carriage. Suddenly, they were set upon by political assassins and knifed to death. An era of conciliation seemed to have begun under Prime Minister Gladstone, and he had recently ordered the release from prison of three Irish Members of Parliament—Parnell, Dillon and O'Kelly. Consequently, the senseless murders by desperate nationalists were viewed with almost universal horror.

When the news was received in Boston a mass meeting was arranged at Faneuil Hall. It was chaired by Patrick Collins, then a member of the State Legislature, and O'Reilly was the principal speaker. He began by declaring his great sorrow and grief at the event but his intense patriotism and love for his people allowed him to be misled and to totally misjudge the crime. He declared before his audience that the deed could not have been done by Irishmen. He argued that in all history there was no instance in which Irishmen had killed premeditatedly with knives or daggers. He was so sure of his ground that he stated the murders had been the work of men in the pay of the government. This was another instance of his tendency to rush to judgement, in part fuelled by his implacable hatred of England and his weakness for interpreting all Ango-Irish politics in stark black-and-white terms.[15] When he learned the facts of the case at a later date he was clearly shocked:

> The wretched men who committed these crimes have no perception of the injury they have inflicted on the cause of Ireland...Secret organisation to commit violent crime is an accursed disease. It has blighted Ireland...It has blasted every country that has resorted to it. Passion and ignorance are its parents, and its children are murder and cruel crime.[16]

Early in June of the same year O'Reilly travelled to Detroit for the reunion of the Army of the Potomac and on the 14th read his poem 'America', especially composed for the occasion. The ageing General Ulysses Grant, one-time President of the United States and hero of the Civil War, was present and was so greatly moved by the poem that he insisted upon shaking the hand of the poet to the renewed applause of all those present.

'America' is a long patriotic ode of 180 lines celebrating the origins and rise of the Republic culminating with a eulogy for those who fought and died in the great battles of the Civil War. The last stanza is remarkable for its political foresight and shows, not for the first time, O'Reilly's happy knack of heralding future events:

> O, this thy work, Republic! this thy health,
> To prove man's birthright to a commonwealth;
> To teach the peoples to be strong and wise,
> Till armies, nations, nobles, royalties,
> Are laid to rest with all their fears and hates;
> Till Europe's thirteen monarchies are States,
> Without a barrier and without a throne,
> Of one grand Federation like our own!

O'Reilly's invitation to compose 'America', and its subsequent popular reception throughout the country (it was widely published), marks a shift in the public regard for the poet. From being perceived purely as an expatriate Irish poet he was henceforward accepted as an American bard who was increasingly called upon to write commemorative poems for public occasions. This was a perception which he himself demanded in answer to a correspondent who unwittingly referred to him as an 'English poet'. 'If I am a poet at all, dear Sir, don't call me a British poet. I am an American or nothing.'[17]

CHAPTER 29

A GENIAL BARD

Joys have three stages, Hoping, Having, and Had:
The hands of Hope are empty, and the heart of Having is sad;
For the joy we take, in the taking dies; and the joy we Had is
    its ghost.
Now, which is the better—the joy unknown or the joy we have
    clasped and lost?

John Boyle O'Reilly

IN the far corner by the window of the reading room in the John J. Burns Library at Boston College stands a white marble bust of O'Reilly by the sculptor, John Donaghue. The light from the window illuminates the whiteness of the stone so that it is impossible, even among the rare books and manuscripts, to avoid being attracted to the quiet dignity and composure of the face. The eyes are deep set and serious, though not severe, the nose is aquiline, and below it a bushy drooping moustache falls either side of the firm line of the mouth. The close-cut hair is beginning to recede above the temples which gives the impression of a high forehead. This is a man, we would guess, in his early forties. There is also, in the possession of the family, a portrait of O'Reilly by Dr Edward Parker which was probably painted in the early 1880s because the full-on face, though very similar to that of the bust, appears slightly younger. The pose is formal. O'Reilly is seated with his right arm resting on the arm of a desk chair and his left is raised nonchalantly to his cheek. It is not difficult to suppose that this is the portrait of an athletic, sporting man.

And this would be right. It may seem surprising that in addition to his literary interests and his political activities, O'Reilly remained throughout his life devoted to athletics, boxing and outdoor sports. The popular image of the literary man is of someone who is mainly sedentary, thoughtful, and generally physically inactive. But O'Reilly was strong and athletic, proficient at fencing and especially devoted to boxing, although to him boxing was a science, a manly sport: he rejected prize-fighting which relied on brute force and, in those days, bare knuckles. He was a familiar figure in the Harvard gymnasium where, for a time, he taught fencing to the students. He participated in field sports and sponsored the annual O'Reilly Hurling Cup. He served on the committee of the Boston Athletics Association and was a prominent member of the Cribb Club (named after the famous English boxer, Tom Cribb) and served as its president for a term. He was also a member of the Boston Union Boat Club.

It is a mystery how he managed so much in so short a time. 'My time is mortgaged away into futurity', he wrote, 'the days are not half long enough'.[1] His restless energy and his frenzied life worked against him in the end. His diversity of interests and the apportioning of his time among such a range of activities may account for the absence of any major literary achievement. O'Reilly wrote much, but he never wrote a masterpiece, either in prose or poetry—a matter regretted by his admirers:

> He was the one man, perhaps, who might have been the Dickens or even the Tolstoy of Ireland's mass migrations and national agitations of the last century. Instead he could never bring himself to give a systematic and realistic depiction of either, nor even sketch the life of the Boston Irish community in which he settled.[2]

But like most frenetically busy people, O'Reilly dreamed of a more leisured existence. He wrote to a friend on holiday on a Pacific island: 'I envy you the laziness, the island and the sun, and the vague future...I long to go and lie down in the clover fields of my boyhood. I long to be listless and dreamy and idle'.[3]

O'Reilly's 'island in the sun'—his holidays, though never listless—were his canoeing trips down the Merrimac and Charles Rivers. His first excursion was in the summer of 1882 and he enjoyed the experience so much that he made a more extended cruise the following July in the company of his friend Dr Guiteras. He revelled in the quiet and the beauty of the surrounding lush country where he felt absolutely free from the conventions of life and free of professional cares and worries. He often swam behind his canoe or coasted along on swift-running waters; he sunbathed on the banks during the afternoon and slept in a tent under the stars at night. He wrote that there was no other joy he experienced equal to this, 'better than honour, fame or riches'. Once discovered, canoeing became a passion with him, and his annual holiday was a canoeing trip—sometimes taken alone, at other times with a companion. He became an authority on canoeing and his last book, published a year before his death, included instructions and advice to canoeists and an account of his own expeditions.

In the year of his first canoeing trip two mass meetings of Irish-Americans took place in Boston. The first was at the Boston Theatre on 17 February 1882 and was addressed by John E. Redmond, Member of Parliament for New Ross, County Wexford. Predictably, John Boyle O'Reilly as chairman opened the proceedings. In his speech he drew attention to the youthfulness of the leaders of Irish nationalism: 'hardly a single man who leads or is foremost in the movement for an Irish National Party has yet seen forty years, and many of them have not seen thirty years'.[4] The second meeting occured after he had returned from holiday. The Irish National League Convention held an altogether bigger affair in the New England Manufacturers' Institute on 15 August which attracted 20,000 and two Irish Members of Parliament: Redmond again, and Thomas Sexton who was later to present a petition in Westminster on behalf of O'Reilly. O'Reilly took an active though unofficial part in the organization.

In the same month the *Boston Daily Globe* commenced serializing a story which proved so popular that it is said to have raised the circulation to 30,000. Entitled *The King's Men*—a line from the 'Humpty Dumpty' nursery rhyme—it was written by four authors, Robert Grant, Frederick Stimpson, John T. Wheelwright, and John Boyle O'Reilly. Said to have been generated at lunches attended by the authors, possibly at the Marliave, it was published by Charles Scribner of New York in the same year with the added subtitle, *A Tale of Tomorrow*.

The authors imagine an England sixty years on, sometime in the 1940s. A revolution has taken place before the story begins and the rightful king, George V, has fled in exile to America. The republican government, headed by a president, was popular at first but has lately become corrupt and authoritarian. Written a full thirty years before Lenin's rise to power, there are fleeting semblances to a Marxist dictatorship in the strong military presence, summary executions, and the Castro-like figure of President Bagshaw who has a coal-black beard, smokes a cigar in a bare room, and is surrounded by minders. The old aristocracy has been divested of power and status but is tolerated, and still inhabits clubs and shabby, run-down stately homes. The story is even-handed and far from being a socialist tract. The aristocrats, who plan a revolt to reinstate the monarchy, are often sympathetically drawn. A conversation between two of the conspirators, Geoffrey Ripon and Sir John Dacre, is particularly telling. Dacre is contending that republicanism is immoral and unnatural and Geoffrey Ripon disagrees, referring to America which, he says, is the happiest, richest and most orderly country in the world. Sir John Dacre replies: 'I speak of republicanism in England, not in America.'

'But where is the difference?' persists Ripon. 'If universal suffrage be a virtue in America, how can it be a vice in England?'

'As the food of one life may be the poison of another', answers Dacre. 'Human society has many forms, and all may be good, but each must be specially protected by its own public morality. England was reared into greatness and flourished in greatness for twenty hundred years on one unvarying order. America has developed under another order, a different but not a better one.'

'That may be, but in less than two hundred years America has reached a point of wealth, order and peace that England has never approached in two thousand.'

'America', continues Dacre, 'had nothing to unlearn. Her people had no royal traditions—we have no democratic ones'.

Dacre and Ripon lead a revolt of the nobles, enlisting the support of royalist army units at Aldershot, but their plotting is overheard by a Mrs Oswald Carey who is in love with one of the conspirators but has been rejected by him. On the principle that 'hell hath no fury like a woman scorned' she seeks an interview with President Bagshaw and tells all she knows. Forewarned, the republicans forcibly suppress the revolt. The old aristocrat commander, Lord Arundel, at the moment of raising the king's standard on the parade ground at Aldershot, is shot on his horse. A pitched battle follows; some are killed and others are taken prisoner and incarcerated in Dartmoor prison. In due time they make a daring escape aided by Sir John Dacre's faithful old retainer who has the family steam yacht awaiting them at Torquay, and from there they sail for Boston and freedom. The one-time George V is also there, living as a commoner, and 'not all the king's horses, nor all the king's men' could put him on the throne of England again.

The Dartmoor scenes are clearly based on O'Reilly's experiences: the digging of ditches on the moors, the heavy manual labour of breaking stones under the supervision of guards, and the prison routine. At one point Geoffrey Ripon and his fellow convicts unearth a stone obelisk with an inscription commemorating the deaths of French and American prisoners of war at Dartmoor in the years 1811–16. One convict explains to the others that a hundred years previously Irish convicts had found the remains of the prisoners while digging in the ditches, and obtained permission to rebury them and erect the simple memorial. This is a neat reference to the actual event of O'Reilly's self-imposed task mentioned on page 86. Another significant allusion is the use of '406' again which was the number given to one of the fictional convicts.

How much each author contributed to the writing of The King's Men is impossible to unravel, but at least we can be sure that O'Reilly wrote the sections set in Dartmoor prison which came directly from his knowledge and experiences. Probably Robert Grant was responsible for the greater part since he is cited as the copyright holder; the others may have contributed only ideas and short sketches.[5] At the time, Robert Grant was on the threshold of two careers: a distinguished one in the law (he eventually became a judge), and the other in literature, in which he had a reputation no less prestigious. The first of his several novels, *The Confessions of a Frivolous Girl*, was published in 1880 and had been well received. His work is characterized by a mellow satirical outlook and a wordly wisdom, both of which are evident in *The King's Men*. This book is now a literary curiosity, rare and largely forgotten, but is of interest to us because of O'Reilly's contribution and, more generally, because it is one of the first in a long and distinguished line of political futurologies of which *1984* and *Brave New World* are only two examples.

Towards the end of the year an opportunity arose for O'Reilly to travel abroad and the question arose as to whether it was safe for him to leave his country of exile, the country of which he was now a citizen.[6]

O'Reilly's detestation of England, so vigorously expressed in his writings and speeches, would not have helped his application of 29 January 1885, addressed to the British Home Secretary in Whitehall, asking for a guarantee of safe passage across the United States' border to Canada. In December 1884 he had been invited to deliver the St Patrick's Day oration in Ottawa on the following 17 March. The Canadian Government had already promised that they would take no action against O'Reilly which encouraged him to accept the invitation.

The American Secretary of State had made an official application on his behalf through the US Legation in London: all to no avail. O'Reilly received his answer through the State Department, Washington, dated 18 February, informing him that the British Home Secretary, 'having due regard to the circumstances of the case...regrets that your request is one that cannot be safely granted'. O'Reilly also received a reply to his personal application, couched in similar terms. The reply gives the impression that he had asked permission to visit not only Canada, but also England and Ireland. The request through diplomatic channels appears to refer only to a visit to Canada.[7]

The matter was not to end there. O'Reilly's name was included in a petition in the Westminster parliament in February, which begged for an amnesty for himself and James Stephens. Mr Sexton, MP argued that every other civilian and military offender had been set free and that there could be no moral distinction between the case of John Boyle O'Reilly and those members of the British Army who had been tried, convicted and sentenced at the same time.

> Mr O'Reilly was one of the most influential men in the United States, and might long ago have occupied a seat in Congress if he could have [been] spared from his literary labours and the duties of journalism.[8]

Mr Sexton then quoted the opinion of the Honourable Member Sir Lyon Playfair, chairman of the Ways and Means Committee, who said after meeting Mr O'Reilly in Boston that he was 'so impressed with his personal qualities and gifts' that he thought the government had a duty to pardon him. The debate continued with Sir William Vernon Harcourt, the Home Secretary, refusing to reconsider his earlier ruling, maintaining that O'Reilly was a special case because he had broken his parole.

The Westminster parliamentary supporters of the petition may not have known that O'Reilly, when informed of the petition to be presented at the request of the Drogheda National League, telegraphed the committee as early as the previous December demanding that they withdraw his name. O'Reilly was a proud man and the notion of petitioning a government which he despised was repugnant to him. Presumably the committee did not act on his request in view of the debate which followed.

The petition and debate were fully reported in America and provoked considerable interest. Subsequently, both Henry Hathaway and the faithful Father Patrick McCabe (then living in Minnesota) denied that O'Reilly had 'broken his parole'. The priest wrote to Roche:

> [He] never broke his parole, never having had one to break. From the day he landed from the convict ship *Hougoumont*, in Fremantle, up to the day of his escape from Bunbury, he had been under strict surveillance, and was looked upon as a very dangerous man and treated as such.[9]

At this distance from the event it is difficult for us to understand and forgive the intransigence of the British Government; but the political climate in the first months of 1885 was hardly favourable to reconciliation. The memory of the Phoenix Park murders and recent attacks by Irish nationalists on Westminster Hall, the Houses of Parliament and the Tower of London—the so-called 'dynamite outrages'—would not have helped. Although no human life was lost in the most recent attacks (the explosions were intended as a symbolic gesture against the Union) public outrage was exacerbated because the targets were beloved bastions of English law and order. Although O'Reilly condemned the outrages in his editorials, he reminded England that she had only herself to blame: '[Ireland] unsurpassed in the world for natural wealth, supports a miserable, unhappy, rebellious people whose children are scattered in all lands'.

Further recriminations were hurled from both sides after the retaliatory shooting of O'Donovan Rossa in a New York street by an English woman, Yseult Dudley. The attempted assassination was greeted in the English press with scarcely disguised pleasure. O'Reilly was shocked at the worsening relations between the two countries and pleaded for reconciliation:

> When thirty million English people wildly cheer a half insane and wholly disreputable murderess, and thirty million people of Irish blood half sympathise

with the desperate lunatics who would burn down London—it is time for both sides to pause. It is time for both England and Ireland to answer this question: *Is it too late to be friends?*

And he concluded by begging England to be the first to make a political concession:

> She [England] is dealing with a generous and proud and warm-hearted race. We know the Irish people; we gauge their hatred and measure their hope; and we profoundly believe that the hour is not yet too late for England to disarm and conquer them by the greatness of her spirit, as she has never been able to subdue them by the force of her enemies.[10]

But O'Reilly's entreaties, if they were noticed at all on the other side of the Atlantic, fell on deaf ears. Another forty years of bitterness and political activity would pass before a significant change was made and the Irish Republic was born: an event O'Reilly was destined never to see.

In June 1886 O'Reilly managed to wrest time from his crippling schedule for 'five tranquil and delicious days—fishing, shooting and canoeing' on the Merrimac. He made his headquarters the summer residence of his friend Father Arthur Teeling which was unoccupied at the time. He revelled in his solitude and was joined occasionally by welcome visitors. He noted in his diary of the trip, 'Boyle's Log', that 21 June was a red-letter day, the day on which he would have been freed in Fremantle after twenty years imprisonment had he not escaped in 1869. 'This is a good place to celebrate the day', he wrote, 'alone— thinking over the changes—the men—the events of twenty years!'.[11]

Later in the year O'Reilly's fourth and last book of poems, *In Bohemia*, was published. The title was that of the first poem in the collection of thirty. Although like all his earlier work it received mixed reviews, *In Bohemia* remains, in many ways, his most pleasing work as it contains some of his most delicate, lyrical poetry.

The majority of the poems in the volume appear to come from a more reflective and mature voice, that of a poet grown tired of materialistic, squabbling society, and who now longs for a simpler more spiritual life. The title poem and 'The Cry of the Dreamer' are two of special quality and deserve to be anthologized and remembered. In the first, the poet declares that he would prefer to live in Bohemia than in any other land, Bohemia being a symbolic place free from hypocritical conventions and where philosophy, art and spiritual values predominate:

> To the empty heart in a jewelled breast
> There is value, maybe, in a purchased crest;

But the thirsty soul soon learns to know
The moistureless froth of the social show;
The vulgar sham of the pompous feast
Where the heaviest purse is the highest priest;
The organised charity, scrimped and iced,
In the name of a cautious, statistical Christ.

'The Cry of the Dreamer' is his most popular poem among his admirers. In it he continues the theme of rejection of the material world and its values but here he probes deeper into his own feelings, and the reader may wonder how accurately the poem describes the poet's own growing despair and disillusionment:

I am tired of planning and toiling
    In the crowded hives of men;
Heart-weary of building and spoiling,
    And spoiling and building again.
And I long for the dear old river,
    Where I dreamed my youth away;
For a dreamer lives for ever,
    And a toiler dies in a day.

I am sick of the showy seeming
    Of a life that is half a lie;
Of the faces lined with scheming
    In the throng that hurries by.
From the sleepless thoughts endeavour
    I would go where the children play;
For a dreamer lives forever
    And a thinker dies in a day.

I can feel no pride but pity
    For the burdens the rich endue;
There is nothing sweet in the city
    But the patient lives of the poor.
Oh, the little hands too skilful
    And the child-mind chocked with weeds!
The daughter's heart grown wilful,
    And the father's heart that bleeds!

No, no! from the street's rude bustle,
    From trophies of mart and stage,
I would fly to the woods' low rustle
    And the meadows' kindly page.

Let me dream as of old by the river,
　And be loved by the dream away;
For the dreamer lives for ever,
　And a toiler dies in a day.

In Bohemia also included some of his public commemorative poems: 'America', 'The Three Queens', and a eulogy on the death of his great friend, the Negro reformer Wendell Phillips.

The critic George Edward Woodbury, writing in the *Atlantic Monthly*, thought the poems were distinguished by force, reality and modernness. Oliver Wendell Holmes wrote and congratulated O'Reilly when he received a copy of the book saying that, 'the poems have heart and soul in them and if they have faults which have escaped my too hasty reading, that is a small matter when a poem has life in it'.[12]

The year came to a close with the unveiling of Bartholdi's great Statue of Liberty in New York harbour and O'Reilly wrote a special poem for the occasion, which was first published in the New York *World*. It is a rousing, patriotic ballad opening with the line, 'Majestic Warder by the Nation's Gate', and includes the warning:

Freedom is growth and not creation; one man suffers, one man is free.
One brain forges a constitution; but how shall the million souls be one?
Freedom is more than a resolution—he is not free who is free alone.

Although not a great poem, and not to be compared with his best in the small, slim volume of *In Bohemia*, the general public took O'Reilly to their hearts as their popular, genial bard and would have crowned him with a laurel wreath had that been the custom of the time.

Chapter 30

'Terribly Overworked'

I am tired of planning and toiling
In the crowded hives of men;
Heart-weary of building and spoiling,
And spoiling and building again.

John Boyle O'Reilly

THE publication of *In Bohemia* with its more introspective poems marks a turning point in O'Reilly's life. It seems that from here on, in the few years left to him, he grew tired—not just physically tired, but tired and strained within himself. As early as 1882 Fanny Parnell had expressed her concern that he had been 'so ill', and in several subsequent letters he mentioned his illnesses, and often the fact that he '[had] been laid up with a dreadful cold'. His handwriting became a hurried scrawl and at times, practically illegible. He complained increasingly of insomnia: 'I am now suffering the consequences of overwork', he wrote to Francis Bowen, 'my poem for your collection I have had mapped out and partially written for over a month; but now I am stopped by an attack of insomnia...the very thought of my inability [to write it] aggravates my sleeplessness'.[1] And in another letter to the same correspondent, 'I am now ill, sleepless again, from overwork; I must go away for two or three weeks at least'. He wrote to Devoy, 'I am terribly overworked and cannot go to sleep'.[2] And yet again, he wrote in a letter to his canoeing friend, Edward Moseley: 'I am tired to death...'.

This great tiredness and a strong sense of ennui is further suggested in a fragment of undated, unpublished poetry found among his papers. It is perhaps not much more than a doodle, but surely significant:

His tongue has grown stale; his heart has grown cold
Till the smile bares his mouth, and the ring leaves his laugh
And he shirks the bright headache when you ask him to quaff.

235

He grows formal with men, with women polite,
And distrustful of both when they're out of his sight.
Then he eats for his palate, and drinks for his head
And loves for his pleasure—and it's time he were dead.

And then he added a scribbled couplet as if an afterthought:

And who, till he weighed it, could ever surmise
That his heart was a cinder instead of a coal?[3]

Was O'Reilly's fire burning out in his last years? If so it was not reflected in his day-to-day work. He was still a young man, comparatively speaking, and certainly the pace of his activities and his continual travelling did not diminish. The change in O'Reilly was internal.

On St Patrick's Day 1887 he read his 'Exile of the Gael' before the Charitable Irish Society of Boston on the 150th anniversary of the foundation of the association. In the poem he returns to one of his constant themes which can be summed up in his saying: 'We can do Ireland more good by our Americanism than by our Irishism'.

No treason we bring from Erin—nor bring we shame nor guilt!
The sword we hold may be broken, but we have not dropped the hilt!
The wreath we bear to Columbia is twisted of thorns, not bays;
But the hearts we bring for Freedom are washed in the surge of tears;
And we claim our right by a People's fight, outliving a thousand years.

William O'Brien, MP was given a public reception before a crowd of 5,000 people in Boston on 29 May, and O'Reilly again presided. In a reference to the ugly reception that was accorded O'Brien in the British dominion of Canada, and the attempt on his life, O'Reilly continued to fire salvos at the British position:

We protest as Americans, against a ruler on this continent, in the adjoining country, who tramples upon the law of the land, who smiles approbation upon passionate mobs, bent upon outrage and murder. We want no mobs or revolutions in America,—and least of all revolutions in the interests of privilege and caste and foreign power.[4]

On 21 June British Americans celebrated Queen Victoria's jubilee with a banquet in Faneuil Hall. On the previous evening O'Reilly joined demonstrators protesting at the use of the hall for such a purpose. He was unprepared to speak but nevertheless was encouraged to do so, and he gave vent to his anger and detestation of the Crown. He said the use of Faneuil Hall for the banquet was a violation of tradition, that the hall was thereby desecrated. He argued that they could not prevent the Englishmen from hiring it because of 'the orders of those whom we elected', but in an intemperate outburst he vowed:

> I will never enter the walls of this hall again. I will never—so help me God—I will never. May my tongue cleave to my mouth if I ever speak a word for man or cause in Faneuil Hall again.[5]

It would have been wiser for O'Reilly to have ignored the jubilee celebrations. By speaking so rashly the Irish protest was interpreted as an attempt to restrict free speech, and the resultant publicity did little for O'Reilly's reputation and the Irish cause. The Faneuil Hall incident was another example of his tendency to impetuous reactions which he regretted on later reflection.

O'Reilly was given to the use of hyperbole, whether in the cause of damnation or praise. When the sculptor John Donaghue, who had carved O'Reilly's bust and received praise from Oscar Wilde during his visit, held an exhibition in Boston in January 1888, O'Reilly lavished praise on the three works exhibited. While he judged all three to have 'grace beauty and eloquent action', he reserved his greatest adulation for *The Boxer* which stood in the central arch 'filling the whole hall with its colossal strength, calmness and beauty... It is a statue once seen can never be forgotten'. He continued:

> It is unlike all other statues in the world—as unlike the glorious 'David' of Angelo is unlike the 'Discobolus' of the Athenian master. Strangers visiting Boston will ask for years to come: 'Where is the statue of The Boxer?'. And should the city be fortunate enough and wise enough to keep this great work in immortal bronze in one of our halls or galleries, it is sure to win international renown as the towering 'Young David' in Florence.[6]

Later that month O'Reilly espoused a more conciliatory approach when speaking at a reception in Boston at which Sir Thomas Esmonde and Mr John Stuart—two of Mr Gladstone's envoys who supported Home Rule—were present. He said he was glad of the opportunity of standing on the platform with an Englishman like Mr Stuart and declared that between such Englishmen and Irishmen there was no quarrel. He said he was reminded in Mr Stuart's speech that there were two Englands, one composed of a few thousand people, and the other of tens of millions. The thousands had all the glory and power and wealth, while the millions had all the darkness, the crowding, the suffering and the labour. Here was the humane O'Reilly strongly contending that it was

237

the British Government, the ruling few, that he abhorred, and that his sympathies were with all oppressed and deprived peoples.

On Monday evening, 28 February, he was again on the platform among distinguished guests. On this occasion, it was a literary gathering at Sanders Theater, Cambridge, the heart of academia, and the purpose was to raise funds for the Longfellow Memorial. According to a report in the Boston *Transcript*, O'Reilly seemed nervous among the literati when he rose to recite some of his poems.

> It seemed rather a trait of audacity for him to read *In Bohemia* before an audience which must have included very few Bohemians, and where he could hardly expect a favourable reception for his sentiments regarding organised charity and statistical Christianity.

But the report went on to say that his audience loved it and cheered him wildly when he had finished.

On Saturday, 5 May O'Reilly set out for Norfolk, Virginia at the southern end of Chesapeake Bay. It was a two-day journey by train from Boston via New York and Washington, and O'Reilly was loaded with equipment including cushions, blankets, cooking utensils, a rifle and a camera. He had arranged to meet his great friend Edward Moseley for one of his canoeing holidays and together they would explore an area a few miles out of Norfolk known as Dismal Swamp. In spite of its unattractive name the water was 'wonderfully pure' and, according to O'Reilly, free from malaria. It was beautiful virgin country which was sparsely populated by the descendants of fugitive slaves.

O'Reilly enjoyed his excursion with Moseley 'immensely', notably the canoeing, the game shooting (there were deer and wild boar in the area as well as deadly copperhead rattlesnakes) and the friendly camp fire conversation in the evenings. They hired the services of a Negro guide and Moseley recounted how O'Reilly engaged in conversation with the local people, 'poor unfortunates whose mentality was about as low as it's possible to imagine', and regaled them with stories of the wrongs and sufferings of Ireland. Moseley wrote of his 'wonderful ability to place himself en rapport with all classes of men, and adapt himself to the capacity of others to understand him'.[7]

Like all professional journalists, O'Reilly was never entirely on holiday. He would make use of his experiences to write an article for the *Herald* and *Sun*, illustrated with his own photographs. He would also describe his canoeing expeditions, including Dismal Swamp, in his forthcoming book, *Ethics of Boxing and Manly Sport*, which was published by Tickner and Company and later republished under the simpler title, *Athletics and Manly Sport*.

The successful orator and Boston newspaper editor. (Courtesy of the Pilot)

The book is an oddity, although in view of O'Reilly's passion for sport and physical wellbeing it is hardly surprising. What *is* surprising is how such a busy man could have found sufficient time to research his subject; the book is in the nature of an authoritative encyclopaedia on the history and evolution of boxing and a treatise on health and physical exercise. It carries the dedication:

To all those who believe that a love for innocent sport, playful exercise, and enjoyment of nature, is a blessing intended not only for the years of boyhood, but for the whole life of man.

O'Reilly's introduction would be applauded by all modern aerobics and physical fitness evangelists. He writes: 'There is a character as well as strength in muscle; and little of either in flabbiness or lard. Fatness and softness are merely sensuous expressions, or symptoms of disease'. The book is divided into three parts. The first is a history and treatise on boxing, illustrated with drawings. Amongst a welter of facts and statistics he calculates the average age at which prize-fighters have died: forty-seven. 'This is not a very bad showing for men whose profession involved numerous severe trainings and exhaustive conflicts and whose lives, in the intervals, were usually dissipated and full of excitement.' Subjects covered in detail in Part One include 'The Sacred Games of Greece', 'The Gladiators of Rome', and 'The Skill of Greek Boxers'.

Part Two deals with the training of athletes and here his advice on diet, sleep and exercise is retold in countless books on the subject today. He advocates only one full meal a day and advises athletes to:

Go to bed at ten and get up at seven. Open your window, and, if possible, make a draught through the room, but not across your bed. Never exercise in a room with closed windows. During exercise, especially walking, keep abdominal muscles well under the will, so that the abdomen may be drawn in, and kept in. The abdomen muscle is the test of condition.[8]

Part Three is an account of his canoeing expeditions and gives general advice on camping and canoeing on the Delaware and Merrimac Rivers.

While *Ethics of Boxing and Manly Sport* was in preparation—it was published towards the end of that year, 1888—O'Reilly's punishing round of public activities and writing commissions continued unabated. On 18 November a monument erected in Boston to the first man killed in the American Revolution, a Negro called Crispus Attucks, was unveiled. O'Reilly's poem, 'Crispus Attucks', was read at the dedicatory service. When the idea of the monument was first suggested there was considerable opposition arising from colour prejudice. But O'Reilly campaigned vigorously for it, and in his poem he includes a scathing indictment of the Tories whom he depicts as denying rights to any minority group:

> Patrician, aristocrat, Tory—whatever his age or name,
> To the peoples' rights and liberties, a traitor ever the same.
> The natural crowd is a mob to him, their prayer a vulgar rhyme;
> The free man's speech is sedition, and the patriot's deed a crime;
> Whatever the race, the land, whatever the time or throne,
> The Tory is always a traitor to every class but his own.

Accepting an invitation from Boston's Negroes, O'Reilly read 'Crispus Attucks' on 18 December at the Charles Street coloured church where he also made a short speech urging the Negroes to act for themselves:

> It is easier to break political bonds than the bonds of ignorance and prejudice. The next twenty-five years can bring many reforms, and by proper training our coloured fellow-citizens may easily be their own protectors. They must, above all things, establish a brotherhood of race. Make it so strong that its members will be proud of it—proud of living as coloured Americans and desirous of devoting their energy to the advancement of their people.[9]

In September 1889 O'Reilly was evidently seriously ill as he was to be found convalescing at Crawford House in the White Mountains of New Hampshire, about 170 miles north of Boston. Uncharacteristically, he refused to accept further commissions and declined an invitation to speak at the forthcoming Catholic Congress in Baltimore. 'I am just recovering from a repeated attack of insomnia', he wrote, 'which so alarmed my wife that I promised her to abstain from all engagements outside my editorial work for a whole year'.[10] O'Reilly did not entirely keep his promise but the number of engagements from then until his death—with one notable exception—were far fewer than previously.

In December he was ill again. On this occasion his entire family and two servants were prostrated at once with a virulent epidemic known as 'la grippe'. 'I was never so sick in my life', he wrote to his canoeing friend Edward Moseley. And no doubt O'Reilly's general debility at that time contributed to the seriousness of his own condition. 'I have never seen such dangerous illness in my house before', he added.

The notable exception to his self-imposed, much reduced work program was an extended speaking tour throughout March 1890, during which O'Reilly travelled as far west as San Francisco. In hindsight it proved ill-advised and probably contributed much to the tragic event later in the year.

He set out on the night train from Boston for Syracuse on 3 March accompanied by his friend, Dr John Young. Throughout the trip he kept a diary of scribbled notes which are now difficult to decipher but which are valuable personal glimpses of people, places, and events en route.[11] He was seen off on the journey by 'dear Molly and uncle Jack' and when they had gone he feared that he had not shown sufficient gratitude for their kindness: that thought and his homesickness 'prayed on me all night and grew into great pain'. The next morning the train arrived in Syracuse and the two travellers walked to the hotel in the bright sun. He was pleased to find a telegram waiting for him from 'Mamsey' with love from the children. That night he lectured to an audience of about 3,000 and attended a banquet afterwards.

The next day he was on the train again, complaining that the journey was monotonous. Evidently his companion was not the sparkling company that the gregarious Irishman needed: 'J.Y.'s nature is singularly grave and plain. He does not understand a joke. He thinks closely and clearly on medical subjects chiefly'. They arrived in Chicago on 7 March three hours late, but they had time for a sightseeing tour before departing again for St Paul. He thought Chicago 'the most crowded city in the main parts I have ever seen'. Dr Young's skills were appreciated when a flying cinder from the engine lodged in his eye; in extracting it the doctor used cocaine 'which deadened the pain'. They reached St Paul that evening and were conducted to a grand banquet at the very splendid Ryan House Hotel—'if only they knew our opinion of banquets!', he scribbled in parenthesis. Among the '100 clever men mostly in evening dress' was Ignatius Donnelly the famous American Bacon-Shakespeare theorist. Whatever O'Reilly might have thought on the subject of Bacon writing Shakespeare, he noted that Donnelly was 'the most eloquent after-dinner speaker I have heard'.[12]

In Minneapolis he lectured at 8.00 p.m.—'the audience was good, not large, around 1100 people'—and attended the inevitable banquet afterwards at an opulent private house full of elaborate works of art, carved wood and stained glass. The hostess was a Mrs Kelly whose ostentation disgusted O'Reilly: 'She was enamelled and painted and blazing with diamonds—Dr Young estimated the value at around $20,000. She simpered and sidled like a silly duchess'. Poor O'Reilly won the honour of taking her into dinner: 'As I glanced round at her I had an unpleasant feeling of disgust and amusement'.

On 10 March he lectured in Butte City, Montana where the Opera House was packed to capacity. The next day he was invited to don a miner's suit and descend a silvermine where he dug out some silver ore to take home to his family. Later that day he boarded the train again for destinations further west, crossed the Yellowstone River on the 11th—'frozen, the whole country covered

in snow'—and arrived in Helena Mint in the Rocky Mountains on the afternoon of the 12th. The diary entries show the easterner's simple delight in the
dramatic scenery of mountains and ravines, and in the enormous distances between one town and another. At one point he met a Belgian missionary priest
on the train who told him his parish extended over 60,000 square miles: 'not
six, or sixteen', he wrote, perhaps for the edification of his daughters when he
returned, 'but 60,000'.

He travelled on to Spokane Falls in 'a magnificent pullman car' and noted
that this luxury changed his opinion of rail travel, which had now become so
comfortable and interesting that he proposed another trip: 'Next year, or this
Fall', he wrote, 'I will take Mary, please God'. This wish was never fulfilled.

He reached Seattle on 16 March where he lectured on Irish history to a large
and appreciative audience. The following day he took the steamer south down
Puget Sound to Tacoma where he was obliged to take part in a St Patrick's Day
procession. After the lecture that night he attended another banquet in his
honour which lasted until 4.00 a.m. He managed only a couple of hours sleep
and then was up again to catch the train to Portland. In his haste he left washing
and a towel in the hotel.

After Portland he enjoyed three days 'great rest' on the San Francisco-bound
steamer, *Oregon*, but admitted he was homesick for his family, 'How plainly I see
them all as I close my eyes'.

In San Francisco the tour began to go horribly wrong. A worrying telegram
from Mary which awaited him did not help. 'Something is wrong', he noted,
although he did not explain what that might be. There were arguments about
the fees and the number of remaining lectures; and lectures were postponed or
not adequately publicized. At Sacramento there were eleven people in the
audience and although O'Reilly agreed to speak to them, the organizer (only
referred to as 'Carroll' by O'Reilly) decided to cancel the engagement.

On his way back on 28 March O'Reilly developed a heavy cold and was
'almost unable to move' but managed to 'keep cool' when meeting the organizing committee to talk about his contract and payments due. Several pages of the
diary are largely indecipherable scribbles relating to arguments about fees.
O'Reilly was willing to settle for $2,700 and waiver $500 to cut the tour short.
He succeeded in getting three cheques, one for $1,000 and two for $500 each.
It is not clear from his notes whether he ever received the balance. Argument
continued with Carroll whom O'Reilly described as 'looking wily and insolent'.
The bad cold and O'Reilly's complaints about headaches and insomnia could
not have helped the relationship.

O'Reilly arrived back in Boston on 5 April and, in spite of the unfortunate
experience towards the end of the trip, was full of admiration and enthusiasm

for the great possibilities of the western region. 'That matchless country, as large as an empire, and filled with all kinds of natural wealth, contains only as many people as the city of Boston', he wrote in the *Pilot*. But the tour had been exhausting which added to the general decline in his health.

CHAPTER 31

'AND WAKING IS DEATH'

Life is a certainty,
Death is a doubt;
Men may be dead
When they're walking about.
Love is as needful
To being as breath;
Loving is dreaming,
And waking is death.

John Boyle O'Reilly

TOWARDS the end of May 1890 the O'Reilly household, as was the custom, removed to their summer residence at Hull and O'Reilly caught the ferry to his city office during the week. Mrs O'Reilly, suffering from bouts of depression and insomnia, was attended regularly by the Hull physician, Dr William Litchfield. Two of the O'Reilly daughters, Betsy and Agnes, remained at their convent school at Elmhurst, Providence until the end of the summer term. The eldest daughter Mollie, aged seventeen, was at the Collegiate College for Women which had recently been established at Harvard (later to be known as Radcliffe College). Under the existing conditions she could not be admitted to a degree course but was allowed to attend lectures on English literature and history, and she also studied languages.

Hull in the 1880s was little more than a small fishing village but the increasing holiday population had resulted in the building of an elegant hotel, the Pemberton. O'Reilly knew all the fishermen and the residents of the village and was a popular figure among them. He greatly admired the heroism of those who manned the lifesaving boats and praised their exploits publicly at a dinner given in their honour by the Hull Yacht Club. Roche tells the story that when O'Reilly's poem, written for the dedication of the Pilgrim Fathers' Monument, was published in the morning paper following the dedication ceremony at

Plymouth, the crew and his fellow passengers on the city-bound ferry held papers aloft and cheered him as he boarded the boat.[1]

The selection of a foreign-born poet for the honour of composing the poem for such an important national occasion resulted in objections being voiced from some quarters. The president of the Pilgrim Society, ex-Governor Long, responded to the criticism when he introduced O'Reilly at the ceremony by reminding his audience that the poet was 'a genuine New England Pilgrim, born not on the mainland, but on a small island out at sea'. He concluded by saying that, 'Nothing could be in better keeping with the comprehensiveness of this occasion than that he should write and speak the poem of the day'.[2]

'The Pilgrim Fathers' is an epic work of 260 lines written for the most part in rhyming iambic pentameters. It explains the reasons for the voyage and celebrates the arrival of the Pilgrim Fathers on the American shore and the establishment of a new, free land:

> Here on this rock and on this sterile soil,
> Began the kingdom not of kings, but men:
> Began the making of the world again.

It also shows that O'Reilly was not unaware of some of the less pleasant characteristics of the Pilgrim Fathers:

> They never lied in practice, peace, or strife;
> They were no hypocrites; their faith was clear;
> They feared too much some sins men ought to fear:
> The lordly arrogance and avarice,
> And vain frivolity's besetting vice;
> The stern enthusiasm of their life
> Impelled too far, and weighed poor nature down;
> They missed God's smile, perhaps, to watch His frown.

'The Pilgrim Fathers' was his crowning work, his last major commemorative poem. While generally well received, it still attracted criticism (in spite of the lines quoted) from those who believed O'Reilly had glossed over the intolerance and cruelty of Pilgrim society; in short, they believed that O'Reilly had confused the Blarney Stone with Plymouth Rock.

During the early summer of 1890, O'Reilly attended few public engagements and concentrated his declining energies in forthright newspaper editorials reflecting his passionately held beliefs. In the issue of 31 May he confirmed that the *Pilot* was truly a Democratic paper, and defined his idea of what democracy was by tabling, among others, the following principles:

Democracy means the least government for the people, instead of most.

It means the spreading and preserving of doubt, distrust, and dislike of all sumptuary and impertinent laws.

It means that law shall only be drawn to disorder, and that all affairs that can be managed without disorder should be managed without law.

It means watchfulness against Federal legislation for such state questions as education, temperance, irrigation, and all other questions that may arise and are sure to arise in the future.

It means antagonism to all men, classes and parties that throw distrust and discredit on the working or common people, and who insinuate or declare that there is a higher, nobler, or safer patriotism among the wealthy and more book-learned classes than the common people possess or appreciate.

He continued with his outspoken defence of the American Negro, and in the *Pilot* of 28 June he wrote a piece celebrating the achievement of Clement Garnett Morgan, the first Negro graduate of Harvard who was chosen to deliver his class oration. He deplored the probability that once Morgan had departed from Harvard and stepped out into the world he would be regarded as 'the nigger' who

could never be invited to one's house or proposed at one's club, who would be refused a room at nearly all leading hotels and would not be tolerated even in the half-empty pews of polite worshippers.

He wished Morgan strength and wisdom to bear his sufferings arising from public prejudice.

In a letter dated 14 July to Mr T.B. Fritz, president of the Catholic Union, O'Reilly expressed his opposition to a proposed National Catholic Convention in Boston. He said that national conventions of citizens, whether Catholics, Baptists or Methodists were of doubtful value, and that worthy papers read before an audience of representatives would be better published in magazines and papers where they would reach a far greater number of people.

In the same month he contributed an article 'Canoes and Boats' to the Boston *Evening Traveler*, in which he expressed the opinion that 'there is no rest so complete and no play so refreshing as that which brings us face to face with primitive nature'. Sadly, he was never to experience canoeing again. His little boat *Blanid*, called after his youngest child, had been wrecked on its moorings during a storm which swept over the Nantasket peninsular and he had not procured another. In any case, it is doubtful whether his declining health would have permitted another expedition. On 6 August, while acting as judge at the National Irish Athletic Association's annual games, he was attacked by a 'weakness and fainting condition' to the extent that he had to retire from the field.

The incident was not serious enough to prevent him from assisting the organizing committee in making arrangements for the Grand Army of the Republic celebrations which were held in Boston the following week. The *Pilot* brought out a special commemorative edition. Neither was his condition serious enough, it seems, to prevent routine editorial work. The front page of the issue of Saturday, 9 August included a reprint of his article, 'Canoes and Boats', from the *Evening Traveler*; a story about the Mining King of Montana who was an Irishman; and news of Mr Gladstone's treaty with the Vatican which culminated in the appointment of a British envoy to the Papal State. Inside was the news that John Donaghue, the sculptor, had sent one of his superb bronzes home to Boston from Paris. O'Reilly's editorial was an appeal to two prominent Irish activists who had quarrelled with one another to settle their differences. On balance, it was not a distinguished edition with which to take his leave.

The editor left his office at about 2.00 p.m. on 9 August, to all appearances looking well but tired. He boarded the 2.30 p.m. boat for Hull and was met on arrival by his little daughter, Blanid. A local resident and witness to his arrival in Hull that afternoon described how the two of them frolicked together happily, 'the witty remarks of the father and the joyous laughter of the child furnishing much amusement'.[3] John Murphy, Mrs O'Reilly's brother, who was staying at the Pemberton Hotel, spent the evening with the family and reported later that John Boyle was in his usual good spirits. At 10.30 p.m. Murphy prepared to leave the house and O'Reilly said: 'I'll walk home with you, John, and see if I can walk myself into a condition of sleep'.[4] The two parted at the hotel and O'Reilly reminded Murphy not to sleep late because they were all to take a carriage drive to mass the following morning.

In the event, John Murphy was up earlier than expected. At about 5.00 a.m. he was summoned back to the O'Reilly residence to find that his brother-in-law was dead.

Shortly after returning home when O'Reilly had prepared himself for bed, his wife asked him to walk over to the doctor's house and obtain for her some more medicine. It was after midnight when O'Reilly returned with Litchfield who diagnosed nothing more serious than nervous tension and left some medicine for her. At about 2.00 a.m. O'Reilly was again sent by his wife to the doctor's house on account of her having spilt the medicine prescribed. Litchfield gave him some more and (according to Litchfield) his caller departed saying that he himself was very tired and had not slept for several nights.

The events of that strange night were reported in the *Boston Daily Globe* of Monday, 11 August. The *Globe* described how Mrs O'Reilly, awaking at 3.00 a.m. after a brief sleep, noticed that her husband had not yet retired. She found him sitting at the table with a book in front of him and his left hand resting on it. He was leaning forward, his right elbow on his knee, and his hand to his mouth holding a cigar. Mrs O'Reilly, thinking him asleep, tried to rouse him, but she was greatly alarmed when unable to do so and sent a servant for Dr Litchfield. When the doctor arrived O'Reilly was said to have rallied for a few moments before he sank back, collapsed and died.

In the first light of the morning Mrs O'Reilly, prostrated by grief and sedated by Litchfield, left her brother and other members of the household to announce to America and the world the shocking and wholly unexpected news of the death of one of America's most celebrated and beloved citizens.

The John Boyle O'Reilly monument in Dowth churchyard, erected 1903.
(Photograph by the author)

CHAPTER 32

O'REILLY—THE LEGACY

The primal truth neither dies nor slumbers,
But lives as the test of the common right,
That the laws proclaimed by the sworded numbers
May stand arraigned in the people's sight.

John Boyle O'Reilly

THE unadorned retelling of that lamentable night of 9 August 1890, and an examination of the various accounts of it which followed—of why and how John Boyle O'Reilly died when he did—have an unsatisfactory ring about them, and raise questions which have been pondered over by his admirers ever since.

Mary O'Reilly can hardly escape the charge of thoughtless self-indulgence in sending her husband out twice in the middle of the night for medicines of questionable necessity; a husband, moreover, who was clearly exhausted and on his own admission had been without sleep for several nights. Would another wife have been more concerned about her husband's condition? What effect did these errands have on his own health and mental condition at the time? And was his concern for his wife connected with what followed?

And what, in fact, had caused O'Reilly's death? The *Boston Herald* stated at the head of a lengthy report on Monday that the cause was simply 'heart failure': a heart attack. It quoted John Murphy as saying that his brother-in-law 'was prone to heart disease'. The *Boston Daily Globe* similarly stated that the cause was heart failure, based on an interview with Dr Litchfield.

Roche's account is somewhat different. He was close to the family and presumably formed his opinions at a later time. He wrote that Mrs O'Reilly found her husband, 'sitting on a couch, reading and smoking', and when she spoke to him and insisted that he went to bed, he answered her: 'Yes Mamsey dear, I have taken some of your sleeping medicine. I feel tired now. I will go to sleep right away'. As he lay down Mrs O'Reilly noticed a strange drowsiness

251

come over him and when she tried to rouse him again, the only answer she received was an inarticulate 'Yes, my love! Yes, my love!'. Roche concluded his account by saying that when the doctor arrived, he tried for an hour to revive O'Reilly but could not prevent his death at about 5.00 a.m.[1]

If the *Boston Daily Globe* quoted Litchfield accurately in the first report, it follows that the doctor changed his opinion later because the death register gives the cause of death as 'accidental poisoning'. There are two known mistakes in the death records: the name of O'Reilly's father, and the place of O'Reilly's birth are both wrong. Could there have been a third mistake?[2]

Roche stated that whatever medicine O'Reilly took contained chloral. Chloral was first used as late as 1869 as an anaesthetic and hypnotic drug, and if administered without proper safeguards it could be dangerous. It had a greasy, somewhat bitter taste and a pungent odour, but provided the raw substance was well diluted the mixture would induce in the patient a deep sleep lasting several hours. In large doses it acted as a depressant on circulation and respiration and sent the patient into a profound coma. It was also habit-forming.

If O'Reilly took chloral he could hardly have been ignorant of what kind of medicine it was. Presumably it was not the first time that Litchfield had prescribed it for Mrs O'Reilly, and it is more than likely that he himself had taken the drug on previous occasions. Surely his doctor friends—and there were several—would have prescribed medicine for him. So why did this dose produce a coma, as it so obviously did? The only satisfactory answer is that Dr Litchfield, in the early hours of the morning, did not prepare the chloral to the required standard or issue proper instructions before he gave it to O'Reilly to take home. O'Reilly may have died from a common cause in those days: medical malpractice.[3] 'Accidental poisoning' in the death register is a neat way of explaining it.

O'Reilly's death at the early age of forty-six gives rise to another possibility: that he suffered a nervous breakdown, and in a moment of acute depression knowingly took an overdose of the medicine in front of him. As unlikely as this may seem in view of his apparently strong religious faith which abjured suicide (and also considering he had the support and love of his family and friends, and his interest in so many causes) it is, nevertheless, worth some consideration. We know that O'Reilly attempted suicide early in his life and that in the months preceding his death he was chronically tired and under immense pressure from overwork. He was also burdened with a sickly child and an invalid wife. In clinical terms he must have been a strong candidate for a nervous breakdown. O'Reilly, like many others constantly in the public eye, also had a private, inner life. As Martin Carroll observed: 'His personality was permanently scarred by what he had experienced in Western Australia'.[4] The public O'Reilly was a strong, humane, self-confident leader respected by all; only a close reading of some of his poems and letters reveals glimpses of the other introspective and despairing O'Reilly.

If any members of the family, or even Doctor Litchfield, suspected that O'Reilly had taken his own life, it is understandable they would have wanted to supress any hint of scandal. Thus John Murphy's statement to the *Boston Herald* that his brother-in-law had been prone to heart disease—clearly untrue from what we know of O'Reilly's athletic interests, and the fact that no mention of such a condition was made in any of the letters to his doctor friends—may have been deliberate obfuscation. But as Roche pointed out when writing about those early morning hours of 10 August, 'What occurred is not known to anybody'. No medical evidence survives. There was no autopsy. The cause of death, as far as it has been described, could point to a heart attack, or to an innocent but mistaken dose of chloral, or to suicide. And that is how the case must rest.

All speculation is set aside as we rejoin the family and friends, stunned with grief on that August morning in Hull. Mrs O'Reilly, we are told, 'was hardly able to bear her bereavement' and was taken to her mother's home in Charlestown, along with little Blanid and Betsy. John Murphy, together with Agnes and Mollie, accompanied the body as it was ferried back to Hull across the bay. A crowd of local villagers and fishermen had gathered, tearful and silent, to see them off. After the body was embalmed it remained at the Charlestown home until the funeral on the following Wednesday morning.

The news spread like wildfire through the city and suburbs; some, disbelieving, thought that it was Mrs O'Reilly who had died rather than her husband. Prayers were offered at masses in O'Reilly's church in Charlestown. Shock and genuine grief were voiced everywhere.

The impact of the news of O'Reilly's death and the subsequent grief which was expressed publicly—not only in America but worldwide—was extraordinary. Perhaps it was only to be expected that Catholics and Irish-Americans should be deeply affected by the loss of their champion, but sorrow was by no means confined to those of his own religion and race. The Boston papers splashed the news over several pages with grieving headlines such as: 'John Boyle O'Reilly Mourned By All'; 'Boyle O'Reilly's Tender Heart'; and, 'None Knew Him But To Do Him Honor'. Extracts of his poems were printed and the story of his daring escape from Western Australia retold. The *Boston Daily Globe* included on the front page a large picture of him surrounded by a black border.

The fact that O'Reilly had become one of the most important public and literary figures in America within the space of twenty years residence is amply born out by the countless obituaries which appeared in weekly and monthly journals, some written by friends, but others by nameless admirers. *Harper's Weekly* described O'Reilly as

> easily the most distinguished Irishman in America. He was one of the country's foremost poets, one of its most influential journalists, an orator of unusual power, and he was endowed with such a gift of friendship as few men are blessed with.[5]

The obituary in the *Literary World* was even more effusive:

> In the sudden death of Mr Boyle O'Reilly, American literature has suffered a great loss. For though he was born and reared to manhood in Ireland, he was a thorough American in spirit and there is probably none among the younger American poets whose verse has expressed with more fervour and intensity, the patriotic feeling which should animate citizens of these United States.[6]

As well as the numerous obituaries, personal messages of sympathy and regret poured into the O'Reilly home after his death. Oliver Wendell Holmes described O'Reilly as 'a man of heroic mould and nature; brave, adventurous, patriotic and enthusiastic. We have been proud of him as an adopted citizen'. Ex-President Cleveland regarded him as 'a strong and able man, entirely devoted to any cause he espoused, unselfish in his activity, true and warm in his friendship, and patriotic in his enthusiasm'.

His great friend Patrick A. Collins, who succeeded in becoming Boston's second Irish-born mayor three years after O'Reilly's death, wrote:

> He was a branded outcast some twenty years ago, stranded in a strange land, friendless and penniless; today, wept for all over the world where men are free and seeking to be free, for his large heart went out to all in trouble, and his soul was the soul of a freeman; all he had he gave to humanity and asked no return.[7]

It was Cardinal Gibbons, head prelate of the Catholic Church in America, who summed up O'Reilly's loss to Catholicism by describing his death as 'a public calamity—not only a loss to the country, but a loss to the Church, and to humanity in general'.

The *Pilot* had to wait until the following Saturday to pay sorrowful tribute to its distinguished editor, and so great was the impact on the paper that the tributes and stories extended over the next three issues.

On Tuesday afternoon, 12 August, his body was taken from his home and down the hill to St Mary's Church on the corner of the street where it lay in state before the high altar. The following morning at 10.30 a.m. his daughters and other relatives, friends, and official guests assembled for the solemn

O'Reilly's grave at the foot of a black basalt rock at the highest point in Holyhood Cemetery, Boston. (Photograph by the author)

Requiem. Among those present were civic dignitaries as well as representatives from Catholic and Irish societies, the Grand Army of the Republic, athletic associations, and the press and literary societies. Only Mrs O'Reilly, distraught with grief, could not leave her bed. The eulogy was preached by Father Robert Fulton, SJ and ended with these words:

> Those who knew him noticed how increasing years enriched his character, and imparted to him readiness to forgive, reluctance to pain, charity of interpretation. He was approximating Christ, for such is our Exemplar.[8]

The funeral cortege moved through Boston to the suburb of Roxbury, where the coffin rested in a temporary vault awaiting a final resting place at Holyhood Cemetery, Brookline. Today the site of the grave, originally selected by O'Reilly, is marked by a huge boulder on which is affixed a copper medallion incorporating a bas-relief of O'Reilly's profile. Inset on the reverse side of the boulder is a stone which was brought from the village churchyard of Dowth, where O'Reilly had once expressed the wish to be buried.

Memorial services in Boston and other cities in America, together with numerous other expressions of communal grief in clubs and societies with which O'Reilly had been associated, continued long after the day of burial. The

The John Boyle O'Reilly Memorial at the Fenway, a busy intersection close to the Charles River, Boston.
(Courtesy of the Pilot*)*

Metropolitan Opera House in New York was filled to capacity for a civic ceremony chaired by the Governor of New York, Leon Abbett, and at which a message was read from President Harrison. A pontifical Requiem Mass was celebrated by Archbishop John Williams on 10 September in the Boston Cathedral of The Holy Cross (he had been away from Boston at the time of O'Reilly's death). Within two years of O'Reilly's death a majestic stone memorial to him, incorporating a bronze bust and symbolic Irish figures, was erected at a busy intersection in Boston and remains there today, as impressive as ever. It was paid for by public subscription. There must be few figures in American history—other than national leaders—whose demise has been attended by such prolonged, universal mourning.

In searching for reasons for O'Reilly's popularity and the esteem in which he was held—phenomenal in view of his humble beginnings as a poor migrant exile in 1870—we should consider two main points. First, he was perceived as a brave, romantic figure who had dared all to win his freedom from the same colonial power from which his American hosts had so recently freed themselves. But that early popular image might have worn thin had O'Reilly remained merely a trenchant Irish nationalist, like others who used America as a base for militant republican activities while staying in their ghettoes. Almost from the start O'Reilly had encouraged nationalist Irish-Americans to move away from ideas of conspiracy and violence. And without in any way betraying his patriotism, he had urged immigrants to become loyal to America, to take part in civil life and society, and to make the most of their new freedoms and opportunities and so earn the respect of their new country. For this he became the acceptable face of 'Irishism' for the native-born Americans. They trusted him: in him they looked beyond the stereotypical squalid, squabbling, aggressive malcontents of the Boston tenements, and saw instead the quintessential, gentlemanly Irish bard of romantic history. They felt safe with him.

Secondly, we must not underestimate the power of O'Reilly's remarkably warm, generous and loving personality which is attested to by everyone who came into his company. It is difficult for us at this distance to imagine the magnetism of the man, and the goodness that radiated from him. Effusive eulogies are off-putting and by their nature deserve the scepticism they generally provoke. But the sheer number and force of the tributes to O'Reilly can only impress even the most cynical. The writer George Parsons Lathrop, neither an Irishman nor a Catholic, wrote from New London, Connecticut a few days after learning of O'Reilly's death:

> Except for the loss of my father, and that of my own and only son, I have never suffered one more bitter than that afflicted by the death of my dear and noble and most beloved Boyle O'Reilly. He is a great rock torn out of the foundations of my life. Nothing will ever replace that powerful prop, that magnificent buttress. Boyle was the greatest man, the finest heart and soul I knew in Boston, and my most dear friend.[9]

Among O'Reilly's many fine qualities, he had his obvious faults. His rush to judgement has already been mentioned together with his implacable and seemingly unchristian hatred of England which was never to soften over the years. His intemperate language and sometimes inaccurate charges when refer- ring to England in his poetry, speeches and prose, are disturbing to the more rational, political and religious ecumenism of the present time. To understand him we must see these in context, and understand the politics of the time. It could be argued that only relentless, passionate invective would have produced the political changes which were so necessary and so eagerly sought then, but which now might be better achieved through negotiation and diplomacy. It must be remembered too that during all his years in America he was still a 'wanted man' in Britain, classed as a common fugitive and liable to be returned to Dartmoor the moment he set foot outside the United States. This was sufficient reason, perhaps, to make him bitter.

We must also understand the lasting influence of his experiences in childhood, of the deprivation and poverty of his people, and of the lessons he learned beside the flowing river of Irish history, the Boyne. From his mother's womb he carried a fanatic heart.

What then has O'Reilly left behind so that we may remember him with gratitude? His legacy to Western Australia may be accounted as his legend as a folk hero, a symbol of that brave, independent, resourceful spirit which marks the Australian character and which finds voice even today in celebrating the escape of the remaining Fenians from their shores. And more importantly there is his poetry which demonstrates that, in spite of his imprisonment, he had a rare understanding, sensitivity and warm regard for the strange environment which he inhabited for a short time.

Among the lasting achievements of John Boyle O'Reilly in America can be numbered the change in American perceptions of the Irish-Americans, and the raising of the consciousness of the Irish immigrants themselves. He fought bravely for social justice for minorities and attacked racial prejudice long before it became respectable to do so.

His legacy to his native country is not only his poetry. He was one of her Wild Geese, one of the many thousands who fought and worked for her independence from a foreign base. Like so many of Ireland's writers and poets he never lost sight of his republican convictions, and may be accounted among those who laid the foundation of the Irish Free State which came into existence thirty-two years after his death.

O'Reilly hated what he termed 'humbug', by which he meant deception, graft and political posturing. He frequently used the word derisively in letters and in his newspaper editorials. He was open and straightforward in his business and social dealings and one cannot imagine him ever being guilty of a dishonest or spiteful action. As James Jeffrey Roche described him in his biography, 'He remained throughout his life a brave, honourable, Christian gentleman, a loyal friend, a generous foe, a lover of God and of his fellow-men'.

ABBREVIATIONS
NOTES AND SOURCES
SELECT BIBLIOGRAPHY
INDEX

ABBREVIATIONS

Note: The abbreviated titles of repositories listed below are used in the Notes and Sources and Select Bibliography which follow.

AAB	Archives of the Archdiocese of Boston
BBC	John J. Burns Library, Boston College
BLP	Battye Library, Perth
BPL	Boston Public Library
HH	Houghton Library, Harvard
LRO	Lancashire Records Office, Preston
MAA	Massachusetts Archives
ML	Mitchell Library, Sydney
NLD	National Library, Dublin
PPL	Preston Public Library
PROD	Public Records Office, Dublin
PROL	Public Records Office, London
PROWA	Public Records Office, Western Australia
WAA	Western Australian Archives

NOTES AND SOURCES

PART 1 THE CRY OF THE DREAMER (1844–1867)

CHAPTER 1   CHILDHOOD BY THE BOYNE

1.   William R. Wilde, *The Beauties and Antiquities of the Boyne*, facsimile edn, Tower Books, Cork, 1978, p. 4. William Wilde was the father of Oscar, the poet and playwright, whom O'Reilly was to meet in Boston in 1882.

2.   From a notice proclaiming the rules and regulations of the Netterville Alms House found recently in the 1877 Alms House cellar. Printed by Alley & Co., Capel Street, Dublin. Date unknown.

3.   W.E. Vaughan (ed.), *A New History of Ireland, Volume V, 1801–1870*, Oxford, 1989, p. 533.

4.   ibid., p. 532.

5.   id.

6.   John Devoy, *Recollections of an Irish Rebel*, facsimile edn, Irish University Press, Dublin, 1969, p. 13.

7.   *A New History of Ireland*, op. cit., pp. 234–235.

8.   National Schools Registers, ED2/34-106 (PROD).

9.   Mary Boyle O'Reilly to J. McCarthy, 10 February 1924 (BBC).

10. Cited in Cecil Woodham-Smith, *The Great Hunger: Ireland 1845–49*, London, 1962, p. 20.

11. ibid., p. 24.

12. ibid., p. 102.

13. Cited in R. Kee, *Ireland*, London, 1980, p. 99.

14. G.M. Trevelyan, *The Life of John Bright*, London, 1913, pp. 162–163.

15. O'Reilly to Anderson, 7 November 1884, cited in James Jeffrey Roche, *Life of John Boyle O'Reilly, Together with his Complete Poems and Speeches Edited by Mrs John Boyle O'Reilly*. New York, 1891, p. 432.

16. Roche, op. cit., p. 375.

17. 'The Dreamer' in *By a Hearth in Erin*, pp. 128–133. Biographical sketch of J.B. O'Reilly. Author and date unknown (BBC).

18. Poem included in O'Reilly's Notebook of Poems and Shorthand Notes, handwritten, 1868 (BLP). For a detailed report on the find, see media release 'Hundred and twenty-four year old stenography lesson to solve a mystery', 6 January 1992, Library and Information Service of Western Australia; also *West Australian*, 16 May 1992.
19. Roche, op. cit., p. 381.
20. ibid., p. 432. The poem quoted was found among O'Reilly's papers after his death and was not published during his lifetime.
21. Brian O'Higgins, 'John Boyle O'Reilly: Glimpses of his boyhood', *Donahoe's Magazine*, no. LIV, August 1905, pp. 182–193.
22. *By a Hearth in Erin*, p. 128.
23. G.M. Trevelyan, *A History of England*, 3rd edn, London, 1945, p. 494.
24. Roche states that O'Reilly 'left home' at 'about the age of eleven' (p. 5). This was later contested by Katherine Conway in an article in the *Catholic World*, vol. L111, April–September 1891, in which she quotes a letter from O'Reilly's sister stating that O'Reilly joined the *Drogheda Argus* at the age of nine. Although it was legally possible in those days to be an apprentice at nine years of age, I have preferred Roche's version in view of O'Reilly's undoubted educational standard at the time.
25. Wilde, op. cit., p. 308.
26. *Drogheda Argus*, 15 March 1858.
27. ibid., 9 January 1858.
28. Roche's estimate that the young John Boyle served nearly four years of his apprenticeship (Roche, op. cit., pp. 5–6) seems likely in view of the established dates of his movements in the immediate future.

CHAPTER 2   THE YOUNG JOURNALIST

1. J.B. O'Reilly, letter to a friend 1881, cited in Roche, p. 7.
2. Census 1861, RG9/3139 (PPL).
3. Roche, op. cit., p. 7.
4. John Boyle O'Reilly, *Moondyne*, facsimile edn, Sydney, 1975, p. 40.
5. John Devoy, op. cit., p. 153.
6. *Preston Guardian*, 13 December 1862.
7. Roche, op. cit., p. 195.
8. Stephan Bull, *Volunteer! The Lancashire Rifle Volunteers 1859–85*, Lancashire County Museums Service, Preston, 1993, p. 8 et seq.
9. Roche, loc. cit.
10. Devoy, op. cit., p. 154.
11. ibid., pp. 152–153.

CHAPTER 3   THE REBEL SOLDIER

1. The Fenian oath is reproduced in several studies of the IRB, sometimes showing slight variations. This one is taken from Seán O Lúing's work, *Fremantle Mission*, Anvil Books, Dublin, 1965, p. 5.
2. S. Pender, *Fenianism: A Centenary Lecture* given on 26 February 1967 at Cork University; published by the University Extension Committee, p. 6.
3. ibid., p. 8.
4. Devoy, op. cit. p. 33.
5. ibid., p. 28.
6. ibid., p. 146.
7. id.

8.   ibid., p. 28.
9.   ibid., p. 152.
10.   ibid., p. 153
11.   ibid., p. 155.
12.   Roche, op. cit., p. 124.
13.   Letter from Michael MacLaughlin published in the United Irishman, New York, 25 February 1888 and cited in Seán O Lúing, op. cit., p. 13.
14.   John Devoy, the elder statesman of Fenianism, survived in exile in America to die at the great age of eighty-six in 1928. His obituary in The Times (1 October 1928) described him as:
      the oldest of Irish revolutionaries and the most bitter and persistent, as well as the most dangerous enemy of this country Ireland has produced since Wolfe Tone, the organiser of the United Irish movement at the end of the 18th century, brought about by the attempted invasion of Ireland by the French under Hoche. Devoy was unremittingly engaged in conspiracies, both in Ireland and America, for the establishment of an Irish republic...

CHAPTER 4   'A TERROR TO THE THRONE'

1.   Leon O Broin, Fenian Fever: An Anglo–American Dilemma, London, 1971, p. 222. Talbot's assailant was captured red-handed and put on trial but acquitted as a result of an able defence by Sir Isaac Butt.
2.   S. O'Hegarty, Ireland Under the Union, London, 1952, p. 451.
3.   Roche, op. cit., p. 18
4.   id.
5.   Regimental records WO12/962 16693 (PROL).
6.   John Boyle O'Reilly, Songs from the Southern Seas and Other Poems, Roberts Bros., Boston, 1873, p. 156.
7.   This and other quotations from the trial in Chapters 4 and 5 are taken from the transcript reproduced at length in Roche, op. cit., pp. 29–47, with additional information given by Devoy in Recollections of an Irish Rebel.

CHAPTER 5   PRISONER 9843

1.   Pilot, 8 July 1871.
2.   Letters quoted in Roche, op. cit., p. 376.
3.   Charles Dickens, American Notes and Pictures from Italy, London, 1907, p. 98.
4.   D.B. Cashman, The Life of Michael Davitt, facsimile edn, Tower Books, Cork, 1979, p. 29.
5.   From an O'Reilly manuscript quoted in Roche, op. cit., pp. 53–55.
6.   Letter from prison in the possession (then) of Mrs Henry of Liverpool, England, reproduced in facsimile in Roche, op. cit., p. 64.
7.   O'Reilly's prison record. Transportation records, Ireland to Australia. Ref. TR14 (BLP).
8.   Robert Grant, Frederick J. Stimpson, John T. Wheelwright and John Boyle O'Reilly, The King's Men: A Tale of Tomorrow. New York, 1884, p. 193.
9.   On his release from Dartmoor Corporal Thomas Chambers went to live in exile in Boston and died prematurely in Carney Hospital where he was constantly attended by O'Reilly. He died on 2 December 1888. O'Reilly wrote his obituary in the Pilot from which this is extracted.
10.   O'Reilly interview shortly before his death, date unknown, quoted by Roche, op. cit., p. 64.
11.   John S. Casey (ed. Martin Kevin Cusack), Journal of a Voyage from Portland to Fremantle on Board the Convict Ship, Hougoumont, Captain Cozens Commander, October 12th 1867, (hereafter Casey Diary), Dorrence & Co., Penn. (ML, BLP).
12.   Roche, op. cit., p. 65.

CHAPTER 6   FENIAN FEVER

1. 'Resolutions of a Meeting held to determine whether Western Australia should apply to become a Penal Settlement'. (Parliamentary Papers on Convict Discipline and Transportation vol. V1, Governor Fitzgerald to Earl Grey, 3 March 1849, enclosure.) (PROWA).
2. Alexandra Hasluck, *Unwilling Emigrants*, Fremantle Arts Centre Press, Fremantle, 1991, p. 134 et seq.
3. Keith Amos, *The Fenians in Australia 1865–1880*, New South Wales University Press, Sydney, 1988, pp. 78-9.
4. Amos, pp. 80-81
5. ibid., p. 79.
6. Quoted in *Fremantle Herald*, 21 December 1867.
7. id.
8. Hampton to Buckingham, 29 January 1868, cited in Amos, op. cit., pp. 93. See also *Perth Gazette*, 20 December 1867.
9. Manning to Crampton, 2 December 1867, Governor's Correspondence, AN395 (PROWA).
10. Hampton to Buckingham, 29 January 1868, cited in Amos, op. cit., p. 97.
11. Lucille M. Quinlan, *Undaunted Spirit*, Melbourne, 1980, p. 150.

CHAPTER 7   ON BOARD THE *HOUGOUMONT*

1. O'Reilly, *Moondyne*, p. 160.
2. ibid., p. 160.
3. ibid., p. 161.
4. Roche, op. cit., p. 66. The incident is also related briefly in Casey's Diary, p. 4.
5. Roche, op. cit., p. 66. O'Reilly also describes the scene in much the same words in his novel, *Moondyne*, even to the use of the uncommon word 'diapason', p. 168.
6. Casey Diary, op. cit., p. 4.
7. ibid., p. 5.
8. O'Reilly, *Moondyne*, p. 168
9. Casey Diary, op. cit., p. 10.
10. O'Reilly, *Moondyne*, p. 168
11. Casey Diary, op. cit., p. 10.
12. O'Reilly, *Moondyne*, p. 172
13. Written on the *Hougoumont*, 12 October 1867, 'published' in the *Wild Goose*, but not included in his collected poems.

CHAPTER 8   THE *WILD GOOSE*

1. Cashman, 'An Obituary', *Boston Herald*, 24 August 1890.
2. ibid.
3. ibid.
4. Denis Cashman, Diary, September 1867 – January 1868 (hereafter Cashman Diary) (ML, BLP).
5. Casey Diary, op. cit., p. 16.
6. *Wild Goose: A Collection of Ocean Waifs*, no. 1 of 7. Original handwritten copies in Mitchell Library, Sydney, MSS1542, 6-446C (ML).
7. ibid.
8. ibid.
9. ibid.
10. ibid.

CHAPTER 9   IN SOUTHERN LATITUDES

1. Cashman Diary, op. cit.
2. Casey Diary, op. cit., p. 18.
3. *Wild Goose*, no. 2, p. 2.
4. Cashman Diary, op. cit.
5. *Wild Goose* no. 2, op. cit. p. 3.
6. The poem was not republished in his collected works.
7. Casey Diary, op. cit., p. 20.
8. Cashman Diary, op. cit.
9. The poem appears in John Boyle O'Reilly's *Songs, Legends, and Ballads*, Pilot Pub. Co., Boston, 1878, p. 83. The volume was dedicated to O'Reilly's wife whose name was also Mary. The original poem was written long before he met her and referred to a Mary he knew in his adolescence. But did Mrs O'Reilly think that the poem was written for her?
10. Coleridge's poem had been published in 1817, fifty years previously, and had gained wide popularity.
11. The poem was not republished and should not be confused with 'My Mother's Memory', published in *Songs, Legends, and Ballads*, p. 79.
12. *Wild Goose*, no. 4.
13. Casey Diary, op. cit., p. 25.
14. *Wild Goose*, no. 5, p. 4.
15. id.
16. Casey Diary, op. cit., p. 27.
17. Cashman Diary, op. cit.

CHAPTER 10   JOURNEY'S END

1. *Wild Goose*, no. 7, p. 2.
2. ibid., p. 12.
3. Casey Diary, op. cit., p. 35.
4. Cashman Diary, op. cit.
5. ibid.
6. O'Reilly, *Moondyne*, p. 203
7. ibid.

PART 2 THE UNWILLING IMMIGRANT (1868–1869)

CHAPTER 11   'THE ESTABLISHMENT'

1. W.H. Knight, Auditor-General, 1870. Quoted in J.K. Ewers, *Western Gateway: A History of Fremantle*, Fremantle City Council, 1948, p. 73.
2. Mrs Edward Millet, 1863, ibid., p. 49.
3. O'Reilly, *Moondyne*, p. 203.
4. *Fremantle Herald*, 11 January 1868.
5. ibid.
6. *Fremantle Herald*, 25 January 1868.
7. Patrick Walle to his parents, quoted in the *Irishman*, 11 April 1868, cited in Amos, op. cit., pp. 122–123.

8. Casey copied out in his diary an official notice announcing the conditions of ticket-of-leave granted to prisoners in Fremantle Prison, 29 December 1867.

> Convicts hereafter sent to Western Australia will be eligible for Tickets of Leave if entirely without offence or complaint of any sort recorded against them when they have served half of the periods of their sentences remaining unexpired at the end of (9) nine months from the date of their original conviction.
>
> If they misconduct themselves their Penal Servitude on the public works is liable to extension limited only by the length of their sentence of penal servitude.
>
> When they have served with uniformly good conduct half the periods of their original sentence remaining unexpired at the time they are granted Tickets of Leave they will be eligible to receive licenses to be at large releasing them from several restrictions to which Ticket of Leave holders in the Colony are subject.

9. Wakeford, 'Report on the Convict Dept. for 1867', 5 March 1868 (CO18-158, PRO1657). Quoted in Amos, op. cit., p. 124 (original not sighted).
10. Anthony Trollope, *Australia and New Zealand*, vol. 2, Chapman Hall, London, 1873, p. 113.
11. 29 January 1868 (CO18-158, PRO1657), Australian Joint Copying Project. Quoted in Amos, op. cit., p. 125 (original not sighted).
12. O'Reilly, *Moondyne*, p. 15.
13. Poem published in *Songs, Legends, and Ballads*.
14. Superintendent's Order Book SO 10, p. 256, ACC419-3 (PROWA).

CHAPTER 12   THE BUSH CAMP

1. Quoted in Martin Carroll, Behind the Lighthouse: A Study of the Australian Sojourn of John Boyle O'Reilly 1844–1890, PhD thesis, University of Iowa, 1954.
2. O'Reilly, *Moondyne*, p. 4
3. Roche, op. cit., p. 70.
4. Survey of non-Fenian *Hougoumont* convicts, Rica Erickson (comp.) *Dictionary of Western Australians*, University of Western Australia Press, Nedlands, passim.
5. Roche, op. cit., p 70.
6. O'Reilly, *Moondyne*, p. 8.
7. Poem published in *Songs from the Southern Seas and Other Poems*.
8. cf. George Russo, A Friend Indeed, Perth, 1996, pp. 232–233.
9. Michael Davitt, *Life and Progress in Australasia*, London, 1898, pp. 132–133.
10. Carroll, op. cit., p. 323 et seq.

CHAPTER 13   'NO RAMBLING POET'

1. O'Reilly, *Moondyne*, p. 11.
2. Published in *Songs from the Southern Seas*, p. 137
3. Quoted by Graeme H.C. McNally, Roads and Bridges Constructed by Convicts 1850–1860, thesis (BLP).
4. Michael J. Bourke, On the Swan, University of Western Australia Press, Nedlands, 1987, p. 222; see also Alexandra Hasluck, op. cit., p. 66.
5. Amos, op. cit., pp. 137–138.
6. Convict Eugene Lombard to his parents, 22 January 1868, quoted by Amos, op. cit., p. 129.
7. Roche, op. cit., pp. 73–74. See also Drake-Brockman, 'Did O'Reilly save this tree?', *West Australian*, 23 August 1952.
8. Roche, op. cit., p. 74.
9. Drake-Brockman, op. cit.

10. *Songs from the Southern Seas*, p. 155.
11. Roche, op. cit., p. 73
12. *Songs from the Southern Seas*, p. 101. O'Reilly uses the old spelling of 'dugite', with a 'k'.
13. Roche, op. cit., p. 76. See also Carroll, op. cit., pp. 253.

CHAPTER 14   THE WARDER'S DAUGHTER

1.   O'Reilly, *Moondyne*, p. 223.
2.   ibid., p. 224.
3.   Davitt, op. cit., p. 458.
4.   Davitt, op. cit., p. 130.
5.   J.B. O'Reilly, Notebook of Poems, and Shorthand Notes, handwritten, 1868 (BLP). (Hereafter O'Reilly Notebook). For a detailed report on the find, see media release 'Hundred and twenty-four year old stenography lesson to solve a mystery', 6 January 1992, Library and Information Service of Western Australia; also *West Australian*, 16 May 1992.
6.   ibid. From the translation of the shorthand by Gillian O'Mara, reproduced by permission.
7.   Davitt, op. cit., pp. 132–133.
8.   O'Reilly, *Moondyne*, p. 5.
9.   O'Reilly Notebook.
10. O'Reilly, *Moondyne*, p. 98.
11. Amos, op. cit., p. 155.

CHAPTER 15   FACING THE ABYSS

1.   Roche, op. cit., p. 76.
2.   William T. Timperley, Private Journal, 1878–79 (hereafter Timperley Journal), ACC2892A MN781 (PROWA).
3.   Timperley to Hare, 28 February 1869, Colonial Police Records, AN5 ACC129 12/962 (PROWA).
4.   Amos, op. cit., p. 154.
5.   Newspaper interview with Henry Hathaway. Annotated cutting found amongst O'Reilly's papers. Date and paper unrecorded by O'Reilly (BBC).
6.   Letter dated 27 December 1876, Governor's Correspondence, AN395 (PROWA).

CHAPTER 16   'TAKEN AT THE FLOOD'

1.   O'Reilly Notebook.
2.   Herman Melville, *Moby Dick*, Penguin Classics, London, 1986, p. 78.
3.   Alexandra Hasluck, *Portrait with Background*, Fremantle Arts Centre Press, Fremantle, 1990, pp. 217–219.
4.   *Perth Gazette*, 7 and 21 February 1868, cited in Carroll, op. cit., p. 311.
5.   Amos, op. cit., p. 159
6.   Timperley to Hare, 20 and 24 February 1869, Colonial Police Records, AN5 ACC129 12/962 (PROWA).
7.   O'Reilly, *Moondyne*, p. 56.
8.   The account of O'Reilly's escape, which follows, is based largely on: O'Reilly's own account published in the *Celtic Monthly* of Boston (date unknown); the account in Roche, op. cit., pp. 75–82 which in turn was reprinted from the Philadelphia *Times*, 25 June 1881; from other accounts, including those published in the *Boston Daily Globe* and other papers immediately after O'Reilly's death; and is supplemented by the author's own researches.

9. One of the Fenians, James Reilly, has been confused in some accounts with John Boyle O'Reilly, particularly in relation to John Boyle's suicide attempt and his affair with Jessie Woodman. After a period of punishment James Reilly and the other six convicts were returned to Perth without working in the district. See Amos, op. cit., p. 141.
10. Amos, op. cit., p. 160.
11. Roche, op. cit., p. 79. Conversation quoted by Roche who would, in turn, have learned it direct from O'Reilly.

CHAPTER 17 FUGITIVE IN THE DUNES
1. See note 8, sup.

CHAPTER 18 'THE UTMOST VIGILANCE'
1. Timperley to Hare, 20 February 1869, op. cit.
2. ibid.
3. Timperley to Hare, 3 March 1869, Colonial Police Records, AN5 ACC129 12/962 (PROWA).
4. Timperley Journal, op. cit.
5. Timperley to Hare, 20 February 1869, op. cit.
6. ibid.
7. Hare to Timperley, 27 February 1869, Colonial Police Records, AN5 ACC129 12/962 (PROWA).

CHAPTER 19 COURAGE REWARDED
1. Annie Stokes, quoted by Martin Carroll and subsequently quoted in Amos, op. cit., p. 158.
2. O'Reilly, Moondyne, p. 10.
3. Roche, op. cit., p. 82.

CHAPTER 20 HUNTING THE WHALE
1. Melville, op. cit., p. 531.
2. Dates, route and ports of call, and other details of the voyage of the Gazelle are taken from the log, Kendall Whaling Museum, Mass.
3. It is highly unlikely that the Gazelle carried explosive guns since these harpoon instruments first appeared on Norwegian whalers only as late as 1866.
4. Melville, op. cit., p. 172.
5. Letter, Hathaway to O'Reilly, 25 November 1869; quoted in Roche, op. cit., p. 95.
6. Melville, op. cit., p. 252.
7. Melville, op. cit., p. 128
8. Poem published in Songs from the Southern Seas, p. 75.
9. Melville, op. cit., p. 343.
10. ibid., p. 341.
11. ibid., p. 393.
12. Letter, Hathaway to Roche, 1887; quoted in Roche, op. cit., pp. 84–85.

CHAPTER 21 THE POLITICAL REFUGEE
1. O'Reilly papers (BBC).
2. Captain Hussey, first officer of the Gazelle, said at the time, 'the governor was not so badly fooled as we thought...'; quoted in Roche, op. cit., p. 89.
3. Roche, op. cit., p. 89.
4. Roche, op. cit., pp. 89–90.

5. Roche, op. cit., p. 90.
6. Letter, Hathaway to O'Reilly, 29 July 1869; quoted in Roche, op. cit., p. 91.
7. O'Reilly to his aunt, Mrs C. Watkinson, 5 April 1870; quoted in Roche, op. cit., pp. 105-106.
8. Lecture delivered at the Music Hall, Boston, January 1870; quoted in Roche, op. cit., pp. 99-100.
9. From the poem 'Liberty Lighting the World', written to commemorate the unveiling of Bertoldi's Statue of Liberty in New York Harbour on 29 October 1886; later published in Roche, op. cit., p. 420.

PART 3 THE EXILE OF THE GAEL (1870–1890)

CHAPTER 22   WAR CORRESPONDENT

1. Roche, op. cit., p. 101.
2. Francis G. McManamin, *The American Years of John Boyle O'Reilly 1870-1890*. Dissertation submitted to the Arts and Science Faculty, Catholic University of America, 1959, later published by the Arno Press, New York, 1976, p. 39.
3. O'Reilly to A.M. Sullivan, 30 December 1869 (NLD).
4. *Pilot*, 12 April 1870, quoting the report from the New York *Irish People*, 2 April 1870.
5. O'Reilly to Sullivan, op. cit.
6. Thomas H. O'Connor, *The Boston Irish: A Political History*, Boston, 1995, p. 70.
7. ibid., pp. 100-101.
8. ibid., p. 63 et seq.
9. ibid., p. xvi.
10. O'Reilly to George Cahill, 27 March 1870 (BBC).
11. Michael Davitt, *The Fall of Feudalism in Ireland*, New York, 1904, pp. 129-130.
12. O'Reilly to Mrs C. Watkinson ('My own dear Aunt'), 5 April 1870; quoted in Roche, op. cit., p. 106.
13. *Pilot*, 11 June 1870.

CHAPTER 23 · A MAN OF INFLUENCE

1. O'Reilly to John Devoy, 2 March 1872 (BBC).
2. O'Reilly to Devoy, 28 January 1871; quoted in *Devoy's Postbag*, Dublin, 1848-53, p. 13.
3. O'Reilly to 'Officers and Members of the Fenian Brotherhood of Boston', 31 July 1871 (BBC).
4. The disparity between the date given for the Battle of the Boyne in Chapter 1 and the date of all subsequent commemorative celebrations is due, in part, to the reforms of the modern (Gregorian) calendar. The Julian calendar, in force at the time of the battle, establishes the date as 1 July and this is the date most historians cite. The Gregorian corrections advance Julian dates by ten, which then means the battle was fought on the 11th. Why the 12th is often cited, and why Orangemen march on this date, is probably due to simple confusion.
5. *Pilot*, 23 July 1870.
6. ibid.
7. Quoted on the office notepaper, and occasionally printed in the newspaper itself.
8. *Pilot*, 26 May 1883.
9. O'Reilly to Devoy, 13 February 1871, *Devoy's Postbag*, op. cit., p. 32.
10. cf. McManamin, op. cit., pp. 46-47 and Roche, op. cit., p. 120.
11. O'Reilly to Devoy, 13 February 1871, *Devoy's Postbag*, op. cit., p. 31.
12. O'Reilly to Mrs C. Watkinson, 7 September 1874; quoted in Roche, op. cit., p. 133.

CHAPTER 24   A PHOENIX TOO FREQUENT

1.   O'Reilly to A.M. Sullivan, 12 April 1881 (NLD).
2.   O'Reilly to Mrs Rossa, 1 February 1872 (BBC).
3.   O'Reilly to Mrs C. Watkinson, op. cit.
4.   Roche, op. cit., p. 132.
5.   *Boston Daily Globe*, 11 November 1872.
6.   Published in *Songs, Legends, and Ballads*, p. 94.
7.   *Pilot*, 14 June 1873.

CHAPTER 25   'A VERY CLUBABLE MAN'

1.   Roche, op. cit., pp. 138–139.
2.   'Loving Cup of the Papyrus', published in *Songs, Legends, and Ballads*, p. 48.
3.   *Boston Daily Advertiser*, 23 September 1886.
4.   A view expressed by O'Reilly's grandson during a conversation with the author, July 1995.
5.   Dr David Boyle, 'John Boyle O'Reilly and the Irish adjustment in America', *Journal of the Old Drogheda Society*, 1995. He writes: '...in 1974, lecturing at Salve Regina College, Rhode Island, on Irish America, I was introduced to a fine huge ancient of a man in his mid-nineties. He had been John Boyle O'Reilly's batman or valet in the years just before the poet's death. His fondness was such, after eighty-five years, that he reversed Napoleon's dictum that "No man is a hero to his valet"'.

CHAPTER 26   TWICE TO THE RESCUE

1.   'Patrick Donahoe, founder of the *Pilot*', *Donahoe's Monthly Magazine*, vol. XXV, no. 2, February 1891.
2.   O'Reilly to Charles Hurd, 27 January 1876 (BPL).
3.   Robert H. Lord, John E. Sexton, Edward T. Harrington, *History of the Archdiocese of Boston*, New York, 1944, p. 394.
4.   Agreement for purchase of the *Pilot*, 14 April 1876; and letter, O'Reilly to Archbishop Williams, 4 August 1886 (AAB).
5.   McManamin, op. cit., p. 134.
6.   ibid., p. 134.
7.   McManamin, op. cit., p. 56.
8.   *Pilot*, 2 September 1876.
9.   *Pilot*, 9 September 1876.
10. Roche, op. cit., pp. 47 and 386.
11. Francis G. McManamin in his excellent study, *The American Years of John Boyle O'Reilly*, (op. cit.) writes in his summary that: '[O'Reilly] had violent prejudices. The most marked sprang from his deep detestation of England. This sentiment became a veritable fixation and rendered his thinking on the subject extremely biased and void of all objectivity. Frequently O'Reilly entered the arena of political, social or even religious controversy swinging a huge club the force of which at times thrust him forward beyond where his cooler judgement would dictate'.

CHAPTER 27   WRITING FOR REFORM

1.   W.F.P. Stockley, 'Reminiscences of John Boyle O'Reilly 1844–1890', *Catholic World*, vol. CXL, March 1935.
2.   Roche, op. cit., p. 177.
3.   O'Reilly to Chambers, 22 December 1877; quoted in Roche, op. cit., p. 179.

4. O'Reilly to Dorr, 11 March 1879. Quoted in McManamin, op. cit., p. 237 (original not sighted). cf. *Sunday Record* (Boston) a similar description of his work in an undated newspaper cutting in O'Reilly's scrapbook (BBC).
5. O'Reilly, *Moondyne*, p. 84.
6. Unpublished and unfinished; quoted in Roche, op. cit., p. 190.
7. *Pilot*, 16 August 1879.
8. O'Reilly to Alfred Webb, 23 October 1889 (NLD).
9. *Pilot*, 20 January 1883.
10. *Pilot*, 15 December 1883.
11. Roche, op. cit., p. 343.
12. ibid., p. 289.
13. ibid., p. 341.
14. W.G. Schofield, *Seek for a Hero: The Story of John Boyle O'Reilly*, New York, 1956, p. 52.

CHAPTER 28   'AN AMERICAN OR NOTHING'

1. *Pilot*, 28 February 1880.
2. MacManamin, op. cit., p. 149.
3. O'Reilly to Archbishop Williams, 18 June 1888 (AAB).
4. O'Reilly to Mrs Anthony, 28 December. The year is omitted from the letter (HH).
5. O'Reilly to Dr Hamilton Osgood, 9 July 1889 (NLD).
6. Conway to McQuaid, 22 January 1890; quoted in McManamin op. cit., p. 143 (original not sighted).
7. McManamin, op. cit., n. 33, p. 146.
8. ibid., p. 249.
9. Richard Ellmann, *Oscar Wilde*, London, 1987, p. 164.
10. ibid., p. 173.
11. Fanny Parnell to O'Reilly, 31 January 1882. Letter in possession of Richard O'Reilly Hocking.
12. Ellmann, op. cit., p. 190.
13. Roche, op. cit., p. 213.
14. ibid., pp. 213-214.
15. cf. McManamin, op. cit., p. 85 et seq.
16. Roche, op. cit., p. 216.
17. O'Reilly to (?), 16 March 1880 in answer to a reader's query (BPL).

CHAPTER 29   A GENIAL BARD

1. O'Reilly to William Onahan; quoted in McManamin, op. cit., n. 4, p. 307.
2. Boyle, op. cit.
3. O'Reilly to Stoddard, 21 June 1882; quoted in Roche, p. 291.
4 ibid., p. 238.
5. A newspaper report among O'Reilly's cuttings under the subheading 'Unseen Hand' describes how the book was written: 'Upon their first meeting, which was naturally for the purpose of selecting a theme, among other ideas presented, was the skeleton of a tale which had been jotted down by Mr Wheelwright...a plan was formed to which each of the four contributed ideas, as they suggested themselves. In this manner the work was apportioned out, each undertaking to write certain chapters entire. Numerous meetings were of course necessary, at which the different portions were read by their authors, in the proper order, all discrepancies effaced, and the continuity of the whole preserved'. (BBC)
6. McManamin's researches indicate that O'Reilly took steps to secure US citizenship on 7 March 1870, in the city of Boston. McManamin, op. cit., n. 75, p. 38.

7.   Lushington to O'Reilly, 19 January 1885 (BBC).
8.   Roche, op. cit., p. 250.
9.   McCabe to Roche, 19 November 1890; quoted in Roche, op. cit., p. 255.
10.   Roche, op cit., p. 258.
11.   ibid., p. 293.
12   O.W. Holmes to O'Reilly, 2 October 1878 (BPL).

CHAPTER 30   'TERRIBLY OVERWORKED'

1.   O'Reilly to Bowen, 13 June 1887; quoted in McManamin, op. cit., p. 298.
2.   O'Reilly to Devoy, 24 July 1886; Devoy's Postbag, op. cit., vol. 2, p. 286.
3.   Unfinished manuscript among O'Reilly's papers (BBC).
4.   Roche, op. cit., p. 304.
5.   ibid., pp. 307–308.
6.   ibid., p. 311.
7.   ibid., p. 317.
8.   John Boyle O'Reilly, Athletics and Manly Sport, Boston, 1890, pp. 162–167.
9.   Roche, op. cit., p. 326.
10.   O'Reilly to Harson, 25 September 1889, quoted in Roche, op. cit., p. 338.
11.   When sighted, the diary was in the possession of Richard O'Reilly Hocking, Madison, New Hampshire; it was later deposited in the Houghton Library, Harvard.
12.   Donnelly claimed that Bacon had hidden among Shakespeare's works a cypher revealing the true authorship of the plays. His frantic but fruitless search in southern England for buried boxes that would, purportedly, prove Bacon's authorship attracted a good deal of attention at the time. cf. Ian Wilson, Shakespeare, the Evidence, London, 1993.

CHAPTER 31   'AND WAKING IS DEATH'

1.   Roche, op. cit., pp. 336–337.
2.   ibid., p. 336.
3.   Unnamed resident of Hull quoted in the Boston Daily Globe, 11 August 1890.
4.   Fire Commissioner John R. Murphy, Mrs O'Reilly's brother, quoted in the Boston Daily Globe, Monday, 11 August 1890.

CHAPTER 32   O'REILLY—THE LEGACY

1.   Roche, op. cit., pp. 355–356.
2.   Death Registers, vols 410, 426 (MAA).
3.   A view suggested by O'Reilly's grandson, Richard O'Reilly Hocking, in conversation with the author.
4.   cf. McManamin, op. cit., n. 71, p. 37.
5.   'John Boyle O'Reilly Obituary', Harper's Weekly, no. XXXIV, 23 August 1890, p. 664.
6.   'John Boyle O'Reilly Obituary', Literary World, no. XXI, 16 August 1890, p. 271.
7.   Roche, op. cit., p. 370.
8.   Roche, op. cit., p. 360.
9.   Roche, op. cit., p. 358. Lathrop (1851–1898) had a distinguished literary career. He wrote several novels and was, consecutively, associate editor of the Atlantic Monthly, editor of the Boston Sunday Courier, and literary editor of the New York Star.

SELECT BIBLIOGRAPHY

BOOKS, POETRY AND ARTICLES

Amos, Keith. *The Fenians in Australia 1865–1880*. New South Wales University Press, Sydney, 1988.

Australian Dictionary of Biography 1788–1850. Melbourne, 1966–90.

Barry, Liam. *Selected Poems, Speeches, Dedications and Letters of John Boyle O'Reilly 1844–1890*. The National Gaelic Publications, Australind, WA, 1994.

Bourke, Michael J. *On the Swan: A History of the Swan District of Western Australia*. University of Western Australia Press, Nedlands, 1987.

Capen, Rev. Dr Elmer H. *The Eulogy: Memorial of John Boyle O'Reilly*. Boston, 1897.

Casey, John Sarsfield. *Journal of a Voyage from Portland to Fremantle on Board the Convict Ship Hougoumont, Captain Cozens Commander, October 12th 1867*. Ed. M.K. Cusack. Dorrence & Co., Penn., 1988.

Cashman, D.B. *The Life of Michael Davitt*. Facsimile edn. Tower Books, Cork, 1979.

Conway, Katherine E. *Watchwords of John Boyle O'Reilly*. Boston, 1891.

Crowley, F.K. *Australia's Western Third*. Melbourne, 1960.

Davitt, Michael. *Life and Progress in Australasia*. London, 1898.

—— *The Fall of Feudalism in Ireland*. New York, 1904.

Devoy, John. *Recollections of an Irish Rebel*. Facsimile edn. Irish University Press, Dublin, 1969.

—— *Devoy's Postbag*, 2 vols. Dublin, 1848–1853.

Foster, R.F. *Modern Ireland, 1600–1972*. London, 1988.

Grant, R., Stimpson, F.J., Wheelwright, J. T. and O'Reilly, J.B. *The King's Men: A Tale of Tomorrow*. New York, 1884.

Handlin, Oscar. *Boston's Immigrants*. New York, 1974.

Hasluck, A. *Unwilling Emigrants*. Fremantle Arts Centre Press, Fremantle, 1991.

—— *Portrait with Background*. Fremantle Arts Centre Press, Fremantle, 1990.

Levine, Edward M. *The Irish and Irish Politicians*. Indiana, 1966.

Lyons, F.J. *Ireland Since the Famine*. London, 1971.

Melville, H. *Moby Dick*. Penguin Classics. London, 1986.

McMahon, J.T. *Success Stories*. Essays and reminiscences including an account of a visit to John Boyle O'Reilly's daughter, Mary. Privately published, Perth, 1987.

McManamin, Francis G. *The American Years of John Boyle O'Reilly 1870–1890*. Arno Press, New York, 1976.

Moody, T.W., Martin, F.X. and Boyne, F.J. (eds). *A New History of Ireland, Volume III, 1534–1691*. Oxford, 1989.

O'Connor, Thomas H. *The Boston Irish: A Political History*. Boston, 1995.

O Lúing, Seán. *Fremantle Mission*. Anvil Books, Dublin, 1965.

O'Higgins, Brian. 'John Boyle O'Reilly: Glimpses of his boyhood'. *Donahoe's Magazine*, no. LIV, August 1905, pp. 182–193.

O'Mara, Gillian. *Convict Records of Western Australia*. Friends of The Battye Library, Perth, 1990.

O'Reilly, John Boyle. *Moondyne*. Facsimile edn. Rigby Ltd, Sydney, 1975.

—— *Songs from the Southern Seas and Other Poems*. Roberts Bros, Boston, 1873.

—— *Songs, Legends, and Ballads*. Pilot Pub. Co., Boston, 1878.

—— *The Statues in the Block and Other Poems*. Roberts Bros, Boston, 1881.

—— *In Bohemia*. Pilot Pub. Co., Boston, 1886.

—— *Ethics of Boxing and Manly Sport*. Tickner & Co., Boston, 1888 (later published as *Athletics and Manly Sport*, 1890).

—— *Selected Poems*. P.J. Kenedy, New York, 1913.

O'Reilly, P. and Tuite, B. (eds). *The Cry of the Dreamer and Other Poems. John Boyle O'Reilly*. Drogheda, n.d.

Paving the Way 1829–1979. History of Road Construction, WA Main Roads Department, Perth, 1979.

Pender, Prof. S. *Fenianism: A Centenary Lecture*. Cork Corporation University Extension Committee, 1967.

Reece, R. and Pascoe, R. *A Place of Consequence*. Fremantle, 1985.

Roche, James Jeffrey. *Life of John Boyle O'Reilly, Together with his Complete Poems and Speeches Edited by Mrs John Boyle O'Reilly*. New York, 1891.

Sanders, Theodora. *Bunbury: Some Early History*. Roebuck, Canberra, 1975.

Sartin, Stephen. *The People and Places of Historic Preston*. Preston, 1988.

Schofield, William G. *Seek for a Hero: The Story of John Boyle O'Reilly*, New York, 1956.

Seddon, George. *Sense of Place*. University of Western Australia Press, Nedlands, 1972.

Shannon, William V. *The American Irish*. New York, 1963.

Trevelyan, G.M. *A History of England*. 3rd edn. Longmans, London, 1945.

Vaughan, W.E. (ed.). *A New History of Ireland, Volume V, 1801–1870*. Oxford, 1989.

Watson, John (ed.). *Catalpa 1876*. Perth, 1976.

Wilde, William R. *The Beauties and Antiquities of the Boyne*. Facsimile edn. Tower Books, Cork, 1978.

Woodham-Smith, Cecil. *The Great Hunger: Ireland 1845–49*. Hamish Hamilton, London, 1962.

UNPUBLISHED DOCUMENTS AND THESES

Carroll, Martin C. Behind the Lighthouse: A Study of the Australian Sojourn of John Boyle O'Reilly 1844–1890. PhD thesis, University of Iowa, 1954.

Cashman, D.B. Diary, September 1867–January 1868 (ML).

Hunt, Charles Cook. Diary, 1866–1867 (BLP).

McNally, Graeme H.C. Roads and Bridges Constructed by Convicts 1850–1860. Thesis (BLP).

O'Reilly, John Boyle. Notebook of Poems and Shorthand Notes. Handwritten. 1867. Dedicated to the Reverend Patrick McCabe, RCC (BLP).

—— Diary of speaking tour, March–April 1890. In possession of Richard O'Reilly Hocking, Madison, New Hampshire.

Timperley, William T. Private Journal, 1878–79 (BLP).

Log of the *Gazelle*, on a voyage from New Bedford, August 1866–April 1870. Kendall Whaling Museum, Kendall, Mass.

Walsh, Francis Robert. The Boston *Pilot*: A Newspaper for the Irish Immigrant, 1829–1908. Dissertation, Boston University, 1968.

NEWSPAPERS AND JOURNALS

Atlantic Monthly, 1870–1890.
Boston Daily Advertiser, 1870–1890.
Boston Daily Globe, 1870–1890.
Boston Herald, 1870–1890.
Bulletin of the Eire Society of Boston, vol. 29, nos 1 and 5, 7 March and 14 April 1971.
Catholic World, 1891 and March 1935.
Celtic Monthly, New York, August 1873.
Donahoe's Magazine, Boston, 1895, 1905.
Drogheda Argus, 1854–1860.
Eire-Ireland, Journal of Irish Studies, St Paul, Minn.
Fremantle Herald, 21 December 1867.
Journal of the Cork Historical and Archaeological Society, vol. XCIII, no. 252, January–December 1988.
Journal of the Old Drogheda Society, Drogheda, 1995.
Sydney Morning Herald, 14 and 31 March 1868.
Pilot, 1870–1890.
West Australian, 1876, 23 August 1952 and 16 May 1992.
Wild Goose: A Collection of Ocean Waifs. Seven handwritten editions 'published' on board the *Hougoumont*. November–December 1867. Ed. John Flood (ML).

INDEX